"This cookbook is not just about good food; it's also about a lifestyle, about a tradition. It's about gathering those you love in the kitchen and cooking together, eating together, and building memories together. These are the traditions that never grow old, that never go out of style. They're classic . . . timeless . . . what memories are made of."

THIS IS SUNDAY DINNER

THIS IS SUNDAY DINNER

52 Seasonal Italian Menus

Lisa Caponigri

STERLING EPICURE
New York

STERLING EPICURE
New York

An Imprint of Sterling Publishing Co., Inc.
1166 Avenue of the Americas
New York, NY 10036

ISBN 978-1-4549-3017-4

Distributed in Canada by Sterling Publishing Co., Inc.
^c/o Canadian Manda Group, 664 Annette Street
Toronto, Ontario M6S 2C8, Canada
Distributed in the United Kingdom by GMC Distribution Services
Castle Place, 166 High Street, Lewes, East Sussex BN7 1XU, England
Distributed in Australia by NewSouth Books
University of New South Wales, Sydney, NSW 2052, Australia

For information about custom editions, special sales, and
premium and corporate purchases, please contact Sterling Special Sales
at 800-805-5489 or specialsales@sterlingpublishing.com.

Manufactured in China

2 4 6 8 10 9 7 5 3 1

sterlingpublishing.com

Interior design by Christine Heun
Cover design by Jo Obarowski

Photographs by Bill Milne (copyright Sterling Publishing, Inc.):
9, 21, 33, 42, 57, 89, 101, 113, 125, 143, 153, 155, 161, 179, 215,
219, 227, 233, 245, 264, 279, 283, 285, 297, front cover
All other photographs © Kelly Rosenhagen

For my parents
Dr. A. Robert Caponigri
and
Winifred Franco Caponigri

The most elegant, dignified couple I have ever known.
Thank you for a lifetime of love.

CONTENTS

———— ✦ ————

INTRODUCTION

Sunday Dinner never goes out of style. Six years ago (I can scarcely believe it has been that long!), I wrote my first cookbook, *Whatever Happened To Sunday Dinner?* Some of the happiest moments of my life have been spent in the kitchen, from cooking with my Sicilian Grandmother, and later cooking with my children from the time they were very small. Building on these wonderful memories, I wanted to help other families create similar memories of cooking together. I'm a "grassroots kind of girl"—I love farmers markets, wine tasting, festivals, street fairs, and Italian festivals. I began selling my first cookbook at these types of events, and the people who bought my book would regale me with how much it meant to have a book like mine, the only book on the market with 52 easy, delicious, authentic Sunday dinner menus. One gentleman even bought six of my books and had me sign them, one for himself and one for each of his five children! Months later, he wrote to tell me that they took turns hosting Sunday dinner every week. I truly believe this is because my cookbook is not just about good food; it's also about a lifestyle, about a tradition. It's about gathering those whom you love in the kitchen and cooking together, eating together, and building memories together. These are the traditions that never get old, that never go out of style. Classic. Timeless. What memories are made of.

So now I bring you *This is Sunday Dinner*, 52 completely new five course Italian menus for another year of delicious, memorable Sunday Dinners with those whom you love. People tease me, how many menus for Sunday Dinners do you have?! My response? Countless! I have done something slightly different and unique in this cookbook. While each menu is still five courses, the way we traditionally eat our Sunday Dinner in Italy, I have organized the 52 menus according to the four seasons and placed each season in a region of Italy that represents that season to me.

There are so many things I love about Italy. One of them is the seasonality of the food in each region. Sicily is known for its citrus, seafood, eggplant, and peppers. And these items are prevalent in Sicilian recipes. For this reason, I've included 13 of the menus in *Summer in Sicily*. Likewise, for me, Tuscany represents the beautiful, harvest–rich Fall: the pressing of the Chianti grapes, roasting chestnuts, the abundant harvest. Raising my children in Tuscany was a hugely important time in my life, and our favorite season was autumn. For this reason, I've brought you 13 of my favorite Tuscan menus, in *Autumn in Tuscany*. Nothing says spring like Campania, the beautiful seaside region that was the ancestral home of my father and, of course, the home of the beautiful city of Naples and the Amalfi Coast. Fresh mozzarella, abundant zucchini, lemons—as you've never seen them before—this is what Campania represents in the spring, and so I've brought you 13 Sunday Dinners from *Spring in Campania*. There is nothing more majestic than winter in the Italian Alps, with the snow-capped mountains, the beautiful town squares covered with snow, and the scent of cappuccino and hot chocolate wafting from the small caffés and pasticcerie. This was the life I led when I worked and lived in Piemonte. It was a new cuisine for me, being a Southern Italian girl, but one that I fell in love with, and have incorporated into my own winter menus. Therefore, I bring you 13 menus from *Winter in Piemonte*.

Italy has been called the most beautiful country on earth. It is a land of drama, from our breathtaking coastlines to our majestic mountains and volcanoes! And the people in Italy, especially Southern Italy, are dramatic, too, from our passion for our food to our incredible zest for life. We live each day to the fullest, in our love of food, and in our love of family life.

This is how I live my Italy, my Italian Sunday Dinners, and I hope you and your family enjoy them and make them part of your life, too, just as my family and I do. And as always, *tutti a tavola e buon appetito*!

My beloved Ponte Vecchio, where I raised my children. *Benvenuti alla mia tavola.*
(Welcome to my table!)

Winter in Piemonte

When I first moved to Piemonte, I wasn't sure I was in Italy. I accepted a position with a multinational company that moved me to Alessandria, a postwar city that resembled absolutely nothing of *my* Italy. Being 100 percent southern Italian I was accustomed to years of living with my parents in Rome, Naples, and Sicily, and, only as far north as Florence. In short, I was used to lots of sunshine, bougainvillea, beaches, and red sauces! Alessandria, on the other hand, greeted me with cloudy skies, dense fog, cold temperatures, and a lot of white food! I still remember my first Sunday afternoon in Alessandria, when my mother called me to make sure that I had arrived safely. I assured her that I had, but I told her I was not sure that I had landed in the right country! But soon I fell in love with the region's rich, hearty, and satisfying cuisine. Full of delicious cheeses, creamy risottos, and decadent desserts, my Piemontese menus are perfect for winter Sunday dinners next to the fireplace!

Lisa's Favorite Wines from Piemonte

Reds

Barolo DOCG: * Full bodied, garnet red, intense, excellent with the rich, comforting food of Piemonte.

Barbaresco DOCG: Great for cooking as well as drinking.

Grignolino: Light-bodied red from the hills of Piemonte—it's like a first cousin to a French beaujolais, and meant to be drunk young, fresh, and slightly chilled. The name comes from the Piemontese dialect for grape seed. Excellent with everything!

Nebbiolo d'Alba DOC: ** Made from the nebbiolo grape and named for the nebbia (Italian for fog), because Piemonte is very foggy. In the fall the fog rolls in every day during the harvest months.

Barbera DOC: from the Barbera grape, this wine is known for its full bodied flavor, excellent with Piemontese food.

Dolcetto: Considered an everyday table wine, like Barbera, Dolcetto is made from the Dolcetto grape, yet it is not sweet at all, as you might infer from the name (dolce means "sweet" in Italian). It is called Dolcetto because the low acidity gives this grape its sweetness when eaten right off the vine. During the vinification process, however, the tannins in the grape balance out the sweetness to produce a crisp, fresh wine with a bite. Also, due to its low acidity (much like the San Marzano tomato, which I use for my tomato sauce), Dolcetto can be made with less sugar, making it a lighter red than other Piemontese reds. It's a great value (about 6 euros in Italy!) and less than $20 in the United States. So indulge!

Whites

Gavi DOCG

Dessert Wines

Asti Spumante
Moscato d'Asti DOCG

---

* DOCG stands for *Denominazione di Origine Controllata e Garantita*, the highest classification of Italian wines. It means that production methods are strictly controlled and the quality of the wine in each bottle is guaranteed.

** DOC on an Italian wine label stands for *Denominazione di Origine Controllata*, and refers to government guarantees of the wine's origin and quality.

Menu 1

SERVES 8

Frutta Ripiena Stuffed Fruit

Linguine all'Aja Linguine with L'Aja

Bistecca in Glassa di Barbaresco Steak in Barbaresco Glaze

Crochette di Patate Potato Croquettes

Sfoglia Ripiena di Mela e Mandorle Apple-Almond Turnovers

This menu features l'aja, the classic Piemontese walnut sauce. It is absolutely delicious on a variety of foods: appetizers, pasta dishes, even meats. Here I use it in my favorite way—in a rich, creamy pasta sauce, with a little bit of arugula to give it just the right kick. Walnut sauce on pasta is one of the most decadent dishes you will ever enjoy. Whenever I prepare it, my children and I reminisce about my youngest son's 12th birthday, when we hiked in the Dolomite Mountains and stopped for lunch at a beautiful *refugio* ("lodge"). That's where we enjoyed this incredible sauce on ravioli—the experience of a lifetime—and I dream about it to this day!

Steak made with a *wonderful* reduction of Barbaresco, the Piemontese signature wine, is the perfect second act after Linguine with l'Aja. The food in this region is exactly like this menu—hearty and delicious!

Finish the meal with scrumptious, yet easy-to-make apple-almond turnovers. They're a perfect example of a recipe that even the most inexperienced cooks in your family, young or old, can help prepare. Cook together and eat together—that is what Sunday dinner is all about!

Buon cibo, buon vino, buoni amici! (Good food, good wine, good friends!)

Frutta Ripiena
Stuffed Fruit

Stuffed Figs

12 figs

6 tablespoons Port wine

8 ounces Gorgonzola cheese, imported from Italy

To prepare and stuff the figs: In a bowl combine the figs and Port wine. Cover the bowl and let the figs soak for 2 hours. Drain the figs from the port wine, and place them on a platter. Cut a slit across the top of each fig and form a small hollow inside the fig with the back of a teaspoon. Cut the Gorgonzola into 12 pieces and fill each fig with a piece of the cheese.

Stuffed Dates

12 dates

8 ounces mascarpone cheese, at room temperature

1 tablespoon heavy cream

2 teaspoons lemon peel, grated

2 tablespoons chopped walnuts

To prepare and stuff the dates: Remove the pits from the dates. Slice the dates lengthwise. Using a tablespoon, beat together the mascarpone cheese, heavy cream, and lemon peel in a small bowl. Fold in the chopped walnuts. Stuff the mixture into the dates. Arrange the dates and figs on a platter and serve.

Linguine all'Aja
Linguine with L'Aja

For l'Aja

1 cup cubed Italian white bread, crust removed

2 cups whole milk

1 cup walnuts, chopped

8 whole cloves of garlic

2 cups extra virgin olive oil

2 teaspoons Sicilian sea salt, fine

1 teaspoon freshly ground black pepper

For the Linguine

2 pounds linguine

2 bunches fresh arugula (approximately 12 ounces)

3 tablespoons unsalted butter

1 cup grated Parmigiano Reggiano

1. *To make l'aja:* Soak the bread in the milk for 30 minutes or until the bread has completely absorbed the milk. Place the soaked bread, walnuts, garlic, oil, salt, and pepper in a blender or food processor and puree.

2. *To complete the dish:* Bring a large pasta pot (6 to 8 quarts of water) to a rolling boil. Cook 2 pounds of linguine according to package directions. While the pasta is cooking, chop the arugula. Place the arugula, l'aja sauce, the butter, and the Parmigiano Reggiano in a large pasta bowl. Toss with the linguine and serve.

Bistecca in Glassa di Barbaresco
Steak in Barbaresco Glaze

For the Barbaresco Glaze

    3 cups Barbaresco wine

    4 whole shallots, peeled

    2 sage sprigs

    2 rosemary sprigs

For the Steak

    ½ cup unbleached flour

    2 teaspoons Sicilian sea salt, fine

    1 teaspoon freshly ground black pepper

    8 (8-ounce) sirloin steaks

    ½ cup extra virgin olive oil

1. *To make the glaze:* In a medium-size saucepan (approximately 2 quarts), bring the wine, shallots, sage sprigs, and rosemary sprigs to a boil for 3 to 4 minutes. Reduce heat to medium. Cook for 14 minutes, or until the liquid is reduced by half. Discard the shallots, sage, and rosemary. Set glaze aside.

2. *To prepare the steak:* In a shallow dish, such as a pie plate, place the unbleached flour with the salt and pepper. Dredge each sirloin steak in the flour on either side. You will need 2 large skillets. In each skillet, place ¼ cup of the extra virgin olive oil and heat until it is smoking, about 2 to 3 minutes. Over medium-high heat, cook 4 steaks in each pan for 2 minutes on either side or until browned. Pour the Barbaresco glaze over the steaks. Cook for 3 minutes.

3. Transfer to a platter, drizzle the glaze on the steaks, and serve.

Crochette di Patate
Potato Croquettes

2 pounds white boiling potatoes, peeled

3 large eggs, separated; reserve the egg whites

¾ cup grated Parmigiano Reggiano

2 teaspoons Sicilian sea salt, fine

1 teaspoon freshly ground black pepper

3 ounces mozzarella, cut into ¼-inch cubes

1½ cups dried breadcrumbs

Canola oil, for frying

1. In a large saucepan filled with water, bring the water to a rolling boil and cook the potatoes until soft, approximately 15 minutes. Drain the potatoes and mash them with a potato masher or in a mixer. Transfer the mashed potatoes to a large bowl. Stir the egg yolks and the Parmigiano cheese into the potato mixture and add the salt and pepper.

2. Using your hands, shape 3 tablespoons of the potato mixture into a 3 × 1-inch log and place it on a platter. Repeat until you've used up all the potatoes. Make a small hole in the top of each log and insert a small cube of mozzarella. Cover the cheese with the potato mixture.

3. Beat the reserved egg whites until frothy and place them in a shallow dish, such as a pie plate. Place the breadcrumbs in another shallow dish, such as a pie plate. Dip the potato logs into the egg whites first, then roll them in the breadcrumbs, and place them on a wire rack to dry for 20 minutes.

4. Pour about ¾-inch of canola oil into a large, deep frying pan over medium heat. Fry the crochette until they're golden brown. Drain them on paper towels and serve.

LISA'S TIP
The potato mixture can be made a day ahead and refrigerated, if desired.

Sfoglia Ripiena di Mela e Mandorle
Apple-Almond Turnovers

4 large Braeburn, Honeycrisp, or Granny Smith apples, peeled, halved, and cored

½ cup apple cider vinegar

½ cup sugar

1 teaspoon pure vanilla extract

1 (14-ounce) package frozen puff pastry, thawed

4 ounces almond paste (imported from Italy; the paste comes in a tube, and can be found at most major grocery stores)

4 tablespoons unsalted butter, cut into small cubes

1 large egg, beaten

Granulated sugar, for decoration

1. Preheat the oven to 400°F.

2. In a large saucepan, approximately 4 quarts, place the apples, vinegar, sugar, ¾ cup water, and vanilla. Cook for 30 minutes over medium heat.

3. Remove the pan from the stove and let the mixture cool. If the apple mixture is watery, drain off some of the liquid—it should resemble applesauce.

4. Roll out the puff pastry on a flat surface to a 14 × 12-inch rectangle and place the puff pastry on a baking sheet lined with parchment paper or a silpat. (A silpat is a nonstick silicone baking mat available at all cooking and major department stores.) Spread a thin layer of the almond paste on the puff pastry. Place the apple mixture horizontally at the center of the puff pastry. Place the butter cubes on the apple mixture.

5. Fold both ends of the puff pastry in over the apple mixture until the puff pastry meets in the center. Crimp the puff pastry with your fingers. Brush the puff pastry with the beaten egg and sprinkle with granulated sugar to decorate. With a paring knife, cut 4 to 6 two-inch-long slits on either side of the seam of the puff pastry to vent the turnover. Bake for 30 minutes.

Menu 2

SERVES 8

Polpettine di Formaggio e Noci Cheese and Walnut Patties
Zuppa d' Inverno Winter Soup
Scalloppine di Vitello Impanato Breaded Veal Scaloppine
Punti di Asparagi con Fontina Asparagus Tips with Fontina
Crostata di Olio di Oliva e Pera Olive Oil and Pear Crostata

Everyone is always surprised by how many soups I prepare, and how many soups we eat in Italy! Zuppa is so popular—and in northern Italy, the zuppe are hearty and warming—the ultimate comfort food! Winter Soup, in this menu, is chock-full of healthy and satisfying vegetables.

Veal Scaloppine is a classic dish of the Piemonte region. The delicate veal, wrapped in crunchy, golden breadcrumbs, is irresistible and comforting.

Fontina cheese, like Gorgonzola, is a northern Italian cheese with a delicate flavor that melts and pairs beautifully with delicate asparagus.

I love desserts made with olive oil, rather than butter, because the flavor is so intense and smooth. Here you have the classic Italian *crostata* (a baked tart or pie) featuring a wonderful pear filling.

Buon appetito!

Polpettine di Formaggio e Noci
Cheese and Walnut Patties

16 ounces fresh, soft goat cheese

3 cups grated Parmigiano Reggiano

1½ cups walnuts, finely chopped

2 cups breadcrumbs

½ cup extra virgin olive oil

2 teaspoons spicy mustard, either imported Italian, or French, such as Dijon

1 teaspoon Sicilian sea salt, fine

½ teaspoon ground black pepper

1. In a medium bowl, using a wooden spoon, mix together the goat cheese, Parmigiano cheese, and chopped walnuts to form a thick paste. Shape the paste into balls, approximately the size of cherries, and flatten them slightly to make little patties. Coat the patties in the breadcrumbs.

2. Place half the olive oil (¼ cup) in a large frying pan and fry the patties for 5 minutes, turning them over once or twice until they are golden all over.

3. In a small bowl with a fork, mix the remaining ¼ cup olive oil with the mustard, salt, and pepper.

4. Place the hot cheese-and-walnut patties on a plate. Drizzle a little of the olive oil/mustard dressing on top, and serve.

Zuppa d'Inverno
Winter Soup

4 pounds mussels, in the shell, scrubbed

1 cup white wine

½ cup extra virgin olive oil

¼ cup Italian flat leaf parsley, chopped

4 garlic cloves, peeled and chopped

3 pounds broccoli rabe, chopped, including the stem

1½ heads escarole, cut in long strips

1 pound gold potatoes, such as Yukon gold, peeled and cut into 1-inch cubes

2 teaspoons Sicilian sea salt, fine

1 teaspoon freshly ground black pepper

1 teaspoon crushed red pepper flakes

2 cups ditalini pasta

1. In a large saucepan (4 quarts), combine the mussels, wine, ¼ cup of extra virgin olive oil, parsley, and ¾ cup water. Simmer and cook until the mussels open (for at least 8 minutes). Transfer the mussels to a bowl using a slotted spoon and save the wine liquid. Discard any mussels that do not open. When the mussels are cool, open them all the way and remove each mussel from the shell. Set aside.

2. Bring 4 cups of water to a boil in a saucepan or a pasta pot. In a large Dutch oven or a heavy pot, place the remaining ¼ cup of extra virgin olive oil and the garlic, and cook until translucent, approximately 3 minutes. Add the broccoli rabe and escarole, and then stir in the potatoes. Cook until all the greens are wilted and the vegetables are well coated in the olive oil, approximately 5 to 6 minutes. Add the wine mixture, in which you cooked the mussels, and then add the 4 cups of water that you just brought to a boil. Add the salt, pepper, and crushed red pepper flakes.

3. Simmer the soup for 10 to 15 minutes. Continue to simmer and stir occasionally, making sure that the potatoes are cooked through. Pour in the ditalini pasta and cook for 10 to 12 minutes more. Serve with a drizzle of olive oil.

Scaloppine di Vitello Impanato
Breaded Veal Scaloppine

> 2 pounds veal scaloppine, sliced to ¼-inch thickness (about 8 pieces)
> Unbleached flour, for dredging
> 4 eggs, beaten
> 3 cups breadcrumbs
> ½ cup extra virgin olive oil
> 4 shallots, finely chopped
> 1 teaspoon Sicilian sea salt, fine

1. Dip each piece of veal scaloppine in the flour, then in the beaten eggs, and then in the breadcrumbs.

2. In a large frying pan, heat the olive oil. Add the shallots and sauté until translucent. Remove the shallots from the pan and set them aside.

3. Arrange as many veal scaloppine as you can fit into the same pan and cook until they're golden brown on both sides. Place the veal on paper towels to drain.

4. To serve, top with the sautéed shallots and sea salt.

NOTE: The recipe below, for Asparagus Tips with Fontina, is used to top the veal and shallots. See instructions below for assembling the dish.

Punti di Asparagi con Fontina
Asparagus Tips with Fontina

- 4 tablespoons unsalted butter
- 4 shallots, finely chopped
- 2 pounds fresh asparagus tips
- ½ cup vegetable broth
- 12 ounces sliced Fontina cheese, imported from Italy

1. In a large frying pan, melt the butter over a low flame. Add the shallots and sauté until they become translucent, for approximately five minutes. Add the asparagus tips and broth, and cook until the broth reduces to about half of what it was, but the asparagus tips are still firm.

2. *To assemble the dish:* On a large platter arrange the veal scaloppine (recipe above), top with the asparagus, and layer the fontina cheese slices on the asparagus tips. The cheese will melt slightly from the heat of the asparagus. Serve warm.

My beautiful 94 year old mother, snapping the asparagus!

This Is Sunday Dinner

Crostata di Olio di Oliva e Pera
Olive Oil and Pear Crostata

For the Crust

¾ cup walnuts, chopped

1 cup cornmeal, very fine (best if it is imported polenta from Italy)

2½ cups unbleached flour

½ cup sugar

½ teaspoon Sicilian sea salt, fine

¾ cup extra virgin olive oil

1 large egg

½ cup water, very cold

For the Filling

3 pounds ripe pears (Bosc or d'Anjou)

4 tablespoons fresh lemon juice

6 tablespoons sugar

3 tablespoons unbleached flour

1. *To make the pastry:* In a food processor or a blender, combine the walnuts, cornmeal, flour, sugar, and salt, and pulse until the walnuts are ground very coarsely. Pour the olive oil into the blender or food processor and blend until the oil is completely distributed through the dough. Add the egg and pulse again. Then sprinkle onto the dough 8 or 10 drops of ice water. Remove the dough and form it into one big ball.

2. Break the dough into 2 balls: one ⅔ of the dough and one ⅓ of the dough. Flatten each ball into a disk, roll the large ball out to a diameter slightly larger than the pie plate, and place it in a 10-inch pie plate. Set aside the small ball of dough.

3. Preheat the oven to 375°F.

4. To make the filling and prepare the crostata: Peel and core the pears, and then cut them into long, thin slices. Place the slices in a medium-size bowl and toss with the lemon juice and sugar. Then sprinkle the pears with the flour and toss until they're well coated. Spread the fruit mixture into the pie crust.

5. Roll out the small ball of dough and cut it into ¼-inch-wide strips. Place the strips on top of the crostata in a lattice pattern. Place the pie dish in the preheated oven and bake for 35 minutes until golden. Serve warm.

Menu 3

SERVES 8

Triangoli di Mortadella Mortadella Triangles

Risotto di Formaggio Fondente Risotto in Melted Cheese

Pollo Fritto Marinato Marinated Fried Chicken

Bietola con Aglio e Peperoncino Schiacciato
Swiss Chard with Garlic and Crushed Red Pepper

Torta di Mela e Zucca Pumpkin and Apple Cake

Mortadella is a bit like Italian bologna. The difference between American bologna and mortadella is that pieces of fat, each of which is about the size of a pea, are visible in mortadella. In addition, mortadella is much wider than bologna (it's approximately 8 or 9 inches in diameter). When you go into a deli or a small grocery shop in Italy, the mortadella is cut fresh for you. It is never sold presliced or prepackaged. When my youngest son Guido was not even 18 months old, and did not speak yet, he would take his little hand and imitate the motion of the meat slicer cutting the mortadella to tell me that he wanted to go to the deli, down the street from our home in Florence, Italy, to buy the mortadella for his snack. He still eats it to this day!

The Risotto in Melted Cheese in this menu brings back so many memories for me. When I first moved to Piemonte, nothing was familiar. Everything was foreign, and I barely felt as if I was in Italy. Being a southern Italian girl, I was used to my red sauces, lots of stuffed peppers, and Sicilian desserts. In Piemonte, I saw nothing but rice dishes, lots of cheese, and polenta. On a cold January Sunday, when the snow is falling outside, nothing is more comforting than a bowl of creamy Italian risotto with gooey melted cheese.

When I moved to Piemonte, I lived in the city of Alessandria. Alessandria is known for its Bagna Cauda (see Menu 6, page 32), as well as the delicious chicken dish in this menu—a marinated fried chicken called Pollo in Carpione. I love the carpione sauce, not only on chicken, but also on fish and vegetables.

When I lived in Alessandria, one of my favorite things to do on a Sunday afternoon was to go to the picturesque town of Asti. Yes, this is the town where the bubbly sweet drink called Asti Spumante was born! I loved the churches in Asti, as well as the town square, and most of all I loved a small, amazing Sicilian bakery in this Piemontese city. I immediately became friends with the owners, a lovely couple from Sicily, and even though I lived way up in Piemonte, up in the Alps and hours away from my beloved island of Sicily, at least on Sundays I could still indulge in cannoli! In this Sicilian bakery, they also made many delicious Piemontese desserts. Among my favorites was Pumpkin and Apple Cake, which always brings back fond memories of fall in the Midwest, where I was born and raised.

Triangoli di Mortadella
Mortadella Triangles

- 1 cup whole milk ricotta
- 2 teaspoons horseradish
- 1 tablespoon Italian flat leaf parsley, chopped
- 1 teaspoon Sicilian sea salt, fine
- ½ teaspoon freshly ground black pepper
- 6 slices mortadella

1. In a bowl, stir together the ricotta and the horseradish. Stir in the parsley. Season with the salt and pepper.

2. Place 1 mortadella slice on a flat surface and spread with ¼ of the ricotta mixture. Then, top with another mortadella slice. Press down gently. Spread another layer of the ricotta mixture and 1 more slice of the mortadella.

3. Cut into 4 pie-shaped wedges. Repeat with the other 3 slices of mortadella and serve.

Risotto di Formaggio Fondente
Risotto in Melted Cheese

- 4 cups Arborio rice, imported from Italy
- 6 tablespoons unsalted butter
- 4 fresh sage leaves
- 1 pound Fontina cheese, cubed, imported from Italy
- ½ cup Parmigiano Reggiano, grated
- 1 teaspoon Sicilian sea salt, fine
- 1 teaspoon freshly ground black pepper

1. Follow the instructions on the box of Arborio rice, cooking it until the rice is al dente. There should be no liquid in the rice when it is done.

2. In a medium-size frying pan, melt the butter, and then add the sage, stirring, until the sage begins to turn color and wilt, and the butter begins to turn brown.

3. In a large serving bowl, combine the hot rice, the melted butter–and–sage mixture, the Fontina cheese and Parmigiano cheese, and the salt and pepper. Toss well and serve.

Pollo Fritto Marinato
Marinated Fried Chicken

For the Chicken

 1 cup extra virgin olive oil

 2 pounds boneless, skinless chicken breasts

 4 eggs, beaten

 2 cups breadcrumbs

For the Carpione Sauce

 4 tablespoons extra virgin olive oil

 2 medium-size red onions, sliced

 2 cups white wine

 2 cups apple cider vinegar

 1 teaspoon Sicilian sea salt, fine

 ½ teaspoon freshly ground black pepper

1. *To make the chicken:* Heat the olive oil in a large frying pan. Dip the chicken breasts in the beaten eggs and then dredge them in the breadcrumbs. Fry the breasts until they're golden brown, approximately 4–6 minutes on each side. Drain the chicken breasts on paper towels and then transfer them to a large ceramic casserole dish.

2. *To make the sauce:* Place 4 tablespoons of extra virgin olive oil in a medium-size frying pan and sauté the onions until they are transparent, for approximately 5 minutes. Add the wine and vinegar, salt and pepper, and simmer for 4–5 minutes.

3. Pour the onion mixture over the fried chicken breasts and serve.

LISA'S TIP
Make a double batch of the Carpione Sauce and freeze half to use later on vegetables or fish.

Bietola con Aglio e Peperoncino Schiacciato
Swiss Chard with Garlic and Crushed Red Pepper

¼ cup extra virgin olive oil

4 cloves of garlic, chopped

4 large bunches of Swiss chard, coarsely chopped, stems removed

1 teaspoon crushed red pepper flakes

Place the extra virgin olive oil in a large frying pan over medium heat. Sauté the garlic for 1 minute. Add all the Swiss chard to the frying pan and cook it for approximately 2–3 minutes, until the leaves are bright green and not too wilted. Add the crushed red pepper and serve.

Torta di Mela e Zucca
Pumpkin and Apple Cake

Butter, for greasing the baking dish

1 cup Marsala wine

½ cup raisins

10 dried figs, chopped

4 cups diced pumpkin (if using canned pumpkin, use 2 cups)

3 cups Braeburn or Honeycrisp apples, peeled and diced

1½ cups whole milk

1½ cups sugar

3 eggs, beaten

6 ounces unsweetened chocolate (if it's in a baking bar, chop it coarsely or use unsweetened chocolate chips)

4 ounces bittersweet chocolate (if it's in a bar, chop it coarsely or use bittersweet chocolate chips)

1 cup amaretto cookies, crushed

1 teaspoon grated lemon zest

1 teaspoon pure vanilla extract

6 tablespoons light rum

1. Preheat the oven to 325°F.

2. Butter a 13 × 9-inch heatproof glass baking dish.

3. In a small bowl, place the Marsala wine and soak the raisins and figs for 15–20 minutes. Drain the fruit and set it aside.

4. Place the pumpkin, apples, milk, and sugar in a large 6-quart pot, and cook over low heat. Simmer the mixture for approximately 15 minutes. (If you're using fresh pumpkin, make sure the pumpkin is cooked all the way through before adding the next ingredients.)

5. Mix the eggs, all the chocolate, the amaretto cookies, lemon zest, vanilla, rum, and the figs and raisins into the pumpkin mixture. Pour the batter into the prepared dish and bake for 2–2½ hours until a toothpick comes out clean.

This Is Sunday Dinner

There are few traditions more prized in Piemonte than hunting for truffles! Here, with my trusted, experienced guide, Ermanno, and his trained dog, Mara, we had a successful day finding these earthy treasures!

Menu 4

Zucca Fritta Fried Squash
Lasagne con Brocoletti e Salsiccie Sausage and Broccoli Rabe Lasagne
Cotoletta di Arista Impanato Breaded Pork Cutlets
Insalata d'Inverno con Pecorino Winter Salad with Pecorino
Prugne al Vino Plums in Wine

In the winter months, the combination of sausage and broccoli rabe is enjoyed all over Italy. I first had this classic combo on the island of Sardinia and included it in my first cookbook, *Whatever Happened to Sunday Dinner?* Until I moved to Piemonte, though, I had only eaten sausage and broccoli rabe on short pasta, which is delicious. But in Piemonte, when I first tasted Lasagne with Sausage and Broccoli Rabe in a creamy, velvety, *besciamella* sauce, the combination was taken to a whole new level of comfort food!

Likewise, the Breaded Pork Cutlets in this menu are comforting and delicious, thanks to the Parmigiano cheese added to the breadcrumbs.

The refreshing, Winter Salad with Pecorino, a unique combination of apples, arugula, and endive is the perfect complement to this winter menu. Walnut oil, instead of olive oil, is commonly used in salads in northern Italy, and gives them a great, nutty flavor.

Fruit, in some form, is the most popular way to enjoy dessert all over Italy. Even we Italian Americans always have fruit on our Sunday dinner table before we indulge in a sweet dessert. Plums in Wine, served with vanilla gelato, are the perfect ending to this delicious Piemontese menu.

Benvenuti a tavola! (Welcome to the table!)

Zucca Fritta
Fried Squash

4 large eggs

3 tablespoons sugar

2 teaspoons Sicilian sea salt, fine

2 cups breadcrumbs

1 cup ground Italian amaretto cookies

Approximately 3 cups canola oil, for frying

4 pounds butternut squash, peeled, seeded, and cut in ½-inch-wide x 4-inch-long slices

Zest of 1 orange

1. In a shallow dish, such as a pie plate, beat the eggs. In another shallow dish, place the sugar, salt, breadcrumbs, and ground amaretto cookies.

2. Place the canola oil in a large frying pan and heat over medium to high heat until small bubbles start to form around the periphery of the pan.

3. Dip each slice of squash, first in the egg, and then in the breadcrumb mixture, coating it evenly. Place the squash slices in the hot oil until they're golden on both sides, approximately 5–6 minutes. Repeat until all the slices are cooked.

4. Place the fried squash on a platter, top it with the orange zest, and serve.

Lasagne con Brocoletti e Salsiccie
Sausage and Broccoli Rabe Lasagne

For the Sausage and Broccoli Rabe Filling

2 tablespoons unsalted butter, melted

1 pound broccoli rabe

½ cup extra virgin olive oil

8 garlic cloves, chopped

1 teaspoon crushed red pepper flakes

2 pounds sweet Italian sausage, loose (not in the casing)

½ cup breadcrumbs

For the Besciamella Sauce

1 stick unsalted butter

½ cup unbleached flour

3 cups whole milk

½ teaspoon Sicilian sea salt, fine

½ teaspoon freshly ground black pepper

1 cup Parmigiano Reggiano, grated

For the Lasagne

2 pounds imported Italian lasagne of good quality, such as De Cecco or DelVerde

2 cups Fontina cheese, imported from Italy, grated

1 cup Parmigiano Reggiano, grated

1. To prepare the sausage and broccoli rabe: Place the melted butter in a deep lasagne pan. Chop the broccoli rabe. In an 8-quart pot of boiling water, cook the broccoli rabe until tender, about 5 minutes. Drain well in a colander and set aside.

2. Add the oil to a large frying pan and cook the garlic, and red pepper flakes, for approximately 3 minutes. Add the sausage and cook, breaking up the sausage with a wooden spoon until the inside of the sausage is no longer pink, approximately 6 minutes. Stir in the broccoli rabe and cook for 4 more minutes. Stir in the breadcrumbs. Remove from the heat. Set aside.

3. To make the besciamella sauce: In another large frying pan, melt the stick of butter and stir in the flour until it is completely absorbed by the butter to form a coarse-textured paste. Add the milk to the flour-and-butter mixture in a slow stream, stirring constantly with a wooden spoon until it forms a velvety, thick white sauce. Stir in the salt and pepper and then remove from heat.

4. *To prepare the lasagne:* Preheat the oven to 325°F. Cook the lasagne according to the instructions on the package. Place two layers of lasagne on the bottom of the prepared pan. Top with the broccoli rabe and sausage filling, then the besciamella sauce, then Fontina and Parmigiano. Repeat until you end with a layer of lasagne. Pour the remaining besciamella on top of the lasagne and bake for 20 minutes.

LISA'S TIP
I like a lot of besciamella in my lasagne, so I usually double the recipe for the besciamella so the lasagne is nice and creamy.

Cotoletta di Arista Impanato
Breaded Pork Cutlets

    4 eggs, beaten
    ¼ cup whole milk
    3 cups breadcrumbs
    1 cup Parmigiano Reggiano, grated
    ¼ cup Italian flat leaf parsley, chopped
    ¼ cup extra virgin olive oil
    6 cloves garlic, chopped
    8 pork cutlets

1. Preheat the oven to 325°F.

2. In a bowl, beat together the eggs and milk.

3. In another bowl, mix together the breadcrumbs, Parmigiano, and parsley.

4. In a large frying pan heat the olive oil. Stir in the garlic and cook until golden. Remove the garlic.

5. Dip each pork cutlet into the egg and milk mixture, and then into the breadcrumbs. Place the cutlets in the frying pan over medium heat and cook until they're golden brown, approximately 5 minutes on each side.

6. Transfer the pork cutlets to a large, ovenproof casserole. Cook for 30 minutes in the preheated oven and serve.

Insalata d'Inverno con Pecorino
Winter Salad with Pecorino

1 cup walnut oil

6 tablespoons red wine vinegar, excellent quality, preferably imported from Italy

1 teaspoon Sicilian sea salt, fine

1 teaspoon freshly ground black pepper

4 bunches arugula

4 Belgian endive, cored and cut into 1-inch-long pieces

3 apples, cored and cut into thin slices

½ pound Pecorino Romano, shaved paper thin

1. In a measuring cup combine walnut oil, vinegar, salt, and pepper.

2. In a large salad bowl place the arugula, endive, and apple slices. Toss with the oil and vinegar mixture.

3. Place in 8 salad bowls and garnish with the Pecorino shavings.

Prugne al Vino
Plums in Wine

3 cups white wine

1 cup sugar

3 cinnamon sticks

Rind of 2 lemons, thinly sliced

16 plums, pitted and halved

½ gallon vanilla gelato

1. In a large saucepan, approximately 4 to 6 quarts, place the wine and sugar. Cook over medium heat, stirring until the sugar has dissolved into the wine. Add the cinnamon sticks and thin strips of lemon rind. Add the plums. Reduce the heat to a simmer and cook the mixture for approximately 12 to 15 minutes.

2. Remove the plums with a slotted spoon and place them in a medium-size serving bowl.

3. Continue to cook the syrup in the saucepan until it is thick enough to coat the back of a wooden spoon.

4. To serve, place 3 or 4 plum halves in a small bowl, top with one scoop of the vanilla gelato, and drizzle the plum syrup on top.

Menu 5

SERVES 8

Bruschetta Verde con Fontina Bruschetta with Greens and Fontina
Lasagne in Bianco White Lasagne
Stufato di Manzo Piemontese Piemontese Stewed Beef
Insalata di Mela, Finocchio e Sedano Fennel, Celery, and Apple Salad
Biscotti alla Nocciola Hazelnut Cookies

In my introduction to Piemonte, I mentioned that I was surprised not to find my beloved southern Italian red sauces when I arrived in northern Italy, and all the food seemed white! This menu features one item of white food I would not change for the world: White Lasagne. Definitely Italian comfort food, the besciamella sauce and the Fontina and Parmigiano cheeses make this dish a creamy, gooey slice of heaven, ideal for a cold, winter Sunday! And the great part of making lasagne is that everyone can be involved—no matter how experienced. Children have great fun layering the cheeses.

This menu ends with a perfect example of simple, rustic Italian baking. With only four ingredients, Hazelnut Cookies are delicious and easy to make. They've become a staple in my kitchen.

Sempre famiglia! (Always family!)

Bruschetta Verde con Fontina
Bruschetta with Greens and Fontina

- 1 loaf of ciabatta (flat, wide Italian bread, sold at all bread shops and in most grocery stores)
- 2 cloves garlic, cut in half
- ¼ cup extra virgin olive oil
- 1 pound fresh spinach
- 1½ cups Fontina cheese, shredded

1. Slice the loaf of ciabatta into ¾-inch-wide slices. Place the bread on a baking sheet under the broiler, set to high, and toast the bread until it is golden brown. Remove it from oven. Rub the cut garlic cloves across the surface of toasted bread slices. Discard the garlic.

2. Preheat the oven to 325°F.

3. In a medium-size saucepan, pour the extra virgin olive oil. Sauté the spinach until it wilts. Drain the spinach very well so that there is no liquid (you can also use paper towels to absorb all the liquid). Arrange the sautéed spinach on the toasted garlic bread and top with the Fontina.

4. Put the bread into the preheated oven for 2–3 minutes until the cheese melts. Serve.

Lasagne in Bianco
White Lasagne

2 pounds excellent-quality lasagne,
imported from Italy

For the besciamella sauce

4 tablespoons unsalted butter

½ cup unbleached flour

4 cups whole milk

1 teaspoon Sicilian sea salt, fine

1 teaspoons nutmeg, grated

For the Lasagne:

12 ounces prosciutto cotto, thinly sliced

12 ounces Fontina cheese, thinly sliced

1½ cups Parmigiano Reggiano, grated

1 teaspoon nutmeg, grated

1. Preheat the oven to 325°F.

2. *To make the pasta:* Put a large 8-quart pasta pot on the stove and bring it to a rolling boil. Cook the lasagne according to the directions on the package. Drain the lasagne in a colander. Immediately place the drained lasagne on clean cotton or linen kitchen towels, on your kitchen table. Lay the lasagne flat on the towels, so they do not overlap, and cover them with another layer of towels.

3. *To make the besciamella sauce:* Melt the butter in a large frying pan. Slowly add the flour and mix it into the butter with a wooden spoon until all the flour has been incorporated into the butter. Slowly begin to pour in the milk (see Note). While the milk is thickening slightly in the pan, add the salt and grated nutmeg. The besciamella should coat the back of a wooden spoon, but still be thin enough to spoon with a ladle over the lasagne.

4. Immediately remove the besciamella from the heat.

5. *To assemble the lasagne:* Ladle some of the besciamella into the bottom of a deep, 13 × 9-inch lasagne pan, then add 2 layers of lasagne noodles, another layer of besciamella, a layer of prosciutto, and a layer of Fontina. Sprinkle some of the Parmigiano on top. Add another layer of lasagne, besciamella, prosciutto, Fontina, and Parmigiano. Repeat until you have filled the pan. You should end with a layer of lasagne topped with besciamella and Parmigiano. Cook the lasagne for 30 minutes until the cheeses on top are completely melted and golden brown.

★ Note: Although the besciamella sauce in this recipe uses the same ingredients in all my recipes for besciamella, you will notice that the proportion of milk to the flour and butter is much greater. That's because you want a thinner besciamella to keep the lasagne from getting too dry as it bakes. In white lasagne, the besciamella is the only sauce used—it is not mixed with tomato sauce—so it needs to be thin.

Stufato di Manzo Piemontese
Piemontese Stewed Beef

  4 pounds chuck roast, cleaned and
    cut into 2-inch cubes

  1 cup, plus 1 tablespoon, extra
    virgin olive oil

  ¼ cup sage, chopped

  ¼ cup thyme, chopped

  ¼ cup rosemary, chopped

  2 teaspoons Sicilian sea salt, fine

  1 teaspoon freshly ground black pepper

  3 large carrots, peeled

  3 large celery stalks

  3 white onions

  5 tablespoons unsalted butter

  4 bay leaves

  1 bottle Barolo wine, excellent quality

  2 cups vegetable or beef bouillon,
    excellent quality

1. Place all the cubed meat in a large bowl and coat with ½ cup (8 tablespoons) of olive oil. Add the chopped herbs, 1 teaspoon of the salt, and the pepper, and mix very well, using your hands. Allow the meat to marinate for 30 minutes.

2. Chop the carrots, celery, and onions.

3. In a large frying pan, melt 3 tablespoons of the butter over medium heat and add approximately 6 tablespoons of olive oil. Sear the chuck roast until all the pieces are brown on the outside, approximately 8–10 minutes.

4. Transfer the meat to a large bowl. Add 2 more tablespoons of butter and 3 more tablespoons of the olive oil to the frying pan, and sauté the carrots, celery, and onions (the *soffritto*, as we call it in Italian) until the mixture becomes golden, approximately 6 minutes. Add the remaining 1 teaspoon salt.

5. Transfer the meat-and-vegetable mixture to a large 6-quart pot. Add ⅔ of the bottle of Barolo and the vegetable or beef stock to the pot. Bring the mixture to a low simmer and cook for 2–2½ hours over a low flame. Serve with Barolo.

Insalata di Mela, Finocchio e Sedano
Fennel, Celery, and Apple Salad

    1 cup plain, organic yogurt, excellent
        quality, such as Greek yogurt
    2 tablespoons chives, chopped
    1 teaspoon Sicilian sea salt, fine
    1 teaspoon freshly ground black
        pepper
    4 fennel bulbs, fronds removed
    2 green apples
    2 celery hearts

1. *To prepare the dressing:* In a medium-size bowl, mix the yogurt and chives, and season with salt and pepper. Set aside.

2. Slice the fennel, and core and slice the apples. Slice the celery hearts into rounds.

3. Combine all ingredients with the yogurt dressing.

Biscotti alla Nocciola
Hazelnut Cookies

    ¾ cup hazelnuts
    1 cup unbleached flour
    ½ cup sugar
    1 stick unsalted butter, cold and
        cut into squares

1. On a small baking sheet, toast the hazelnuts in a preheated 350°F oven for 5 minutes. Let the nuts cool completely.

2. In either a blender or a food processor, chop the nuts until finely ground. In a medium bowl, add the nuts to the flour and sugar until well combined. In a stand mixer, or with a hand mixer, mix the butter with the flour and nut mixture and process until the dough can be formed into a ball.

3. Divide the dough into 2 or 3 pieces and shape the cookie dough into logs, approximately 1 inch in diameter. Wrap each log in plastic wrap and chill for 1 hour.

4. Slice the logs into ½-inch slices and arrange on 2 baking sheets. Bake at 350°F for 12 minutes.

Menu 6

SERVES 8

Bagna Cauda Piemontese Dipping Sauce
Penne con Zucca Invernale Penne with Winter Squash
Filetto alla Gorgonzola Filet Mignon with Gorgonzola
Cipolline Caramellizati Caramelized Cipolline
Torta di Noci Walnut Cake

Bagna cauda, meaning "Piemontese Dipping Sauce," is fun for everyone at the table! Dipping raw veggies into a rich olive oil–and–butter sauce is a wonderful example of Piemonte cuisine, which combines a warm, comforting sauce with healthy veggies.

Living in Piemonte, I vastly expanded my knowledge and use of squash and other winter vegetables. Squash is a typical northern vegetable—hearty, versatile, and definitely a northern Italian comfort food served on pasta, as in this dish.

Cheeses are plentiful in this part of Italy, and Gorgonzola is a perfect example of a rich, northern Italian cheese that becomes creamy when used as a sauce. Combined with a filet, there is nothing more decadent!

When my children were little, one of their favorite vegetables was cipolline, a round, delicate-tasting, disk-shaped onion. Caramelizing is a delicious way to prepare them, as the savory sweet sauce makes a nice contrast to the bite of the cipolline.

What made me really fall in love with Piemonte were the desserts. The hearty walnut cake in this menu exemplifies the region's food, which can only be described as rich and wholly satisfying!

Tutti a tavola! (Everyone to the table!)

Bagna Cauda
Piemontese Dipping Sauce

- ¾ cup extra virgin olive oil
- 10 garlic cloves, peeled and finely chopped
- 4 ounces anchovy fillets with the liquid
- 6 tablespoons unsalted butter
- 1 cup raw carrots, peeled and cut into 4-inch spears
- 1 cup raw red and yellow bell peppers, cleaned and cut into spears
- 1 cup cleaned celery sticks, cut into 4-inch spears
- 1 loaf Italian country rustic bread (page 186), sliced into 1-inch-thick slices

1. In a medium saucepan, combine the extra virgin olive oil, garlic, and anchovies, with their liquid. Cook over medium heat for approximately 6 minutes and while cooking mash the anchovies with a fork. Add the butter until the butter is completely melted.

2. Pour the sauce into a fondue pot or a heat-resistant bowl that you can set over a candle or another warming device.

3. Dip the raw vegetables and crusty bread into the sauce and enjoy.

Penne con Zucca Invernale
Penne with Winter Squash

- 6 tablespoons unsalted butter
- 6 tablespoons extra virgin olive oil
- 2 white onions, chopped
- 4 cloves garlic, chopped
- 2 pounds winter squash, cubed (or use butternut or acorn squash or pumpkin)
- 1 cup vegetable bouillon
- ¼ cup Italian flat leaf parsley, chopped
- 1 teaspoon Sicilian sea salt, fine
- 1 teaspoon freshly ground black pepper
- 2 pounds penne rigate (excellent quality, such as De Cecco, Racconto, Del Verde, or Garafolo)
- ½ cup Parmigiano Reggiano, grated

1. In a large saucepan, heat the butter and the oil. Sauté the onions and garlic until they're translucent. Add the squash and cook for 3 to 4 minutes. Add the bouillon, parsley, and salt and cook for 20 minutes on low heat, stirring occasionally. The sauce will cook down almost into a puree. Add the pepper.

2. Meanwhile, cook the penne according to the instructions on the package and toss with the squash puree. Top with the Parmigiano Reggiano.

Filetto alla Gorgonzola
Filet Mignon with Gorgonzola

    6 tablespoons extra virgin olive oil

    8 filets mignon, approximately
       6 ounces each

    1 tablespoon freshly ground black
       pepper

    Dried rosemary

    ½ cup white wine

    8 generous tablespoons of Italian
       Gorgonzola, excellent quality

    5 tablespoons heavy cream

    2 tablespoons unsalted butter

    ½ cup beef bouillon, excellent quality

1. Place 4 tablespoons of the extra virgin olive oil in a large, heavy frying pan over a medium to high flame. When the oil is hot, after approximately 1 minute, sear the filets on each side for no more than 2 minutes each side, until they are brown. Remove the filets from the stove and place them on a platter. Cover both sides of the filets with a generous amount of black pepper and dried rosemary. Cover with aluminum foil.

2. Add the remaining 2 tablespoons olive oil to the frying pan and blend all the drippings from the filets, and the salt and pepper, with the oil. Pour in the wine and allow it to bubble in the pan, over medium to high heat, until it has reduced by at least half. Turn the heat down, spoon in the Gorgonzola and blend it into the liquids in the pan with a wooden spoon. When the cheese has become liquidy, pour in the cream.

3. Place the filets mignon back in the frying pan with the cream and cheese sauce. Cook the filets for 2 more minutes on each side, and then re-plate them, topping the filets with the gorgonzola sauce.

Cipolline Caramellizati
Caramelized Cipolline

    1 teaspoon dried thyme

    3 teaspoons sugar

    1 teaspoon Sicilian sea salt, fine

    2 tablespoons extra virgin olive oil

    2 tablespoons balsamic vinegar,
       excellent quality

    2 pounds cipolline onions, exterior
       skins removed

1. Preheat the oven to 400°F. In a glass measuring cup, whisk together the thyme, sugar, sea salt, olive oil, and balsamic vinegar.

2. In a medium to large bowl, place the cleaned cipolline onions and coat them with the oil and vinegar mixture.

3. Arrange the onions in a 13 × 9-inch heat-resistant glass casserole dish and roast in the oven for 20 minutes. Serve.

Torta di Noci
Walnut Cake

3 cups walnuts

    Butter, for greasing the cake pan

4 eggs, separated

1 cup sugar

1 tablespoon lemon zest

    Confectioner's sugar for decoration

1. Preheat the oven to 375°F.

2. In a blender or a food processor, chop the walnuts until they are very coarse, almost the texture of breadcrumbs.

3. Butter the bottom and sides of a 9-inch round cake pan and line it with parchment paper.

4. In a small bowl, beat the egg yolks with the sugar until creamy. Add the lemon zest and the pureed walnuts.

5. In a separate bowl beat the egg whites until they form stiff peaks. Fold the egg whites into the walnut mixture until well combined.

6. Pour the mixture into the prepared cake pan and bake for 45 minutes. Slice the cake into pie-shaped wedges and sprinkle with confectioners' sugar.

LISA'S TIP

An easy way to fit parchment paper into the bottom of a cake pan is to flip the cake pan over, place a piece of parchment paper on the bottom of the pan, and with a pencil draw a circle around the pan. Then, using a pair of scissors, cut the circle out of the parchment paper and place it in the bottom of the cake pan.

Fonduta Cheese Fondue

Risotto al Barolo Risotto with Barolo Wine

Pollo Ripieno alla Piemontese Stuffed Chicken Piemontese

Cavolini di Bruxelles con Mandorle Brussels Sprouts with Almonds

Torta alla Nocciola Hazelnut Cake

Piemonte is right next to the French border, separated by the famous Monte Bianco. When I first arrived in Piemonte, I was amazed that so many people in this large region in northern Italy speak Italian with the French guttural "r." It completely changes the sound of the Italian language! I grew up all over southern and central Italy, and am accustomed to the classic, romantic, exaggerated, rolling "r." But I quickly learned that the French influence is seen not only in the Italian language, but also in the food!

The antipasto in this menu is a classic example of French influence. It is an Italian version of French fondue, with one of the most well-known cheeses from northern Italy—Fontina. We southern Italians call Fontina the northern version of mozzarella. This antipasto is a fun and delicious way to begin Sunday dinner.

In my wine suggestions for Piemonte, I strongly recommend Barolo. It is a hearty, affordable, full-bodied red, frequently used in meat sauces in northern Italy. I instantly fell in love with Barolo the first time I had it in creamy risotto!

The Stuffed Chicken Piemontese in this menu is not for the faint of heart, but there is nothing more satisfying on a cold January night than this dish. The creamy cheeses pair well with the prosciutto to create the ultimate chicken roll-up!

And if the pine nut is the nut of southern Italy, the hazelnut is the nut of the north.

Rich and buttery, hazelnuts are perfect in desserts, and with chocolate, like the famous Gianduja chocolate from this region.

Buon Appetito!

Fonduta
Cheese Fondue

2 pounds Fontina cheese, cubed

2 cups whole milk

4 egg yolks, lightly beaten

4 cups excellent-quality Italian bread, cubed

1 tablespoon of truffle oil

Imported Italian breadsticks

1. Preheat the oven to 375°F.

2. In a medium-size bowl, combine the cheese with the milk. Place the cheese mixture in the top of a double boiler over medium heat or in a heatproof glass bowl over a saucepan of boiling water. Allow the cheese to melt, whisking it into the hot milk, but do not let the milk boil.

3. Very gently, add each egg yolk, one at a time, to the milk and cheese mixture, stirring constantly over medium heat, until the egg yolks are well incorporated. The fondue should have a glossy color and a creamy, smooth texture.

4. Transfer the cheese mixture to a fondue pot or to a clean bowl placed over a heating element (such as a hot plate).

5. Meanwhile, place the cubed bread on a baking sheet and toast for 8 minutes in the preheated oven. Add the truffle oil to the cheese mixture and serve with the breadsticks and cubed bread.

Risotto al Barolo
Risotto with Barolo Wine

1 cup unsalted butter

2 onions, 1 whole and 1 chopped

2 celery sticks, chopped

2 carrots, chopped

4 cups Arborio rice from Italy

4 cups Barolo wine

2 cups vegetable bouillon, excellent quality

2 teaspoons Sicilian sea salt, fine

1 teaspoon freshly ground black pepper

1½ cups Parmigiano Reggiano, grated, plus a little extra for serving

1. Place ½ cup of the butter in a large frying pan and sauté the chopped onion, chopped celery, and chopped carrots for approximately 5 minutes until the onions are golden. Add the rice and toast it in the hot butter-and-onion mixture until it is well coated and shiny, approximately 4 minutes.

2. Transfer the rice mixture to a large 6-quart pot set on medium heat. Add the Barolo, 1 cup at a time, stirring it into the Arborio rice until it is completely absorbed. Continue to cook the rice in this way, adding the wine and vegetable bouillon alternately, stirring thoroughly, until the rice is cooked, approximately 15 minutes. Add the salt and pepper, then add the remaining ½ cup butter and the Parmigiano Reggiano.

3. Mix well and serve with a little extra Parmigiano Reggiano on top.

This Is Sunday Dinner

Pollo Ripieno alla Piemontese
Stuffed Chicken Piemontese

8 boneless, skinless chicken breasts,
  6 ounces each

1 stick unsalted butter

2 cups dry white wine, such as Gavi

1 cup balsamic vinegar

8 slices provolone cheese

8 slices prosciutto crudo

16 asparagus spears

8 slices bacon

1 teaspoon Sicilian sea salt, fine

½ teaspoon freshly ground black
  pepper

1. Preheat the oven to 350°F.

2. Pound the chicken breasts between 2 sheets of plastic wrap until they're very thin.

3. Place the butter, white wine, and balsamic vinegar in a large frying pan. Over medium heat, cook each chicken breast in the liquid for approximately 2 minutes on each side. Remove the chicken breasts from the wine and balsamic vinegar mixture and place them on a cutting board.

4. Top each chicken breast with a slice of provolone, a slice of prosciutto, and two asparagus spears. Roll up the chicken breast and wrap 1 slice of bacon around the chicken breast.

5. Place each roll-up in a buttered, 13 × 9-inch casserole. Sprinkle with the salt and pepper. Repeat with all the chicken breasts. Bake them for 15 minutes and serve.

Cavolini di Bruxelles con Mandorle
Brussels Sprouts with Almonds

  2 pounds Brussels sprouts, stems trimmed, and cut in half
  1 stick unsalted butter
  ½ cup sliced almonds
  2 garlic cloves
  1 tablespoon lemon zest
  1 teaspoon Sicilian sea salt, fine
  ½ teaspoon freshly ground black pepper
  ¾ cup breadcrumbs

1. Place the halved Brussels sprouts on a large baking sheet or jelly-roll pan and roast them in a preheated 350°F oven for 10 minutes.

2. In the meantime, melt half the butter in a large frying pan. Add the almonds and garlic and cook for 3 minutes. Add the lemon zest, salt, and pepper, and cook for 1 more minute.

3. Remove the Brussels sprouts from the oven and place them in the frying pan, tossing them well with the almond mixture. Add the remaining butter and the breadcrumbs to the frying pan and cook with the Brussels sprouts until the breadcrumbs are golden brown. Serve.

Torta alla Nocciola
Hazelnut Cake

  2 eggs
  1 cup sugar
  1½ sticks unsalted butter, melted
  1¾ cups unbleached flour
  1 teaspoon baking powder
  ½ cup whole milk
  ½ teaspoon Sicilian sea salt, finely ground
  2 cups hazelnuts, toasted and chopped
  Confectioners' sugar for decoration

1. Preheat the oven to 350°F.

2. Line a 9-inch round cake pan with parchment paper.

3. With a hand mixer, beat the eggs and sugar until the mixture is pale yellow. Beat in the butter and then slowly beat in the flour, incorporating it very well. Add the baking powder, milk, and salt. Beat in the hazelnuts.

4. Pour the mixture into the prepared pan and bake for 35 minutes. Sprinkle with confectioners' sugar and serve.

Menu 8

SERVES 8

Torta di Risotto e Spinaci Spinach and Risotto Torta
Cannelloni di Formaggio e Funghi Cheese and Mushroom Cannelloni
Pollo al Marengo Chicken Marengo
Pepperoni con Capperi Roasted Peppers with Capers
Bonet al Cioccolato Chocolate Bonet

As a child, I grew up on cannelloni—except we called it manicotti! My grandmother and my mother frequently made this incredibly satisfying and easy dish. It has always been a go-to dish for my children and me as well. But living in Piemonte, I learned the difference between the two pastas: cannelloni are a smooth, tubular pasta, approximately ¾ inch in diameter, while manicotti are ridged, tubular pasta, and about 1½ inches in diameter. Each is approximately 4 inches long. But both these dishes make for velvety, hearty, comforting stuffed pasta! Cannelloni alla Piemontese are incredibly rich as a result of the mascarpone cheese, and I love that the sauce is a red sauce, rather than a cream sauce—a departure for recipes from this region—but one that pairs well with the creamy stuffing.

Chicken Marengo is a dish from the town of Alessandria, where I lived and worked in Piemonte. It is the Piemontese version of a rustic, country chicken dish—and, with the addition of tomatoes, mushrooms, and onions, it is especially hearty and delicious. Although it is traditional in Italy to make Chicken Marengo in a Dutch oven, you can use a slow cooker instead, if you prefer. That way, you can put all the

ingredients for the dish in the pot on Sunday morning and forget about it until dinner. It will come out just as beautifully!

Chocolate Bonet is perhaps the signature dessert of Piemonte. It is a delicious dessert, cooked in a *bagnomaria* (explained in the recipe) that yields a smooth, rich, chocolate custard with a crunchy sugar crust. Delicious! And remember, everyone can help prepare this dessert, as well as the other dishes, so Sunday dinner becomes a relaxed day of cooking and eating together.

A tavola—che non si invecchia! (No one grows old at the table!)

Torta di Risotto e Spinaci
Spinach and Risotto Torta

6 tablespoons unsalted butter, plus a little extra for greasing the pie plate

1 pound spinach, washed and dried with paper towels

1 cup Arborio rice from Italy

1 white onion, chopped

1 teaspoon salt

4 cups vegetable bouillon

3 large eggs

¾ cup heavy cream

1 cup Parmigiano Reggiano, grated

½ teaspoon nutmeg, grated

½ teaspoon freshly ground black pepper

1. Preheat the oven to 350°F. Butter a 9-inch pie plate. Place 2 tablespoons of the butter in a large saucepan, add the spinach, and cook the spinach until it is wilted, for approximately 3 minutes. Drain and cool the spinach. Using paper towels squeeze the water and butter out of the spinach. Finely chop the spinach and place it in a bowl.

2. In the same pan used to sauté the spinach, place 2 more tablespoons of butter. Add the Arborio rice and sauté it in the butter over medium heat, until the rice is shiny and slightly golden. Transfer the sautéed rice to a 6-quart pot.

3. In the same frying pan in which you sautéed the Arborio rice, add 2 more tablespoons of butter and sauté the onion until translucent, for approximately 4 minutes. Place the onion in the bowl with the spinach. Add the salt. Place the pot containing the sautéed Arborio rice over medium heat and begin to ladle the vegetable broth onto the rice, one ladleful at a time, stirring constantly, and waiting for the broth to be fully absorbed by the rice before adding more broth.

4. While you are cooking the rice, beat together the eggs, cream, cheese, nutmeg, and pepper in a medium bowl. Stir the spinach into the mixture, and then add it to the risotto. Pour the egg, spinach, and risotto mixture into the prepared pan and smooth out the top with the back of a large spoon. Bake the mixture for 30 minutes in the preheated oven. Slice and serve.

This Is Sunday Dinner

Cannelloni di Formaggio e Funghi
Cheese and Mushroom Cannelloni

For the Filling

½ stick (4 tablespoons) unsalted butter, melted, plus more for greasing the pans

2 (9-ounce) boxes of cannelloni, imported from Italy, excellent quality, such as De Cecco

½ cup extra virgin olive oil

2 garlic cloves, chopped

2½ pounds white button mushrooms, chopped

4 onions, chopped

½ teaspoon Sicilian sea salt, fine

½ teaspoon freshly ground black pepper

1 cup mascarpone cream

For the Sauce

16 ounce can crushed San Marzano tomatoes, imported from Italy

2 teaspoons Sicilian sea salt, fine

1 teaspoon freshly ground black pepper

1 tablespoon sugar

2 cups heavy cream

3 cups Parmigiano Reggiano cheese, grated

16 basil leaves, chopped

1. Preheat the oven to 325°F. Butter the bottom and sides of two 13 × 9 × 1½-inch baking dishes. Fill a large 6- to 8-quart pasta pot with water and bring to a rolling boil. Cook the cannelloni according to the directions on the package. Place 4 cotton or linen dish towels on your kitchen table. Drain the cannelloni in a colander and place them side by side on the dish towels to cool. Cover the cannelloni with towels.

2. In a large frying pan, heat ¼ cup of the olive oil. Add the garlic until golden. Remove the garlic and discard. Add 2 tablespoons of unsalted butter to the garlic-infused oil and place the chopped mushrooms and chopped onions in the saucepan. Cook until softened, approximately 8 minutes. Place the onion-and-mushroom mixture in a medium-size bowl and season with salt and pepper. Gently stir in the mascarpone.

3. *To assemble the cannelloni:* In your left hand, pick up 1 cannelloni tube. With an espresso spoon, or any small spoon that fits through the opening of the cannelloni, fill the cannelloni with the mushroom-onion mixture. When all the cannelloni are filled, place them in the buttered baking dishes.

4. *To prepare the sauce:* Place the remaining ¼ cup of extra virgin olive oil and the remaining 2 tablespoons of butter in a large frying pan. Add the San Marzano tomatoes. Cook for 12 minutes. Season with salt and pepper, and add the sugar. Slowly pour in the heavy cream and stir in half the Parmigiano Reggiano and all the basil.

5. Immediately remove the sauce from the heat and pour it over the filled cannelloni. Sprinkle with the remaining Parmigiano cheese and bake for 15 minutes until bubbly. Serve.

Pollo al Marengo
Chicken Marengo

2 teaspoons Sicilian sea salt, fine

1 teaspoon freshly ground black pepper

2 chickens, cut up

½ cup extra virgin olive oil

1 cup dry white wine

6 garlic cloves

8 ounces pearl onions (may be frozen)

½ cup unbleached flour

4 cups vegetable bouillon

8 tomatoes on the vine (small)

16 ounces button mushrooms

¼ cup Italian flat leaf parsley, chopped

1. Rub the salt and pepper all over the skin of the chicken pieces. In a large Dutch oven or a deep pot with a lid, pour the olive oil and heat until bubbly. Brown the chicken on all sides. Pour in the white wine and stir, deglazing the bottom of the pan. Simmer for 15 to 20 minutes. Toss the garlic and pearl onions in the flour and add to the chicken mixture. Stir. Then pour in the vegetable bouillon. Cover the Dutch oven or pot and simmer for 30 minutes over medium heat.

2. While the chicken is simmering, chop the tomatoes into quarters. Cut the mushrooms in half, and, after the chicken has simmered for 30 minutes, add the vegetables to the chicken. Turn the heat to low and simmer the mixture for another 30 minutes.

3. Sprinkle with parsley and serve.

Pepperoni con Capperi
Roasted Peppers with Capers

8 large bell peppers (4 red and 4 yellow)

2 large tomatoes, chopped

2 cloves garlic, chopped

½ cup fresh basil leaves, chopped

½ cup mint leaves, chopped

½ cup extra virgin olive oil

½ teaspoon Sicilian sea salt, fine

½ teaspoon freshly ground black pepper

4 tablespoons capers, rinsed

1. Roast the peppers according to the directions on page 128. Set the roasted peppers aside in a casserole and let them rest for 20 minutes.

2. Meanwhile, combine the tomatoes, garlic, basil, mint, and oil in a bowl, mixing well and seasoning with salt and pepper.

3. Pat the peppers dry with a paper towel and then slice them into strips. Place them in a medium-size salad bowl.

4. Pour the tomato mixture over the peppers, add the capers, toss well, and serve.

Bonet al Cioccolato
Chocolate Bonet

For the Bonet

6 eggs

6 tablespoons sugar

4 tablespoons unsweetened cocoa

1 cup crushed amaretto cookies

4 tablespoons rum

1 cup milk

For the Caramelized Sugar

½ cup sugar

¼ cup warm water

1. Preheat the oven to 325°F.

2. *To make the bonet:* Using a stand mixer, or with a hand mixer, beat the eggs and stir the sugar, cocoa, cookie crumbs, rum, and milk into the mixture. Set it aside.

3. *To prepare the caramelized sugar:* Pour the sugar into a medium-size saucepan, set over very low heat. Move the pan around the burner, tilting it until the sugar melts and begins to turn golden. Very slowly, add the warm water, a few drops at a time. Be careful not to let it splatter.

4. When the sugar liquid is light brown (caramelized), pour it into the bottom of a 9 × 5-inch loaf pan, making sure that it completely coats the bottom of the pan.

5. Pour the bonet mixture into the loaf pan on top of the caramelized sugar. Cover the pan with aluminum foil. Place the loaf pan in a larger baking dish, filled with 2 inches of water to form a *bagnomaria* (also known as a water bath or a double boiler, in which a receptacle is placed in a pan or baking dish filled with hot water in order to heat or cook the food). The point of using the *bagnomaria* is to gently cook the dessert and protect it from the direct heat of the oven, so the warm water actually cooks it, not the heat from your oven.

6. Bake for 40 minutes in the preheated 325°F oven. Remove the *bagnomaria* from the oven, lift out the loaf pan, and put it in the refrigerator for a minimum of 2 hours. After you remove the pan from the refrigerator, run a paring knife around the edges of the bonet inside the loaf pan. Place a platter on top of the loaf pan and flip it over.

7. Serve the bonet at room temperature.

Menu 9
SERVES 8

Sfoglia di Funghi e Gorgonzola Mushroom and Gorgonzola Puff

Macaroni Gratinato Macaroni au Gratin

Trota al Piemontese Trout, Piemontese Style

Broccolini con Quadretti di Polenta Fritta
Broccoli Rabe with Fried Polenta Squares

Crêpes Crepes

I consider this menu northern Italian comfort food at its best! Macaroni au Gratin (again, because of the location of Piemonte, you can see the influence of the French, even in the name of this dish) uses creamy, decadent, *besciamella* sauce for a grown-up, Italian-style macaroni and cheese.

Another French influence on this menu comes in the form of dessert crepes, which have actually become very popular all over northern Italy. Here they are filled with classic Nutella®, a chocolate-hazelnut spread that was originally manufactured in Piemonte and has become popular almost everywhere in the world. Bread with Nutella was my favorite after school snack as a child in Italy.

Crepes are one of my favorite desserts to make with my children, and we frequently have "crepe night" at our house, where we fill the crepes with both savory and sweet fillings. This is such a fun idea—even for Sunday dinner—as everyone can participate in making the crepes, selecting the fillings, and then building their own crepes. All the while, you are building memories together.

Alla nostra! (To us!)

Sfoglia di Funghi e Gorgonzola
Mushroom and Gorgonzola Puff

16 medium-size mushrooms

6 ounces Gorgonzola cheese, imported from Italy

6 ounces mascarpone cheese

3 tablespoons heavy cream

Walnut halves, for decoration

1. Preheat the oven to 325°F. Cut the stems off the mushrooms and reserve for another use. Wash the mushroom caps, and set them aside.

2. In a medium-size bowl, crumble the Gorgonzola cheese. Add the mascarpone cheese to the Gorgonzola in the bowl, along with the heavy cream, and beat with a hand mixer or spoon until the mixture is smooth.

3. Arrange mushroom caps in a 13 × 9 inch casserole. Spoon the cheese mixture into the hollow of each cap and top with a walnut half. Bake for 7 minutes.

Macaroni Gratinato
Macaroni au Gratin

Butter, for greasing the pans

4 cups besciamella sauce (page 58)

6 tablespoons unsalted butter

4 egg yolks

1½ cups Parmigiano Reggiano, grated

2 (16-ounce) boxes elbow macaroni

2 teaspoons Sicilian sea salt, coarsely ground, for preparing the macaroni

1. Preheat the oven to 425°F. Butter two 13 × 9-inch ovenproof baking dishes.

2. In a medium-size bowl combine the *besciamella*, butter, and egg yolks. Gently beat the mixture with a spoon.

3. Cook the elbow macaroni according to the directions on the package, making sure to salt the water. Drain the macaroni. Stir half the *besciamella* mixture into the macaroni and pour it into the prepared casserole dishes. Spoon the remaining *besciamella* mixture on top with the grated Parmigiano Reggiano.

4. Bake the macaroni in the oven for 20 minutes until golden brown.

Trota al Piemontese
Trout, Piemontese Style

½ cup extra virgin olive oil

½ cup celery, chopped

½ cup onion, chopped

8 sage leaves

2 rosemary sprigs

3 garlic cloves, chopped

4 pounds trout fillets

2 teaspoons Sicilian sea salt, fine

1 teaspoon freshly grated black pepper

4 teaspoons white wine vinegar

2 cups fish bouillon (if you cannot find fish bouillon cubes, vegetable bouillon cubes may be substituted)

1 cup golden raisins

1 cup zucchini, sliced in rounds

2 tablespoons balsamic vinegar

1. In a large frying pan, heat half the olive oil over medium heat and sauté the celery, onion, sage, rosemary, and garlic for 5 minutes. Arrange the fish fillets over the vegetables in the frying pan. Season the top of the fish with one teaspoon of the salt and ½ teaspoon of the pepper and pour the white wine vinegar over the fish fillets. Cover the frying pan and cook for 15 minutes—do not touch. Pour in the fish bouillon, add the raisins, and cook for 5 more minutes.

2. In a separate frying pan, sauté the zucchini, season with the remaining salt and pepper, and cook over medium to high heat until the zucchini has softened. Add the balsamic vinegar to the zucchini.

3. Arrange the zucchini in the center of a large platter. Place the trout fillets on top of the zucchini. Pour the chopped vegetable mixture over the trout fillets and serve.

Broccolini con Quadretti di Polenta Fritta
Broccoli Rabe with Fried Polenta Squares

1 14-ounce box instant polenta, imported from Italy

½ cup extra virgin olive oil, plus 8 tablespoons and more for greasing the pan

2 teaspoons Sicilian sea salt, fine

1 teaspoon freshly ground black pepper

4 bunches broccoli rabe, stems cut off and chopped into 1-inch pieces

½ teaspoon crushed red pepper flakes

1. Prepare the instant polenta according to the instructions on the box. Spread the cooked polenta into an oiled 13 × 9-inch glass baking dish. Cool in the refrigerator for 20–30 minutes.

2. Remove the baking dish from the refrigerator. With a paring knife or a small sharp knife, cut the polenta into approximately 2-inch-long triangles. (You should be able to get at least 18 triangles from the polenta.) Set the polenta triangles on a plate.

3. In a large frying pan, heat ½ cup olive oil until it forms small bubbles along the edge of the pan. Place the polenta triangles in the hot oil and fry on each side until golden. Place the fried polenta triangles on paper towels to drain, and generously salt and pepper them.

4. Preheat oven to 350°F.

5. On a jelly-roll pan, place 8 tablespoons of extra virgin olive oil. Add the chopped broccoli rabe to the pan and roast in the preheated oven for 15 minutes.

6. On an oval-shaped platter, toss the fried polenta triangles with the roasted broccoli rabe and red pepper flakes.

Crêpes
Crepes

For the Crepe Batter

4 large eggs

2½ cups whole milk

2 cups unbleached flour

2 tablespoons unsalted butter, melted

½ teaspoon salt

For Cooking the Crepes

¼ cup canola or vegetable oil

1. In a blender, mix together all 5 crepe ingredients. Place the mixture in the refrigerator and chill for 30 minutes.

2. Place 1 tablespoon of canola or vegetable oil in an 8-inch nonstick sauté pan over medium heat. Cover the bottom of the pan with a very thin coating of crepe batter. Tilt the sauté pan until the crepe batter completely covers the bottom of the sauté pan. When the edge of the crepe begins to turn light brown, in approximately 2 minutes, loosen the edge of the crepe with a rubber spatula, and quickly flip it. Cook 1 minute more.

3. When the crepe is cooked on both sides, transfer it to a plate. Cover the plate with plastic wrap and continue making the crepes, stacking each one on top of the other, separated by a piece of plastic wrap.

4. Place Nutella, jam, powdered sugar, orange marmalade, fruit, or any other filling on the surface of the crepe. Fold the right and left side toward the middle, overlapping slightly, roll up, and serve.

Menu 10

SERVES 8

Piemontese Agliata Piemontese Green Sauce

La Famosa Zuppa di Funghi con Sherry di Lisa
Lisa's Famous Sherried Mushroom Soup

Arista di Maiale con Salsa di Noccioli Pork Loin with Hazelnut Sauce

Insalata di Radicchio con Ceci Ceci Beans with Radicchio Salad

Fette di Mele Fritti con Uvette Fried Apple Slices with Raisins

The first time I had *agliata*, I was in Piemonte, and it immediately reminded me of our Sicilian green sauce. *Agliata* has a similar bite, but the Piemontese combine basil with parsley, which gives the sauce a very fresh taste. Combined with creamy goat cheese, the flavors complement each other marvelously.

I am known for my mushroom soup, which I first made in college. The one in this menu was inspired by another memorable Piemontese touch—sherry, which gives this wonderful, creamy mushroom soup a velvety texture and a rich, warm taste. I have been adding sherry to the soup ever since!

The second course in this menu is a perfect example of the versatility of hazelnuts, which are scrumptious in sweet dishes. Here they are just as delicious in a decadent, rich, buttery, cream sauce served over pork.

The family-friendly dessert featured here is one that children adore: fried apple slices. It is not only yummy to eat, but fun to make, and everyone can participate! Cooking together and eating together—that's the best part of Sunday dinner!

Auguri! (Cheers!)

Piemontese Agliata
Piemontese Green Sauce

12 celery leaves

12 basil leaves

1 cup Italian flat leaf parsley

4 garlic gloves, peeled

1 teaspoon freshly ground black pepper

10 ounces fresh goat cheese

1 tablespoon fresh lemon juice

1 teaspoon Sicilian sea salt, fine

10 or 12 slices of toasted Italian country rustic bread

1. In a blender or a food processor, combine the celery leaves, basil, parsley, and garlic. Add the pepper to taste and blend. Break the goat cheese into small chunks. Add it to the herb mixture and process until smooth. Season to taste with the lemon juice and salt.

2. Stir the mixture together in a medium-size bowl. Serve with slices of toasted Italian bread.

La Famosa Zuppa di Funghi con Sherry di Lisa
Lisa's Famous Sherried Mushroom Soup

For the Soup

½ pound white button mushrooms, stems removed

½ pound cremini mushrooms, stems removed

4 tablespoons unsalted butter

1 cup chopped onion

½ teaspoon Sicilian sea salt, fine

½ teaspoon freshly ground black pepper

1 cup good red wine (Italian red wine such as Barolo or Chianti)

3 cups vegetable broth, excellent quality

½ cup excellent quality sherry, such as Harveys Bristol Cream

For the Besciamella Sauce

6 tablespoons butter

3 tablespoons unbleached flour

2 cups whole milk

½ teaspoon Sicilian sea salt, fine

¼ teaspoon freshly ground black pepper

1. *To make the soup:* Before chopping all the mushrooms, select 12 mushroom caps and set them aside. Chop the rest of the mushrooms.

2. In a large frying pan, melt the butter and sauté the chopped mushrooms and onions until the onions are translucent and the mushrooms are soft. Season with salt and pepper.

3. Place the onion, chopped mushrooms, wine, and broth in a large, 6-quart pot. Bring the mixture to a boil, reduce the heat, and cook at a slow boil for 20 minutes.

4. *To make the besciamella sauce:* In a large frying pan, melt the butter, stir in the flour,

and gradually add the milk. Cook the sauce until it is very smooth and coats the back of a wooden spoon. Season with salt and pepper.

5. Allow the onion-and-mushroom mixture to cool. When it's cool, puree the mixture in a blender and return it to the large pot. Stir the besciamella sauce into the mixture. Add the sherry.

6. Heat the soup over medium heat, being careful not to allow it to boil. Cut the reserved mushroom caps in half. Pour the mushroom soup into a tureen and float the mushroom cap halves on top. Serve.

Arista di Maiale con Salsa di Noccioli
Pork Loin with Hazelnut Sauce

4 tablespoons unsalted butter

6 tablespoons extra virgin olive oil

4 cloves garlic, chopped

2 sprigs fresh rosemary

4 bay leaves

1½ cups heavy cream

1½ cups beef both, excellent quality

2 teaspoons Sicilian sea salt, fine

1 teaspoon freshly ground black pepper

One 4-pound pork loin

4 cups hazelnuts, toasted and chopped

1. Preheat the oven to 350°F. Heat 2 tablespoons of the butter and 3 tablespoons of the olive oil in a large roasting pan on top of the stove over high heat. Sear the pork on all sides.

2. In a large frying pan, heat the remaining butter and olive oil and sauté the garlic, rosemary, and bay leaves. Add the cream, broth, salt, and pepper. Pour the mixture over the pork loin in the roasting pan. Bake in the preheated oven for 40 minutes.

3. Remove the pork loin from the oven and place it on a large platter. Discard the rosemary sprigs and the bay leaves.

4. Pour the juices from the roasting pan into a large frying pan on top of the stove over medium heat and add the hazelnuts to this liquid. Slice the pork loin into ¼- to ½-inch-thick slices and place the slices in the frying pan. Cover the meat with the sauce. Cook for 5 minutes. Serve.

Insalata di Radicchio con Ceci
Ceci Beans with Radicchio Salad

  6 red potatoes

  3 heads radicchio

1½ cups ceci beans, drained and rinsed
     (canned is fine)

  ¼ cup extra virgin olive oil

  ¼ cup balsamic vinegar

  2 teaspoons Sicilian sea salt, fine

  1 teaspoon freshly ground black
     pepper

  ½ cup Parmigiano Reggiano, grated

1. Fill a medium-size saucepan with water and
boil the potatoes for 15 minutes. Drain, cool,
and cut the potatoes into 1-inch chunks.

2. Cut the radicchio into strips and place them
in a large salad bowl. Add the ceci beans and
the potatoes.

3. In a glass measuring cup, mix the oil,
vinegar, salt, and pepper and pour the dressing
over the salad. Sprinkle with the Parmigiano
and serve.

Fette di Mele Fritti con Uvette
Fried Apple Slices with Raisins

  4 apples

  1 tablespoon lemon juice

  2 cups unbleached flour

  2 eggs

  ½ cup sugar

  ½ teaspoon Sicilian sea salt, fine

  1 cup cold whole milk

     Canola oil, for frying

  ½ cup raisins for garnish

     Confectioners' sugar, for decoration

1. Peel and core the apples. Cut the apples in
horizontal slices to create circles. Put the apple
circles in a bowl with the lemon juice to keep
them from turning brown.

2. In a medium-size bowl, mix together
the flour, eggs, sugar, and salt. Add the milk
very slowly, little by little, until you have a
nice batter.

3. In a large frying pan, heat an inch of canola
oil. Dip the apple slices in the batter, one at a
time, and place them in the hot oil.

4. Cook until they are golden on each
side. Top the apple slices with raisins and
confectioners' sugar.

Menu 11

SERVES 8

Svolti di Olive e Formaggio Olive Cheese Twists
Polenta Lasagne Lasagne with Polenta Layers
Polpettone Ripieno Stuffed Meat Loaf
Zucchini in Besciamella Zucchini in Besciamella Sauce
Crostata di Nutella Nutella Crostata

This menu highlights one of the most creative dishes I learned to prepare in Piemonte—lasagne that is literally made from polenta. When I make this dish for my family and friends in America, everyone is enthralled. It is so very satisfying and warming, and what could be better than combining cheese with cornmeal?

Leave it to the Piemontese to stuff a meat loaf!! When my children were little, they begged me to make "the meat loaf with cheese inside." It is gooey, fun, decadent, and delicious!

If my children's friends know me for one thing, it is my Nutella Crostata. When my children were at university (in the same city where I now live), their friends would actually ask them if they could request a dessert whenever they were coming to dinner. And, yes, Nutella Crostata was the request! Make two of them; they freeze beautifully.

Mangia bene! (Eat well!)

Svolti di Olive e Formaggio
Olive Cheese Twists

Makes 14–16

Butter, for greasing the cookie sheet

12 ounces goat cheese, crumbled

⅓ cup Italian flat leaf parsley, chopped

⅓ cup black olive pâté (preferably imported from Italy)

2 large egg whites

1 (17-ounce) package frozen puff pastry (2 sheets), thawed

1. Preheat the oven to 350°F. Grease a large cookie sheet with butter. In a medium-size bowl, combine the goat cheese, parsley, olive pâté, and egg whites. Mash the mixture with a fork until all the ingredients are well combined.

2. Remove a puff pastry sheet from the package. On a lightly floured surface, unfold the sheet. With a floured rolling pin, roll it into a 14 × 16-inch rectangle. Cut the pastry sheet in half, crosswise, and spread the cheese mixture evenly within ¼ inch of the edge of the sheet. Top with the other half of the pastry sheet. Gently pat to seal the filled pastry and cut it into half-inch strips with a long, sharp knife. Hold each end of a strip and twist it 4 to 6 times.

3. Place the cheese twist on the cookie sheet. Repeat with remaining sheet of pastry. Bake the cheese twists, 1 inch apart, on the cookie sheet for 12 minutes or until they are nicely browned.

Polenta Lasagne
Lasagne with Polenta Layers

For the Polenta

1 (1-pound) box of instant polenta, imported from Italy

4 teaspoons salt

For the Besciamella Sauce

6 tablespoons unsalted butter

½ cup all-purpose flour

2 cups whole milk

½ teaspoon Sicilian sea salt, fine

½ teaspoon freshly ground black pepper

For the Lasagne

2 (14-ounce) cans San Marzano tomatoes, crushed

1 cup Pecorino Romano cheese, grated

½ cup Fontina cheese, grated

1. Preheat oven to 375°F. Make the polenta according to the directions on the package, adding salt. Set the polenta aside.

2. *To make the besciamella sauce:* Melt the butter in a large frying pan and stir in the flour until the butter has absorbed all of it. You will have small balls of flour. Slowly pour all the milk into the pan, stirring constantly until the flour and butter absorb all the milk. This will take 6–7 minutes. You should have a thick sauce that coats the back of a spoon. Season the besciamella with salt and pepper.

3. *To assemble the lasagne:* Spread ⅓ of the tomatoes on the bottom of a 13 × 9-inch deep lasagne pan. Spread the polenta to form a layer on top of the tomatoes, approximately ½-inch thick. Sprinkle the Pecorino Romano and Fontina cheese on top of the polenta. Top it with a layer of besciamella sauce and then another layer of polenta, a layer of tomato sauce, a sprinkle of the cheeses, and then the besciamella sauce.

4. Bake for 30 minutes or until bubbly. Cut the lasagne into squares and serve.

LISA'S TIP

If the polenta is too hard to smooth out, pour olive oil on either side of a spatula and use it to smooth out the polenta.

Polpettone Ripieno
Stuffed Meat Loaf

- 4 tablespoons olive oil, for greasing the loaf pans
- 1 cup whole milk
- 6 slices Italian bread, ½ inch thick, crusts removed
- 2 pounds ground beef (85% lean/ roughly 15% fat)
- 3 large eggs
- 1 teaspoon Sicilian sea salt, fine Freshly ground black pepper
- 1 teaspoon dried oregano
- 1 cup Parmigiano Reggiano, grated
- 1 pound cherry tomatoes, halved
- 2 large fresh mozzarella balls, approximately 8 to 10 ounces, whole

1. Heat oven to 350°F. Prepare two standard-size loaf pans by placing 2 tablespoons of olive oil in each pan. Set the pans aside.

2. Pour the milk into a large bowl and soak the bread until it completely absorbs the milk. Add the ground beef to the bowl and completely incorporate the bread into the meat. Add the eggs, salt, pepper, oregano, and ¾ cup Parmigiano to the meat mixture and combine well. Divide the mixture into 4 equal-size meatballs. Flatten 1 ball into each of the loaf pans. Top each of the meatballs with the cherry tomatoes and the mozzarella, and flatten a meatball on top of the tomatoes and mozzarella.

3. Bake the two stuffed loaves in the oven for 20 minutes. Remove them from the oven, top the loaves with the remaining ¼ cup Parmigiano, and return them to the oven for an additional 10 minutes. Allow the loaves to cool for 5 minutes.

4. Slice and serve.

Zucchini in Besciamella
Zucchini in Besciamella Sauce

Oil or butter, for greasing the baking dish

3 pounds zucchini, cleaned and cut into circles

2 teaspoons Sicilian sea salt, fine

1 cup Parmigiano Reggiano, grated

For the Besciamella Sauce

6 tablespoons unsalted butter

6 tablespoons unbleached flour

4 cups whole milk

1 teaspoon grated nutmeg

½ teaspoon Sicilian sea salt, fine

1. Preheat the oven to 325°F. Grease a 13 × 9-inch baking dish with butter. Layer the sliced zucchini in the baking dish, top with the salt, and cook for 25 minutes.

2. *To make the besciamella:* Melt the butter in a large frying pan and stir in the flour until it is fully incorporated. Slowly pour the milk into the butter and flour mixture, stirring constantly until it is fully incorporated. The sauce should be smooth and thick enough to coat the back of a wooden spoon. Stir the nutmeg and salt into the sauce.

3. Remove the pan of zucchini from the oven, top it with the besciamella sauce, sprinkle the Parmigiano over the top, and bake for 5 more minutes. Serve.

Crostata di Nutella
Nutella Crostata

Lisa's Pasta Frolla (pastry dough, page 99)

1 (33-ounce) jar of Nutella or 2 (16-ounce) jars of Nutella

Fresh whipped cream, for serving (optional)

1. Preheat the oven to 350°F.

2. Spread the pasta frolla (pastry dough) into a 9½-inch pie plate. Cover the dough with the Nutella. Roll out the remaining small ball of pasta frolla and cut it into ¼-inch strips. Layer the strips over the Nutella to form a lattice.

3. Bake the pastry in the preheated oven for 30 minutes. Delicious served with a dollop of fresh whipped cream.

Frittata di Carciofi e Taleggio Artichoke and Taleggio Frittata

Zuppa di Piselli Green Pea Soup with Spinach

Filetto Strip Steak

Insalata Russa con Sedano Warm Potato Salad with Celery

Budino di Frutta e Ulivette Fruit and Raisin Budino

There are so many delicious cheeses from northern Italy and the regions of Piemonte and Lombardia. Taleggio is definitely one of my favorites! The first time I had this cheese, I ate it as Italian street food at a fun and incredibly quaint food festival in the Piemontese countryside. It was served there on warm, crunchy toast and I remember thinking how mild and flavorful this cheese is. I started to purchase it in the local cheese shops and learned that it is named for the Valley of Taleggio, in Lombardia, north of Piemonte, and is very popular across northern Italy. Taleggio, like Fontina, another of my favorite semi-soft white cheeses from Piemonte, melts beautifully, so it is popular in baked pasta, risotto, and polenta.

Frittate, flat Italian omelets, are popular all over Italy. My maternal grandfather was famous in our family for his *frittate*, and he taught me how to cook them—only on the stovetop—which is exactly how I cook them to this day! We begin this menu with a delicious *frittata* featuring Taleggio, blending the creamy taste of the cheese with delicate artichoke hearts.

When people visit Italy, they are always amazed at how many soups we eat! From north to south, soup is a staple in Italy. As I mentioned in my first cookbook, *Whatever Happened to Sunday Dinner?*, my mother always had a big pot of soup on the stove, no matter what the season. She made green pea soup frequently, as it was one of my father's favorites. Here, I add fresh spinach to the mix, as they do in Piemonte, which not only tastes delicious, but looks inviting, too!

The strip steak in this menu, which is marinated in onions and olive oil, is perfect with the typical Piemontese warm potato salad that you find in *trattorie* (small family-run restaurants) all over the region. Simple and delicious.

We end this menu with one of my favorite puddings, which I loved on a cold evening when I lived in Alessandria. Chock-full of fruit and cinnamon, every bite is creamy and chunky.

Who wouldn't love this Sunday dinner?

Tutti a tavola! (Everyone to table!)

This Is Sunday Dinner

Frittata di Carciofi e Taleggio
Artichoke and Taleggio Frittata

- 1 (12-ounce) package frozen artichoke hearts
- 4 tablespoons extra virgin olive oil
- 1 yellow onion, sliced in half moons
- 3 garlic cloves, chopped
- 1 teaspoon Sicilian sea salt, fine
- 6 large eggs
- 1 cup whole milk
- 1 ¼ cups Taleggio cheese, grated

1. Allow the artichoke hearts to thaw. In a medium-size frying pan, place the olive oil and sauté the onion and garlic. Add the artichokes. Sauté the mixture for approximately 6 minutes. Sprinkle in the salt.

2. In a bowl, beat the eggs, milk, and Taleggio. Pour the egg mixture over the vegetables in the pan. Using a spatula, gently push the egg mixture away from the edge of the pan, gliding the spatula under the edge of the frittata. This allows the frittata to cook evenly.

3. When the bottom of the frittata is set and only the center is a little wet, place a dinner plate on top of the frying pan. Flip the frittata and slide it back into the pan to cook the other side until it is golden, about 2 more minutes.

4. Slide the frittata onto a serving platter, slice it into wedges, and serve.

Zuppa di Piselli
Green Pea Soup with Spinach

- 4 cups shelled fresh peas or frozen peas
- 1 leek, finely sliced
- 3 garlic cloves, chopped
- 2 quarts vegetable bouillon
- 6 tablespoons extra virgin olive oil
- 2 cups fresh spinach, shredded
- 2 stalks celery, chopped
- ½ cup Italian flat leaf parsley, chopped
- 4 teaspoons fresh mint, chopped
- 1 teaspoon Sicilian sea salt, fine
- ½ teaspoon freshly ground black pepper

1. Place the peas, leeks, garlic, and bouillon in a large 6–8-quart soup pot. Bring it to a boil, lower the heat, and simmer for 20 minutes.

2. Meanwhile, in a large frying pan, heat the oil over low to medium heat. Add the spinach, celery, parsley, and mint. Cover the pan and cook the mixture over low heat until the vegetables are soft.

3. Run the pea mixture through a blender until it is smooth.

4. Add the pea mixture to the pan with the sautéed vegetables and herbs, and heat through. Season the soup with salt and pepper and serve.

Filetto
Strip Steak

- 1 medium white onion
- 7 tablespoons extra virgin olive oil
- 8 (8-ounce) strip steaks, 1 inch thick
- 2 tablespoons Sicilian sea salt, coarse
- 1 teaspoon freshly ground black pepper

1. Place the onion and 4 tablespoons of the extra virgin olive oil in a food processor or a blender and puree until smooth. Rub the onion puree all over the steaks. Cover the steaks and refrigerate them for 1 hour. Remove the steaks from the fridge and discard the onion puree.

2. Heat a large sauté pan and add 3 tablespoons of the extra virgin olive oil. Cook the steaks in the pan for 3–5 minutes per side for medium rare. Season with salt and pepper, and let the steaks rest for 5 minutes before serving.

Insalata Russa con Sedano
Warm Potato Salad with Celery

- 3 pounds potatoes, such as Yukon gold, cleaned and quartered
- 2 teaspoons Sicilian sea salt, fine
- ½ cup extra virgin olive oil
- ½ cup Italian flat leaf parsley, chopped
- 6 inner stalks of celery (the very pale green ones with leaves chopped)
- Freshly ground black pepper, to taste

1. Place the potatoes in a large saucepan and fill it with water to cover the potatoes. Bring it to a boil, add the salt, and cook until the potatoes are just tender, approximately 25 minutes. Drain and cool the potatoes for a few minutes and then cut them into bite-size pieces.

2. While the potatoes are still warm, toss them in a medium-size bowl with the oil parsley, and celery. Season the mixture with salt and plenty of pepper. Serve warm.

Budino di Frutta e Ulivette
Fruit and Raisin Budino

1½ cups raisins

1½ cups white Italian desert wine,
    such as Moscato

2 firm medium Bosc or D'Anjou pears

1 large Braeburn or Honeycrisp apple

1 stick unsalted butter, plus more
    for greasing the pan

1½ cups granulated sugar

3 cups coarse breadcrumbs

4 cups whole milk

1 teaspoon pure vanilla extract

½ teaspoon cinnamon

3 large eggs

Zest of 1 lemon

½ teaspoon Sicilian sea salt, fine

1. Soak the raisins in the wine overnight. Peel, core, and quarter the pears and the apple. Then, cut the quarters into ¼-inch thick slices.

2. In a large frying pan, melt the butter over medium heat, add the sliced fruit and sugar, and bring the mixture to a boil. Stir. Reduce the heat and simmer until the fruit is very tender, approximately 15 minutes. With the back of a wooden spoon, mash the fruit in the pan and simmer until the liquid is thickened and resembles a chunky apple sauce, approximately 10 minutes more. Transfer the mixture to a shallow dish and let it cool to room temperature.

3. Preheat the oven to 400°F.

4. Butter the bottom and sides of a springform pan and sprinkle the bottom of the pan with ½ cup of breadcrumbs.

5. Stir together the milk, vanilla, and cinnamon in a bowl and add the remaining 2½ cups of the breadcrumbs. Soak the breadcrumbs for at least 15 minutes.

6. Whisk together the eggs, lemon zest, and sea salt in a large bowl, then stir in the milk, the raisin mixture, and the fruit puree. Pour the combined mixture into the prepared pan.

7. Bake the pudding until it turns golden, approximately 50 minutes. Let it cool completely in the pan and serve.

Menu 13

Polpettoni di Gorgonzola Gorgonzola Patties
Pasta con Ragù di Vitello Pasta with Veal Ragù
Agnello con Castagne Leg of Lamb with Chestnuts
Torta Piemontese Piemontese Cake
Gianduiotto Chocolate Almond Log

Veal is eaten in southern Italy, more often than not, simply because there is not enough land to let the animals graze and grow into large cows. Hence, there are very few beef dishes in Sicily. And although the beef and pork in northern Italy is outstanding, delicious ragùs (meat-based sauces), like the one in this menu, are made with veal.

You'll find chestnuts roasting on every corner of Piemonte during the cold winter months—and you'll find them in a number of wonderful desserts, as well as savory dishes, like the leg of lamb in this menu. The chestnuts give the lamb an outstanding, roasted taste.

The vegetable side dish, a rich, fluffy custard, is a classic Piemontese dish. The texture of the smooth, creamy, cheese custard, paired with the earthiness of the chestnuts and lamb, make a perfect dish for brisk winter days.

Gianduiotto is historically a dessert from the city of Torino, known for its amazing chocolate stores and decadent chocolate desserts. But this dessert is now found all over Piemonte and Lombardia in northern Italy, and is an ideal way to finish a winter Sunday dinner anywhere.

Salute! (To your health!)

Polpettoni di Gorgonzola
Gorgonzola Patties

  1 cup self-rising flour

  ½ cup cold butter, plus more for
  greasing the baking sheets

  4 ounces Gorgonzola cheese, imported
  from Italy, crumbled

  2 ounces Fontina cheese, shredded

  1 cup sesame seeds

1. Place flour in a bowl and, using 2 knives or a pastry cutter, cut the butter into the flour until the mixture resembles coarse crumbs. Add the Gorgonzola and sprinkle in the Fontina. With your fingers, thoroughly mix the ingredients to form a dough. Cover and refrigerate the dough for 30 minutes.

2. Place the sesame seeds in a dry frying pan and stir them constantly over medium heat until they turn light brown. Remove the sesame seeds from the heat and let them cool.

3. Preheat the oven to 400°F.

4. Grease 2 baking sheets with butter. Shape the chilled dough into 24 equal-size balls. Toss each ball in the toasted sesame seeds and press the balls flat with the palm of your hand to coat them well with the seeds. Arrange the flattened balls on the greased baking sheets and press lightly with a fork.

5. Bake the patties for 10 minutes or until golden around the edges. Serve.

Pasta con Ragù di Vitello
Pasta with Veal Ragù

  ¼ cup extra virgin olive oil

  4 tablespoons unsalted butter

  3 pounds ground veal

   Salt and pepper, to taste

  12 fresh sage leaves, sliced very thinly

  ⅛ teaspoon ground nutmeg

  2 small onions, chopped

  4 cloves garlic, chopped

  6 tablespoons tomato paste,
  preferably imported from Italy
  (*concentrato di pomodoro* comes
  in a tube)

  1 cup white wine

  2 cups vegetable bouillon or broth

  1 cup heavy cream

  2 pounds *strozzapreti* pasta or *pici*
  pasta or another sturdy short-cut
  pasta

  1 cup Parmigiano Reggiano, grated

1. Bring a large pot of water to a boil.

2. Meanwhile, in a Dutch oven, heat the olive oil and melt the butter into the olive oil. Add the ground veal and cook, breaking it up with a wooden spoon until the meat is lightly browned, approximately 5 minutes. Season with salt and pepper.

3. Add the sage and nutmeg. Raise the heat to medium-high, stir in the onions and garlic, and partially cover the pan with a lid. Cook the mixture, stirring, until the vegetables soften, 9–10 minutes. Add the tomato paste and cook for 1 minute more. Add the wine, scraping the bottom of the pan, and then add the broth and the cream. Reduce the heat to medium-low and simmer the veal ragù while you cook the pasta.

4. Salt the boiling water and cook the pasta according to package directions for *al dente*. Drain. Toss the pasta with the ragù.

5. Top with the grated cheese.

Agnello con Castagne
Leg of Lamb with Chestnuts

- 1 (4-pound) leg of lamb, preferably from New Zealand
- 6 tablespoons extra virgin olive oil
- 1 teaspoon Sicilian sea salt, fine
- ½ teaspoon freshly ground black pepper
- 1 rosemary sprig
- 2 garlic cloves, sliced into halves
- 2 carrots
- 1 onion
- 2 celery ribs
- ½ pound chestnuts, packaged and already cooked
- 1 cup Marsala wine
- 8 tablespoons butter, melted
- 2 tablespoons sugar

1. Preheat the oven to 400°F.

2. Place the leg of lamb in a large roasting pan. Add the oil, and season the meat with salt, pepper, and rosemary. With a paring knife, cut small slices all around the leg of lamb and stuff them with the garlic slices. Peel and chop the carrots and dice the onion and celery ¼ inch, and place them around the leg of lamb.

3. Roast the meat in the oven for 1 hour, turning the leg of lamb once. Remove the lamb from the oven and crumble the cooked chestnuts on top of the meat. Roast the leg of lamb for another 10 minutes.

4. Remove the pan from the oven and pour the Marsala, melted butter, and sugar over the leg of lamb. Roast the meat for 5 more minutes, and then remove it from the oven.

5. Allow the roast to rest for 10 minutes before slicing and serving it.

This Is Sunday Dinner

Torta Piemontese
Piemontese Cake

Butter, for greasing the baking dish

¼ cup unbleached flour

2 tablespoons unsalted butter

2 onions, sliced

6 large eggs

2 egg yolks

4 cups whole milk

1 cup heavy cream

6 tablespoons Parmigiano Reggiano, grated

4 tablespoons fresh sage leaves, chopped

⅛ teaspoon grated nutmeg

1 teaspoon Sicilian sea salt, fine

½ teaspoon freshly ground black pepper

1. Preheat the oven to 400°F.

2. Butter and flour a 13 × 9-inch casserole dish.

3. Melt the unsalted butter in a large frying pan over low heat. Add the onions and sauté until golden.

4. In a large bowl, beat the eggs and egg yolks together with the milk, cream, Parmigiano Reggiano cheese, sage leaves, nutmeg, and salt and pepper. Add the sautéed onions to the bowl and stir them in.

5. Pour the mixture into the prepared casserole dish, and then place the dish in a deep roasting pan. Make a *bagnomaria* by pouring water into the roasting pan until it comes halfway up the sides of the ovenproof dish.

6. Bake the custard for 30 minutes or until it is set in the middle and looks golden and crisp on top. Serve.

Gianduiotto
Chocolate Almond Log

- 4 eggs, lightly beaten
- 2 cups sugar
- 2 cups unsweetened cocoa
- 2 sticks unsalted butter
- 6 tablespoons toasted almonds, ground
- 4 cups crushed amaretto cookies
- 1 cup heavy cream, whipped

1. In a large bowl, beat the eggs and sugar until the mixture is foamy. Stir in the cocoa, making sure there are no lumps.

2. Cut the butter into small pieces and melt them slowly, over low heat, in a small saucepan.

3. Whisk the melted butter into the sugar mixture, until it forms a thick batter. Fold in the ground almonds and amaretto cookie crumbs until well combined.

4. Line two 8½ × 4-inch loaf pans with wax paper. Divide the mixture in half and pour an equal amount into each loaf pan. Put the loaf pans in the refrigerator and chill the mixture for 3–4 hours, or until it has set. When you are ready to serve, simply lift the loaves out of the pans by gently tugging on the wax paper.

5. Place the loaves on a platter and peel off the wax paper. Garnish with the whipped cream.

Spring in Campania

*C*ampania is a fascinating region of Italy, framed by the sea on one side and the beautiful snow-capped Apennine Mountains on the other. But perhaps Campania is best known for the famous Amalfi Coast, which runs for over 300 miles with breathtaking views and hairpin turns high above the sea. Dotted with idyllic towns like Positano and Amalfi, it literally looks like a postcard!

Naples is the largest and best-known city in Campania, and considered the most vibrant city in Italy, full of exaggeration and contradiction. Rustic and elegant at the same time, it sits directly across the bay from the iconic island of Capri, where I spent a great deal of time as a child.

Neapolitans love life, and this is reflected in their extraordinary love of food! Blessed with the famous San Marzano tomato, grown in San Marzano sul Sarno, it is considered *the* sauce tomato in Italy.

My father came from a small town, high in the hills above Naples, where his mother learned the famous *cucina povera* of Campania—hearty, peasant cuisine. She cooked this way for her 13 children while raising them on Taylor Street in Chicago. In fact, the province from which my father's family hails is famous for people living to be over 100 years old. Their diet may be called *povera*, but it is rich in pasta, vegetables, legumes, extra virgin olive oil, and some fish.

Rivaled only by Sicily for its abundant produce, Campania is known for artichokes, figs,

apricots, San Marzano tomatoes, and citrus. It is the home of huge lemons, which are made into the famous limoncello liqueur. And, of course, Naples is best known as the birthplace of pizza!

Few areas of the world are richer in culinary tradition than Campania, my father's ancestral region, or blessed by more natural beauty. Spring is bountiful in Campania and these menus—from my Neapolitan table to yours—are unique and delicious!

Cent'anni! (May you live for 100 years!)

Lisa's Favorite Wines from Campania

The wines from the region of Campania are highly respected, both in Italy and in the United States, and it is said that the Greeks and Romans planted many of the vines in the region. The beauty of the wines from all over Italy is that they are excellent and not very expensive. Campania is no exception to this rule.

Much like the wine grapes grown around Etna in Sicily, the wines of Campania benefit from the rich, fertile, volcanic soil around Mt. Vesuvius, which produces outstanding grapes. For example, a red wine such as Taurasi, frequently called the "Barolo of the South" (I feature Barolo in the Piemonte section of this cookbook), is a strong, full-bodied red with no bitterness. Campania's red wines are delicious with the pasta and meat dishes that are featured in this section.

Another red wine from Campania that I love is Aglianico del Taburno. Rich and fruity, it goes with everything and is affordable at $16–$22 a bottle.

White wines from Campania are also refreshing, light, and not at all expensive. The best known is Greco di Bianco (note the name, Greco, meaning "Greek," which is a reference to the belief that the vines were first planted by the Greeks). This wine goes splendidly with all the fish dishes featured in this section of this book. Another wonderful white is Falanghina, from the breathtaking Amalfi Coast, where the vines grow up the hillsides—a spectacular sight to behold!

But my personal favorite wines from Campania have to be the Lacryma Christi del Vesuvio. There are three: a red, a rosé, and a white—all exceptional wines. I have been drinking them for years and have never been disappointed. Grown in the fertile soil of Vesuvius, the red is full-bodied, while the rosé and the white are light and crisp. These wines, like most vintages from southern Italy, are intelligently priced and range between $16 and $30 a bottle.

Salute!

Menu 14

SERVES 8

Torte di Risotto Risotto Cakes

Zuppa di Spaghetti Spezzati Broken Spaghetti Soup

Giambotta con Uove Fritte Giambotta with Fried Eggs

Insalata del Nonno Grandfather's Salad

Albicocche in Miele Apricots in Honey

As a southern Italian girl, when I think of Italian food, warm, comforting, satisfying dishes come to mind. Those qualities are the hallmarks of authentic Italian food—you taste the ingredients, and the flavors are true and real. This is the type of traditional food I was raised on, and this menu exemplifies that cucina. I can still see my Sicilian grandmother standing at the stove, breaking the spaghetti into the zuppa that is featured in this menu. I've continued this tradition with my own children, and when they were little they would squeal with delight when I let them stand on a step stool and break the spaghetti into the zuppa. I love the history of Italian food, and this dish is no different. Do you wonder why Italian home cooks came to put broken spaghetti into zuppa? Well, now, we buy packaged spaghetti and break it for fun, but spaghetti did not always come to Italian kitchens unbroken. Historically, pasta was packed and stored in large wooden barrels and then sold in general stores, in villages much like Castelvetrano, Sicily, where my great-grandfather lived. Inevitably, some of the spaghetti would break and settle at the bottom of the barrel. Grocers like my great-grandfather did not want to throw the pieces of pasta away,

so they put it in small bags and sold it for next to nothing. Creative southern Italian cooks put it in their soups!

Few dishes more aptly portray the wide range of fresh, yet hearty vegetables that are grown in Campania than Giambotta, a delicious dish made with fried eggs. In southern Italy, we frequently eat eggs as a main course, and this is by far my favorite main dish.

Evviva! (Cheers!)

Torte di Risotto
Risotto Cakes

- 4 cups freshly made breadcrumbs, or, if store bought, excellent quality
- ½ teaspoon salt
- ½ teaspoon freshly ground black pepper
- ½ teaspoon cayenne pepper
- 4 teaspoons fresh Italian flat leaf parsley, chopped
- 4 eggs
- 4 cups leftover risotto, chilled
- ½ cup provolone cheese, diced
- 4 cups canola oil, for frying
- 8 lemon wedges, for garnish

1. Mix the breadcrumbs, salt, pepper, cayenne pepper, and parsley together in a small bowl. Beat the eggs in a separate, shallow bowl.

2. Place ½ cup chilled risotto in the palm of your hand and fill it with 1 tablespoon of the provolone. Cover the cheese with a tablespoon of risotto, forming a ball, and then flatten the ball in your hand, so that it looks like a small disk.

3. Dip the risotto cake into the egg, on both sides, and then dip both sides of the cake in the breadcrumbs. You should have 12–16 cakes.

4. Pour enough oil into a large frying pan to reach a depth of about ½ inch. On medium-high heat, cook each risotto cake on each side until golden, approximately 3 minutes per side.

5. Remove the cakes from the pan and place them on paper towels to drain. Serve warm.

Zuppa di Spaghetti Spezzati
Broken Spaghetti Soup

- 4 tablespoons butter
- 4 tablespoons extra virgin olive oil
- 1 large white onion, chopped
- 6 cloves garlic, chopped
- 8 cups vegetable broth
- 1 herb bundle (1 bunch flat leaf Italian parsley and 1 bunch fresh thyme, tied together)
- 1 pound spaghetti
- ½ teaspoon freshly ground black pepper

1. In a 6- to 8-quart pot, melt the butter and heat the olive oil. Add the onion and garlic. Sauté until translucent. Add the broth and bring it to a medium boil. Add the herb bundle to the mixture and let it cook for 5 minutes. Then, remove the herb bundle.

2. When the broth comes to a medium boil, break the spaghetti into 1-inch pieces and drop them into the broth. Add the pepper. Cook for 7 minutes. Serve with warm foccacia (recipe below).

Lisa's Famous Foccacia

  1 package active dry yeast

  1½ tablespoons sugar

  5 cups unbleached all-purpose flour, plus more if necessary for kneading

  About 2 tablespoons Sicilian sea salt, coarse

  1½ cups extra virgin olive oil

1. In a small bowl, combine 2 cups of warm water, yeast, and sugar. Allow the yeast to bubble for at least 15 minutes.

2. In a mixer, combine the flour, 1 tablespoon sea salt, and ¾ cup olive oil. Knead the dough on a floured surface for 8 minutes. If it is too sticky, add a teaspoon of flour.

3. Coat the bottom of a large mixing bowl with 1 tablespoon of the olive oil and place the ball of dough in the bowl. Cover the bowl with plastic wrap and place it in a warm location until the dough doubles in size (this should take approximately 1 hour).

4. Coat a jelly-roll pan with ½ cup olive oil and place the dough in the center. With your fingers, press the dough outward until it covers the entire jelly-roll pan. With your fingers, or the end of a kitchen tool, make ¼-inch holes in the focaccia, approximately 1 inch apart. Cover the jelly-roll pan with plastic wrap and allow the dough to double in size once again, for approximately 1 hour.

5. Preheat the oven to 425°F. Sprinkle the top of the focaccia with the remaining sea salt and the rest of the olive oil. Bake for 30 minutes until golden on top. Cut into squares and serve.

Giambotta con Uove Fritte
Giambotta with Fried Eggs

- 6 tablespoons extra virgin olive oil
- 4 Italian frying peppers, seeded and thinly sliced
- 4 medium zucchini, thinly sliced
- 4 large tomatoes, chopped
- 1 medium eggplant, peeled and diced into ½-inch cubes
- 1 medium red bell pepper, seeded and diced
- 2 white onions, chopped
- ½ pound mushrooms, thinly sliced
- 1 teaspoon Sicilian sea salt, fine
- ½ teaspoon freshly ground black pepper
- 2 tablespoons unsalted butter
- 8 large eggs
- 10 –12 (4-inch) squares of focaccia, cut 1-inch thick (recipe above)

1. Heat 4 tablespoons of the olive oil in a large frying pan. Add the frying peppers, zucchini, tomatoes, eggplant, bell pepper, onions, and mushrooms, and cook the mixture over low heat, stirring it occasionally for approximately 20 minutes. Season the mixture with salt and pepper, and keep it warm.

2. In a large skillet, place the butter and 2 tablespoons of extra virgin olive oil, and crack the 8 eggs, or as many as you can fit in the pan. Cook the eggs sunny side up over low heat for 3 to 5 minutes, or until the white is hard, but the yoke is still runny.

3. Place the vegetable mixture on a platter and spoon the eggs on top. Serve with the squares of focaccia.

LISA'S TIP

Italian frying peppers are long, thin peppers that look a little like the "banana peppers" that are marketed in the United States. Italian frying peppers are red and green, however, and are available at all supermarkets.

Insalata del Nonno
Grandfather's Salad

    6 large tomatoes, diced
    4 large celery stalks, chopped
    2 garlic cloves, chopped
    8 basil leaves, chopped
    1 teaspoon dried oregano
    ½ green bell pepper, seeded and
      chopped
    1 teaspoon Sicilian sea salt, fine
    ½ teaspoon freshly ground black
      pepper
    ¼ cup extra virgin olive oil

Toss all the ingredients together in a large
bowl and serve.

Albicocche in Miele
Apricots in Honey

    2 cups high-quality honey
      Zest of 1 lemon
      Juice of 2 lemons
    24 fresh apricots, halved and pitted
      Vanilla ice cream or freshly whipped
      cream, for serving

1. Combine honey, lemon zest, lemon juice,
and ½ cup water in a large saucepan. Bring the
mixture to a boil and then reduce the heat to
medium-low. Place the apricots in the liquid
for 3 to 5 minutes until they're soft.

2. Remove the apricots from the liquid with a
slotted spoon. Serve the fruit with a dollop of
vanilla ice cream or freshly whipped cream.

Menu 15
SERVES 8

Crostini di Pesto Napoletani alla Lisa Lisa's Neapolitan Crostini Pesto

Capellini con Gamberi Cappellini with Shrimp

Peperoni Ripieni alla Salernitana Stuffed Peppers, Salerno Style

Indivia Grilliata Grilled Endive

Il Famoso Tiramisù al Limoncello di Lisa
Lisa's Famous Limoncello Tiramisù

In Italy, tiramisù is really more like a pudding than a cake; it should be moist and light, never dry or heavy. The limoncello tiramisù in this menu, one of my signature dishes, features the famous lemons that grow along the Amalfi Coast in the Campania region. I began to make this tiramisù for my daughter Felicia, who adores all things with lemon.

We Italians savor our stuffed peppers and you can find them, made a little differently, in every region of Italy. I love stuffed peppers the way they are prepared in the province of Salerno, outside of Naples, the ancestral home of my father. There I learned to soak the bread before adding it to the rest of the mix whenever I make stuffed peppers or meatballs.

Salute! (To your health!)

Crostini di Pesto Napoletano alla Lisa

Lisa's Neapolitan Crostini Pesto

 1 eggplant, peeled and cubed

 6 peppers (3 red, 3 yellow), seeded and sliced

 2 red onions, sliced

 8 garlic cloves

 3 fennel bulbs, sliced

 1½ cups extra virgin olive oil

 2 teaspoons Sicilian sea salt, fine

 2 teaspoons black pepper

 2 teaspoons dried oregano

 1 baguette, sliced and toasted

 2 teaspoons crushed red pepper

1. Preheat oven to 375°F.

2. Toss all the ingredients in a large bowl with 1 cup of the olive oil. Spread the mixture on 2 baking sheets (jelly-roll pans) and roast for 30 minutes. Allow the mixture to cool.

3. Run the mixture through a blender or food processor until pureed, but not completely smooth. Leave some chunks. Stir in the remaining ½ cup of olive oil.

4. Spread the pesto on toasted Italian bread and serve.

Capellini con Gamberi

Cappellini with Shrimp

 6 tablespoons extra virgin olive oil

 2 pounds large deveined shrimp, peeled and uncooked

 6 large garlic cloves, minced

 ½ teaspoon dried oregano

 ¼ teaspoon freshly ground black pepper

 1 cup sweet vermouth

 2 (15-ounce) cans diced San Marzano tomatoes, drained

 1½ cups heavy cream

 1 teaspoon fresh lemon juice

 2 pounds cappellini

1. Place the olive oil in a large frying pan and sauté the shrimp, garlic, oregano, and pepper for approximately 2–3 minutes. Stir in the vermouth and the tomatoes, scraping up any brown bits from the bottom of the frying pan. Add the cream and briskly simmer the mixture until the sauce has thickened slightly, about 2 minutes. Stir in the lemon juice.

2. Meanwhile, boil the water and cook the cappellini al dente. Top the cappellini with the shrimp and sauce.

Peperoni Ripieni alla Salernitana
Stuffed Peppers, Salerno Style

8 cups stale Italian bread, cubed

¾ cup whole milk

1 cup Parmigiano Reggiano, grated

1 cup Pecorino Romano, grated

1 cup black olives, pitted and halved

½ cup salted capers, chopped

4 anchovies, rinsed and chopped

2 tablespoons garlic, chopped

1 cup flat leaf Italian parsley, chopped

8 medium red bell peppers

4 eggs

½ teaspoon Sicilian sea salt, fine

½ teaspoon freshly ground black pepper

1 cup extra virgin olive oil

1 pound ground veal

1. Preheat the oven to 400°F.

2. In a large bowl, soak the bread in the milk. In another bowl, combine the cheeses, olives, capers, anchovies, garlic, and parsley. Slice the peppers in half. Remove the stem, seeds, and the white membrane. With your hands, squeeze the milk out of the soaked bread and crumble it into the bowl with the other ingredients. Add eggs, salt, and pepper. Mix very well with a fork.

3. In a medium-size frying pan, pour ½ cup of the olive oil and sauté the ground veal for 4–5 minutes. Do not overcook the meat.

4. Combine the veal with the stuffing mixture. Fill each pepper to the brim with the mixture, without packing it down.

5. Place the stuffed peppers in a large casserole dish. Drizzle about 2 tablespoons of olive oil on top of each one and bake for 45 minutes. These peppers are delish warm or at room temperature.

LISA'S TIP

In my father's town, in the province of Salerno, it is traditional to soak bread in milk before adding it to the other ingredients in meatballs, much as my grandmother did whenever she made her famous meatballs. This method makes the meatballs very moist, while holding them together.

Indivia Grilliata
Grilled Endive

- 4 large heads Belgian endive, halved through the core
- 4 tablespoons olive oil
- ½ cup Gorgonzola cheese, imported from Italy
- 4 tablespoons walnuts, chopped
- 3 tablespoons balsamic vinegar

1. Brush the endive with 2 tablespoons of the olive oil. Set the grill on medium-high. (If you are not using a grill, set the oven to 375°F.) Place the endive directly on the grill or on a cookie sheet and grill for 4 minutes or roast for 10 minutes, turning the endive once, halfway through the cooking time.

2. Place the endive, cut side up, on each plate. Top with cheese and walnuts, and drizzle with balsamic vinegar and the remaining olive oil.

LISA'S TIP
Being Sicilian, I love lemon zest. If you are using a cheese grater, instead of a lemon zester, be very careful not to get any of the white pith of the lemon into the dish, as the pith is bitter.

Il Famoso Tiramisù al Limoncello di Lisa
Lisa's Famous Limoncello Tiramisù

- 30 ounces mascarpone cheese
- 9 tablespoons sugar
- 4 eggs, separated
- 1 cup limoncello liqueur, imported from Italy
- 24 ladyfinger cookies (Savoiardi, imported from Italy)
- 2 tablespoons lemon zest

1. Put the mascarpone, sugar, and egg yolks in a bowl and beat together well.

2. In a separate bowl, beat the egg whites until stiff. Fold the egg whites into the mascarpone mixture.

3. Cover the bottom of a serving or trifle bowl with a few spoonfuls of the mascarpone mixture. Pour the limoncello into a pie plate or a shallow dish. Place one ladyfinger in the limoncello for 10 seconds, turning it so that it becomes well soaked, but still retains its shape. Do not allow the ladyfinger to get soggy.

4. Place the ladyfinger over the mascarpone mixture and sprinkle a little lemon zest on top. Repeat this process until you've filled the bowl. End with the mascarpone mixture and lemon zest.

The Amalfi Coast is world renowned for its beautiful, gigantic lemons. And when life gives you lemons, make limoncello! That's what I do in beautiful Sorrento at the well known Limonoro.

Menu 16

SERVES 8

Fritti di Mozzarella e Provolone Mozzarella & Provolone Fritters

Gnocchi in Sugo di Vodka e Pancetta
Gnocchi in Creamy Vodka Sauce with Pancetta

Salsiccie in Sugo di Pomodoro Italian Sausage in Lisa's Classic Tomato Sauce

Cipolle Ripiene Stuffed Onions

Torta di Ciliege Amare Sour Cherry Pie

One of my most popular sauces, which I now jar and sell across the United States, is Lisa's Creamy Vodka Sauce. It's the perfect combination of a rosé sauce (tomato and cream), with just the right amount of crushed red pepper to give it a kick, and enough vodka to give the sauce its smooth, distinctive taste. You can make my Creamy Vodka Sauce with gnocchi, as in this menu, but it is excellent on any kind of pasta, especially stuffed pasta like ravioli!

We Italians stuff everything, and onions are no exception. The region of Campania, which is known for its amazing produce, is especially famous for the sweet onions that are grown along the coastline. We pick the largest ones we can find; carve out the center; stuff them with breadcrumbs, raisins, and cheese; and get the classic savory-sweet taste of southern Italian cuisine.

I end this satisfying, wholly Neapolitan menu with a typical crostata, which is considered the hallmark dessert for rustic cooking all over Italy.

Cin cin a tutti! (Cheers to all!)

Fritti di Mozzarella e Provolone
Mozzarella & Provolone Fritters

16 ounces mozzarella cheese, sliced,
   ¼ inch thick

16 ounces smoked provolone cheese,
   sliced ¼ inch thick

½ cup unbleached flour

3 eggs, beaten

2 cups excellent-quality breadcrumbs

Canola oil, for frying

1. Coat each slice of mozzarella and provolone in flour. Dip the slices in the beaten egg, and then dip them in the breadcrumbs.

2. Heat ¾ inch of canola oil in a frying pan over medium heat. When the oil is hot, fry the cheese fritters for 5 minutes, until the coating is crisp and golden. Carefully turn the fritters, halfway through the cooking time, using a spatula.

3. Drain the fritters on paper towels and serve.

Gnocchi in Sugo di Vodka e Pancetta
Gnocchi in Creamy Vodka Sauce with Pancetta

Lisa's Homemade Gnocchi (recipe below)
   (or 2 pounds store-bought gnocchi,
   imported from Italy, of excellent
   quality, such as Rana or Buitoni)

8 medium potatoes, preferably
   Yukon gold

1 egg yolk

1 tablespoon Sicilian sea salt, fine

2 to 2½ cups all-purpose flour

1. Preheat oven to 350°F.

2. *To make the gnocchi:* Puncture the potatoes in several places with a fork. Bake the potatoes for 1 hour or until tender. Scoop out the flesh and discard the skins.

3. Push the hot potatoes through a ricer or food mill, into a large bowl; let the potatoes cool slightly. Add the egg yolk, salt, and 2 cups of the flour; mix well. Put the potato mixture on a work surface or a wooden board and knead it into a ball. The mixture should be soft, pliable, and slightly sticky. If it is too sticky, add a little more flour.

4. Lightly flour a work surface and your hands. Break the dough into pieces, about the size of large eggs. Shape the pieces into 6-inch logs, about as thick as your thumb. Cut the rolls into 1-inch pieces. With your thumb, roll the dough down the tines of the fork and then repeat on the other side of the dough. The grooves made by the fork will absorb any sauce. Repeat with the remaining gnocchi. Arrange on a floured tray or large plate and set it aside.

5. In a large pot, filled with water, bring water to a boil and gently place gnocchi in it. When the gnocchi are cooked, they float to the top of the pot.

My son Guido rices the potatoes while my daughter Felicia rolls out the gnocchi. Making gnocchi together is a wonderful Sunday Dinner tradition!

Lisa's Creamy Vodka Sauce

- 8 tablespoons unsalted butter
- 1 onion, chopped
- 4 cloves of garlic, chopped
- ¼ teaspoon Sicilian sea salt, fine
- ¼ teaspoon freshly ground black pepper
- 1 teaspoon crushed red pepper flakes
- 1 (26-ounce) can crushed San Marzano tomatoes
- ½ cup vodka
- 2 tablespoons sugar
- 1 cup heavy cream
- 8 basil leaves, chopped
- ½ cup Parmigiano Reggiano, grated

1. Melt the butter in a large frying pan. Sauté the onion and garlic until they're translucent. Add the salt, pepper, and red pepper flakes. Add the crushed tomatoes and the vodka. Cook the mixture for 5 minutes. Lower the heat to a low simmer. Add the sugar, and stir well. Slowly stir the cream into the sauce until it is well blended, making sure not to allow the sauce to boil after the cream is added. Top the sauce with fresh basil leaves.

2. Place the cooked gnocchi directly into the tomato sauce, transfer it to a serving bowl, and top with the Parmigiano Reggiano.

Salsiccie in Sugo di Pomodoro
Italian Sausage in Lisa's Classic Tomato Sauce

- 1 pound hot Italian sausage, in links
- 1 pound sweet Italian sausage, in links
- ½ cup extra virgin olive oil
- 3 tablespoons chopped garlic
- 2 tablespoons fennel seeds
- 2 cups chopped red onions
- 1 tablespoon Sicilian sea salt, fine
- 1 tablespoon crushed red pepper
- 4 cups Lisa's Classic Tomato Sauce (recipe below)

1. Either grill the Italian sausages on medium-high for 30 minutes, or bake them in a preheated 350° oven in a 13 × 9-inch casserole dish, in 1 cup of water for 30 minutes. Transfer the cooked sausages to paper towels and let them drain.

2. Pour the olive oil into a large frying pan and sauté the garlic, fennel seeds, crushed red pepper, and red onions for 7 minutes, until they're soft, but not brown. Add the sausages and sauté them over medium heat for 12 minutes. Lower the heat to simmer, pour 4 cups of Lisa's Classic Tomato Sauce (recipe below) over the sausages, and let them simmer for 15 minutes more. Serve.

Lisa's Classic Tomato Sauce

- 6 cloves garlic, cut in half, green sprouts removed, if necessary
- ½ cup extra virgin olive oil
- 4 (28-ounce) cans crushed tomatoes, preferably San Marzano
- 1½ tablespoons sugar

1½ tablespoons dried Italian oregano

1½ tablespoons chopped fresh basil

½ tablespoon Sicilian sea salt, fine

½ tablespoon freshly ground black pepper

In a large pot, heat the garlic in the olive oil over low heat for 3 minutes. Don't allow the garlic to brown. Add the remaining ingredients and simmer the sauce over very low heat for 2–4 hours.

Cipolle Ripiene
Stuffed Onions

8 medium-size white onions

6 tablespoons unsalted butter

16 ounces breadcrumbs

¼ teaspoon thyme

¼ teaspoon sage

¼ teaspoon oregano

1 teaspoon Sicilian sea salt, fine

½ teaspoon freshly ground black pepper

2 ounces raisins

6 eggs

1½ cups grated Parmigiano Reggiano

Preheat the oven to 350°F.

1. Slice off the top of the onions and remove the outer skin. Rinse the onions under cold water. With a paring knife, cut a hole in the center of each onion, removing the center section, and leaving at least 2–3 outer layers. Chop the center section of the onion.

2. In a medium-size frying pan, melt the butter. Brown the chopped onions in the butter for 4–5 minutes. Add the breadcrumbs, thyme, sage, oregano, salt, pepper, and raisins.

3. Stuff the onion "shells" with the mixture and place them in a large ceramic or heatproof baking dish.

4. In a separate bowl, beat the eggs with 1 cup of Parmigiano Reggiano and spoon the mixture over each onion. Bake for 30 minutes.

5. Remove the onions from the oven and top with the remaining ½ cup of Parmigiano cheese. Broil for 3 minutes under the broiler. Serve.

Torta di Ciliege Amare

Sour Cherry Pie

For Lisa's Pasta Frolla (Pastry Dough)

1¼ cups all-purpose flour

¼ teaspoon baking powder

Pinch salt

⅓ cup sugar

1 stick, plus 1 tablespoon unsalted butter, cold and sliced

1 egg yolk

For the Filling

20 ounces sour cherry jam, excellent quality, preferably imported from Italy, such as Casa Giulia

Zest of 2 oranges

2 tablespoons confectioners' sugar

1. *To make the pastry dough:* Combine flour, baking powder, salt, and sugar. Make a well in the center of the flour mixture and add the butter and egg yolk. Knead the mixture into a soft dough, adding a few drops of ice water. This can be done by hand or in a mixer. Separate the pastry dough into 2 balls, 1 large and 1 small. Roll out the large ball and line a 9½-inch fluted tart pan or a pie pan with the dough. Prick the dough with a fork and chill it for 30 minutes in the refrigerator. Refrigerate the small ball of dough as well.

2. Preheat the oven to 400°F.

3. *To make the filling:* In a bowl mix together the sour cherry jam and the orange zest. Pour the mixture into the piecrust.

4. Roll out the small ball of dough into a rectangle and cut it into ¼-inch strips to form a lattice over the jam. Bake the pie for 30 minutes.

LISA'S TIP

Depending on your oven, this pie may also be done after 20 minutes, because you are only cooking the crust, so keep an eye on it and adjust the cooking time accordingly.

Antipasto di Spiedini Napoletani Neapolitan Spiedini

Perciatelli Napoletani Perciatelli, Naples Style

Pollo alla Francese Chicken alla Francese

Panzanella Tomato Salad with Cucumber, Onion, and Bread

Biscotti di Anisetta Anisette Cookies

Perciatelli, a larger form of bucatini, is a fun, fat, tubular pasta with a hole down the middle. I always explain to Americans that every shape of Italian pasta is made for a reason: to ensure that the particular kind of sauce you happen to be making will adhere to the type of pasta you are serving. Naples-style perciatelli is no exception. (For a more detailed explanation of pasta cuts and the appropriate sauces, see my how-to video at lisacaponigri.com.) With every bite you taste the luscious interplay of the chunky, hearty, Neapolitan ragù and the pasta.

Being a good southern Italian girl, I love my anisette. Some of you may know it as Sambuca Romana, which is sold everywhere in the United States. Anisette is a licorice-flavored liqueur, which is very popular in Italy. I grew up watching my maternal grandfather, who was from Campania, drink what we called caffe corretto every night after dinner. Caffe corretto, which literally means "correct coffee," is an espresso with a shot of anisette liqueur. I am known for my anisette cookies—the perfect ending to any meal, as well as this menu from Campania.

Sempre famiglia! (Family first!)

Antipasto di Spiedini Napoletani
Neapolitan Spiedini

2 (15-ounce) cans cannellini beans, imported from Italy

1 cup sliced black olives, preferably imported from Italy

2 tablespoons fresh basil leaves, chopped

1 teaspoon Sicilian sea salt, fine, plus more for brushing the skewers

½ teaspoon ground black pepper, plus more for sprinkling on the skewers

½ cup extra virgin olive oil, plus more for sprinkling on the skewers

2 tablespoons lemon juice

3 cloves garlic, chopped

1 loaf country rustic Italian bread (page 186)

8 ounces salami

8 ounces provolone

16 (6-inch) wood or metal skewers (spiedini)

2 cups grape tomatoes

2 (6-ounce) jars quartered artichoke hearts

1. Preheat the oven to 400°F.

2. Line a jelly-roll pan (a cookie sheet with a rim) with parchment paper or aluminum foil.

3. In a large bowl, combine the cannellini beans, black olives, basil, salt, and pepper. Toss this mixture with the olive oil, lemon juice, and garlic. Set aside.

4. Cut the bread, salami, and provolone into 1-inch cubes.

5. *To make the spiedini:* Thread each skewer, first with a piece of cheese, followed by a piece of salami, a tomato, an artichoke, and, finally, a cube of bread. Brush the skewers with extra virgin olive oil and a sprinkle of salt and pepper, if desired.

6. Place the skewers on the prepared baking sheet and bake them for 4 minutes, or until the bread turns golden. Do not let the cheese melt too much.

7. To serve, spoon the bean mixture in the center of a small plate and place 2 spiedini on the bean mixture.

Perciatelli Napoletani
Perciatelli, Naples Style

½ cup extra virgin olive oil, plus
   2 tablespoons

4 cloves garlic, thinly sliced lengthwise

½ pound chicken livers

1 pound green peas, frozen or fresh

1 teaspoon Sicilian sea salt, fine

4 cups Lisa's Ragù (page 286)

2 pounds perciatelli pasta

½ teaspoon crushed red pepper flakes

2 cups fresh mozzarella (2 large balls,
   cut into ¼-inch cubes)

1 cup freshly grated Parmigiano
   Reggiano

1. In a large frying pan, heat ½ cup of the olive oil. Add the garlic and chicken livers. With the back of a wooden spoon, break up the chicken livers as you cook them. Cook until chicken livers are no longer pink. Depending on whether the chicken livers were frozen or not, you may get an excessive amount of water in the frying pan. At this point, pour the chicken livers and garlic into a colander to drain off the water. After draining off any excess water, add 2 tablespoons of oil to the frying pan before putting the cooked chicken livers back into pan.

2. Add the peas to the chicken liver–and–garlic mixture. Add the salt and cook the mixture for 7 minutes.

3. Heat the ragù in a separate large saucepan.

4. Cook the pasta according to the directions on the package and then drain it. Add the pasta to the saucepan with the ragù. Add the chicken livers and peas and toss over high heat until well mixed. Remove the mixture from the heat. Add the red pepper flakes and mozzarella and toss until the mozzarella begins to melt.

5. Pour the pasta into a serving bowl and serve immediately. Top with Parmigiano Reggiano.

Pollo alla Francese
Chicken alla Francese

- 8 boneless, skinless chicken breasts
- 1 cup unbleached flour, for dredging
- 1 teaspoon Sicilian sea salt, fine
- ½ teaspoon freshly ground black pepper
- 4 eggs
- 1 cup extra virgin olive oil
- 6 tablespoons unsalted butter
- 1 lemon, sliced in thin rounds
- 1 cup white wine
- Juice of 1 lemon
- ½ cup Italian flat leaf parsley, chopped

1. Pound the chicken breasts until they are ¼–½-inch thick. Put the flour and the salt and pepper into a flat bowl, such as a pie plate.

2. In another shallow bowl or dish, beat the eggs.

3. Dredge each chicken cutlet in the flour on both sides, and then dip it in the egg wash.

4. Heat the olive oil and butter in a large frying pan. Fry the cutlets for 2–3 minutes on each side until golden brown. Remove the chicken cutlets to a platter and cover with aluminum foil.

5. In the same pan used to cook the chicken, toss the lemon slices and cook them until they've turned golden from the remaining flour in the bottom of the frying pan. Scrape any bits of flour from the bottom of the pan and mix them together with the lemon slices

for approximately 2 minutes. Add the white wine and lemon juice and simmer with the lemon slices. Reduce the heat to medium-low and allow the sauce to thicken slightly, 3–4 more minutes.

6. Return the chicken cutlets to the sauce in the pan. Simmer for a minimum of 5 minutes over medium heat.

7. To serve, place the chicken cutlets on a platter, pour over the sauce, place the lemon slices from the sauce on top, and finish with a sprinkle of the chopped parsley.

Panzanella
Tomato Salad with Cucumber, Onion, and Bread

- 2 red onions, cut in ½-inch-thick slices
- 8 Roma tomatoes, slice ¼ inch thick.
- 9 tablespoons extra virgin olive oil
- 4 cups good-quality Italian bread, cubed
- 2 teaspoons dried thyme
- 1 teaspoon Sicilian sea salt, fine
- ½ teaspoon freshly ground black pepper
- 8 wood or metal skewers
- 2 cucumbers (preferably English cucumbers, which are seedless, cut into ½-inch slices)
- ½ cup fresh basil, chopped
- 4 tablespoons red wine vinegar, excellent quality, preferably imported from Italy

1. Preheat the grill or, if you are not grilling, preheat the oven to 350°F.

2. Brush the onion slices and tomato slices with 3 tablespoons of the extra virgin olive oil and set them aside.

3. In a large bowl, place the cubed bread and toss it with 3 tablespoons of olive oil, the thyme, and salt and pepper, until the bread is well coated. Thread the bread cubes onto the skewers. Grill the bread on the preheated grill for approximately 3 minutes, or until the bread is golden on all sides.

4. Place the onions and tomatoes on the grill and grill for approximately 5 minutes until soft. (If you are not using a grill, you can place the bread skewers, the onions, and the tomatoes on a cookie sheet and roast them for 10–12 minutes at 350°F.)

5. Chop the grilled or roasted onions and tomatoes into big pieces and place them in a large salad bowl with the toasted bread, cucumber, and fresh basil.

6. Whisk together the vinegar, and the 3 remaining tablespoons of olive oil in a small bowl. Pour over the salad and toss.

Biscotti di Anisetta
Anisette Cookies

For the Dough

¾ cup sugar

1 stick unsalted butter, melted

2 large eggs

¼ cup whole milk

2 teaspoons anise extract

2¾ cups unbleached flour

2½ teaspoons baking powder

¼ teaspoon salt

For the Glaze

1 cup confectioners' sugar

6 teaspoons whole milk

1 teaspoon anise extract

1 (2-ounce) jar multicolored nonpareils

1. Preheat oven to 325°F.

2. *To make the cookies:* Beat on high the sugar, butter, eggs, milk, and anise extract in a large bowl with a handheld or stand mixer. After they are well incorporated, lower the mixer speed to low and slowly mix in the flour, baking powder, and salt.

3. Butter a large cookie sheet. With a teaspoon or a small cookie scoop, drop the dough onto the baking sheet, 2 inches apart. Bake for 8–10 minutes until the bottom of the cookies are golden. Remove the cookies from the oven and let them cool.

4. *To prepare the glaze:* Whisk the confectioners' sugar, milk, and anise extract in a small bowl until the mixture is smooth.

5. Dip the top of the cookies in the glaze and immediately sprinkle with the nonpareils. Allow the cookies to rest until the glaze dries before serving.

Menu 18

SERVES 8

Fichi con Formaggio di Capra e Miele
Warm Figs with Goat Cheese & Honey

Spaghetti con Pomodori e Nocciole
Spaghetti with Tomato and Hazelnuts

Pollo alla Romana Roman Style Chicken

Fagiolini Fritti Fried Green Beans

Strudel di Datteri e Pera Pear and Date Strudel

The vegetables in Campania are known for their deep flavor and freshness. Southern Italy is called *Il Mezzogiorno*, which literally means "noon." This nickname is due to the region's constant, sunny, warm climate and intense heat. But the vegetables reap all the benefits of so much light and heat, which you can taste in every flavorful bite! They are never picked before they are perfectly ripe or trucked for thousands of miles and allowed to mature on grocery store shelves. Italy is a small country, and foods are served fresh and at the peak of the season. This is particularly the case with vegetables in southern Italy. In this menu, I share one of my favorite chicken dishes, with some of the most beautiful vegetables from Campania: red peppers, yellow peppers, Roma tomatoes, onions, and garlic, in Pollo alla Romana.

The second course in this menu is equally delicious—a pasta dish that combines fresh, juicy tomatoes with the toasted crunch of hazelnuts, which are delicious in both sweet and savory dishes in southern Italy.

In my cookbooks, I take great pride in bringing to you truly authentic menus that you might not find anywhere else. This is the food that real Italian families eat in Italy. From all my years of living there, both as a child and as an adult raising my own family, I am so happy to share these recipes, so that you can make them with your own family!

Alla nostra! (To us!)

Fichi con Formaggio di Capra e Miele

Warm Figs with Goat Cheese & Honey

- 24 fresh figs, black or green, halved lengthwise (starting at the stem, cut down)
- 1 cup crumbled goat cheese
- 2 tablespoons balsamic vinegar, excellent quality, preferably imported from Italy
- 3 tablespoons honey

1. Preheat the oven to 350°F.

2. Arrange the figs on a baking sheet, cut side up. Spoon ½ teaspoon of the goat cheese on each fig half, and then brush it with the vinegar. Drizzle with the honey.

3. Bake for 8–10 minutes until the figs are warm.

FROM THE VINES OF VESUVIUS

The San Marzano tomato, largely considered the best in the world, is grown outside Naples on the Sorrento peninsula, in the region's fertile soil, which is enriched by Mt. Vesuvius. The San Marzano is the perfect sauce tomato: It is thin-skinned, vibrantly red, and the flesh is dense, yet tender. But, most importantly, its acidity and sweetness are perfectly balanced. It is the only tomato used in Italy for sauce, and the only tomato you will find in my recipes! San Marzano tomatoes are available, imported and canned, everywhere in the United States.

I love the roadside trucks on the Amalfi Coast featuring regional specialties!

This Is Sunday Dinner

Spaghetti con Pomodori e Nocciole
Spaghetti with Tomatoes and Hazelnuts

1 cup hazelnuts, blanched

2 pounds cherry tomatoes, halved

2 teaspoons Sicilian sea salt, fine

2 large round tomatoes, chopped

4 garlic cloves, crushed

2 teaspoons crushed red pepper flakes

2 cups fresh basil leaves

2 pounds spaghetti

1 cup extra virgin olive oil

1 teaspoon freshly ground black pepper

1 cup ricotta salata, grated

1. Place the hazelnuts in a large, dry frying pan and cook them over medium to low heat until they are golden brown, 8–10 minutes. Do not let the hazelnuts burn. Allow them to cool and then chop them coarsely.

2. Place the halved cherry tomatoes in a large bowl and toss them with the salt.

3. In a blender or food processor, puree the tomatoes, garlic, crushed red pepper flakes, 1 cup of the basil leaves, and half of the chopped hazelnuts until smooth. Add this mixture to the bowl of the salted cherry tomatoes.

4. Cook the spaghetti according to the directions on the package. Toss the spaghetti with the hazelnut-tomato mixture in the large bowl, adding the olive oil, the remaining half of the hazelnuts and the remaining 1 cup of basil leaves.

5. Top with ricotta salata and serve.

Pollo alla Romana
Roman Style Chicken

2 cups unbleached flour, for dredging

1 teaspoon freshly ground black pepper, plus more for seasoning at the end

1 cup extra virgin olive oil

2 large chickens, cut up

6 ounces pancetta, diced (if you cannot find pancetta, good-quality bacon will do)

4 garlic cloves, chopped

2 onions, chopped

2 red bell peppers and 2 yellow bell peppers, seeded, white interior seem removed, and diced

1 cup white wine

6 cups chopped Roma tomatoes

2 teaspoons fresh marjoram

2 teaspoons Sicilian sea salt, fine

1. Place the flour in a 13 × 9-inch heatproof glass baking dish and mix in 1 teaspoon of black pepper.

2. Pour the olive oil into a large frying pan and warm it over medium heat. Dredge the chicken pieces in the flour. Brown the chicken pieces for 5 minutes on each side. Transfer the chicken to a platter and cover it with aluminum foil.

3. Over medium heat, stir the pancetta into the same olive oil in the large frying pan that was used to brown the chicken. Reduce the heat to medium-low and add the garlic and onions. Cook for approximately 3 minutes. Add the peppers and sauté for approximately 8 minutes until the peppers soften. Remove half of this mixture from the frying pan and set it aside.

4. Return the chicken to the frying pan (you may have to use 2 frying pans since you are preparing this dish for 8 people) and toss the chicken with the vegetables. Pour the wine over the chicken and cook for 5 minutes, allowing the wine to evaporate. Add the tomatoes, marjoram, salt, and pepper. Bring to a boil. Reduce the heat to medium and simmer for approximately 30 minutes.

5. Five minutes before the chicken is done cooking, add the red-and-yellow-pepper mixture, which you had set aside, to the chicken. Serve.

LISA'S TIP

Only dredge as many pieces of chicken as you are going to fry at one time. When you dredge chicken and allow it to sit for a while, the flour becomes moist and does not form a crispy crust when fried. See more cooking tips at lisacaponigri.com

Fagiolini Fritti
Fried Green Beans

> 2 pounds fresh green beans, ends cut off
>
> 1 cup extra virgin olive oil
>
> 4 eggs
>
> 1 teaspoon Sicilian sea salt, fine
>
> ½ teaspoon freshly ground black pepper
>
> 1 cup Parmigiano Reggiano, grated
>
> 1 cup unbleached flour for dredging

1. Bring a large 4-quart pot of water to a rolling boil. Drop the green beans into the water for 2 minutes. Drain them immediately.

2. Heat the olive oil in a large frying pan over medium heat. Beat the eggs and add the salt, pepper, and cheese to the egg mixture. Coat the green beans in the flour and dip them in the egg mixture.

3. Drop the coated beans into the hot oil one at a time and fry for 2 minutes until golden.

4. Place the beans on paper towels to let them drain.

Strudel di Datteri e Pera
Pear and Date Strudel

For the Filling

    3 cups sliced pears

    2 cups dates, chopped

    ½ cup sugar

    ½ cup walnuts, chopped

For the Puff Pastry

    1 sheet frozen puff pastry, thawed

    1 egg slightly beaten

    Sugar for sprinkling over the pastry

1. Preheat the oven to 400°F.

2. Line a jelly-roll pan (a baking sheet with ¼-inch-high sides) with parchment paper.

3. In a blender or food processor, combine all the filling ingredients until a coarse paste forms.

4. Place the puff pastry dough on the jelly-roll pan and spoon the filling mixture into the center of the puff pastry. Fold in the sides and roll the pastry, placing it seam-side down on the parchment paper. Brush the top and both ends of the puff pastry with the beaten egg and sprinkle the sugar on top of it.

5. Bake the strudel for 20 minutes or until golden brown. Let the strudel cool completely before slicing and serving.

There are few places on earth more beautiful than Positano, in the heart of the Amalfi Coast. And few restaurants are more well known then Buca di Bacco! It features delicious food and overlooks the Mediterranean Sea. Here I help prepare the coveted Risotto and Red Sauce with Chef Giuseppe!

Menu 19

SERVES 8

Bruschetta con Basilico e Formaggio Bruschetta with Basil & Cheese

Manicotti di Salmone Cremoso Creamy Salmon Manicotti

Pesce Spada con Agrumi Citrus Swordfish

Torta di Zucchini e Ricotta Zucchini & Ricotta Tart

Torta di Riso e Limone Lemon Rice Crostata

Since Campania has hundreds of miles of coastline, fish plays a central role in our diet, and there is nothing more elegant than a stuffed pasta dish with a creamy salmon sauce. The saltiness of the salmon, paired with the smoothness of the cream filling, is a perfect combination.

Campania is also known for its citrus fruit—so the swordfish dish in this menu, which is topped with lemons and oranges, is typical of the Campania region and one of my favorite secondi. The saffron in the recipe is evidence of Arab invasions in Italy, which left their influence on our food, and melds beautifully with blood oranges to make a distinctive, rich sauce.

The rice in pastry dishes in Campania, like the delicious Lemon Rice Torte, in this menu, reduces the amount of flour in the pastry and gives it a moist, delicious texture. And, since lemons are featured so often in our desserts in Campania, the hearty and refreshing Lemon Rice Torte is the perfect way to end this Campania menu. It is exceptionally good!

I will end with a saying that my brother loves to use, and which is now a motto in our family:

Mangia bene, bevi piu! (Eat well and drink more!)

Bruschetta con Basilico e Formaggio
Bruschetta with Basil & Cheese

    4 tomatoes (roma or beefsteak)

    2 (2-ounce cans) flat anchovies

    ½ cup extra virgin olive oil, plus 1–2
        tablespoons for greasing the pan

    16 slices Italian filone bread (similar in
        shape and size to a baguette)

    2 cups Fontina cheese, shredded

    1 teaspoon Sicilian sea salt, fine

    ½ teaspoon freshly ground black
        pepper

    ½ cup fresh basil leaves, chopped

1. Thinly slice the tomatoes in rounds.
Drain the anchovies and cut them into strips.
Set the tomatoes and anchovies aside. Grease
a 13 × 9-inch baking dish or jelly-roll pan (a
cookie sheet with a rim) with 1–2 tablespoons
of olive oil.

2. Preheat the oven to 400°F. Arrange the
sliced bread on the oiled baking dish or
jelly-roll pan and sprinkle it with the cheese.
Arrange the anchovy strips over the cheese
and top each slice of bread with 1 or 2 tomato
slices. Sprinkle salt, pepper, and extra virgin
olive oil on top.

3. Bake the bruschetta for 12 minutes.
Remove it from the oven and sprinkle with the
chopped basil.

Manicotti di Salmone Cremoso
Creamy Salmon Manicotti

    4 tablespoons unsalted butter,
        cut into pieces

    ½ teaspoon salt

    ½ teaspoon freshly ground black
        pepper

    8 center-cut salmon fillets,
        approximately 6 ounces each,
        skin removed

For the Besciamella Sauce

    8 tablespoons unsalted butter, cut into
        pieces, plus extra for greasing the
        casserole dishes

    ½ cup unbleached flour

    1 cup whole milk

        Handful of Sicilian sea salt, coarse

    2 pounds excellent-quality manicotti
        (such as DeLallo, Da Vinci, or
        De Cecco)

    ½ cup heavy cream

    4 teaspoons lemon zest

        Salt

    ½ teaspoon freshly ground black pepper

1. *To prepare the salmon:* Either in a preheated
350°F oven or in a large frying pan on the
stove, melt 4 tablespoons of the butter in a
13 × 9-inch baking dish (for the oven) or in a
frying pan (for the stove). Generously salt and
pepper the salmon fillets and cook them for
8 minutes (if you're using the oven) or cook

them in the butter over medium-high heat (if you're cooking them on the stovetop) for 4 minutes on each side. Set the salmon fillets aside and cover with aluminum foil.

2. When the salmon fillets have cooled, use a fork to flake the fish (you do not have to flake it until it resembles minced fish; the flakes should be approximately 1 inch long and ½ inch wide). Put the flaked salmon in a medium-size bowl.

3. *To prepare the besciamella sauce:* Melt the butter in a large saucepan. Slowly spoon in the flour, mixing it with the butter as you go. This will look like a paste. Gradually add the milk, stirring the entire time over low heat, while the flour and butter mixture absorbs the milk, until you get a beautiful, smooth white sauce. Add the besciamella to the bowl of salmon and mix it well, coating all the flaked salmon with the sauce.

4. *To cook the pasta:* Fill a large 8-quart pot with water and bring it to a rolling boil. Add a handful of coarse Sicilian sea salt to the water and cook the manicotti for 2–3 minutes less than the instructions on the package. Drain the manicotti, rinse them in cold water, and place them on a linen or cotton dishcloth on your kitchen table.

5. Preheat the oven to 350°F. Prepare two 13 × 9-inch casseroles by buttering them generously.

6. In the same saucepan used to make the besciamella, heat the heavy cream and add the lemon zest, salt, and pepper. Coat the bottom of each casserole with 3 or 4 tablespoons of the cream sauce. Fill each of the manicotti with the salmon mixture, using a teaspoon, and place it in the cream sauce in the casserole. When all the manicotti are filled and have been placed in the casserole, top the manicotti with the remaining cream–and–lemon zest sauce.

7. Bake the manicotti in the preheated oven for 20 minutes.

Pesce Spada con Agrumi
Citrus Swordfish

6 tablespoons extra virgin olive oil

4 tablespoons unsalted butter

2 cloves garlic, chopped

1 teaspoon saffron threads

4 blood oranges (if you cannot find blood oranges, regular oranges or red grapefruit will do)

4 tablespoons fresh mint, chopped

1 tablespoon Sicilian sea salt, fine

1 teaspoon freshly ground black pepper

8 (4-ounce) swordfish fillets, 1 inch thick

2 lemons, sliced in rounds

1. In a medium-size saucepan, heat 4 tablespoons of olive oil and 2 tablespoons of butter and sauté the garlic for 2 minutes. Remove the saucepan from the stove and crumble the saffron threads into the butter and oil. Let the mixture rest, off the heat, while the saffron is infused. Clean the oranges, peel off the skin with a knife, making sure to remove all the white pith, and cut the fruit into sections. Remove the seeds.

2. In a large bowl, toss the orange sections with the saffron-infused butter-and-oil mixture. Stir in the mint, salt, and pepper. Brush each swordfish fillet with the remaining 2 tablespoons of olive oil on each side and sprinkle with a little salt and pepper.

3. Heat the grill to medium, and cook the swordfish fillets for 8–10 minutes, turning them halfway through the cooking time. (If you are not grilling the swordfish fillets, cook them in a preheated 350°F oven for 8 minutes.)

4. Plate the swordfish fillets and top with the lemons and the saffron sauce.

Torta di Zucchini e Ricotta
Zucchini & Ricotta Tart

For Lisa's Pasta Salata (Savory Crust)

1 cup flour

½ cup butter

Pinch Sicilian sea salt, fine

3 tablespoons whole milk

For the Filling

3 pounds zucchini, sliced in ¼-inch-thick rounds

1 cup unsalted butter, softened

4 eggs, beaten

1 cup whole milk ricotta cheese

12 ounces mozzarella cheese, diced

1½ cups Parmigiano Reggiano, grated

Sicilian sea salt, fine

Freshly ground black pepper

1. *To prepare the pastry dough*: Thoroughly mix together all the ingredients. Refrigerate the pastry dough for 1 hour. Divide the pastry dough into 1 large ball and 1 small ball. Roll out the large ball into a circle, and place it in a buttered pie plate. Reserve the small ball, refrigerated, for making lattice strips (step 4).

2. *To prepare the filling:* In a medium-size pot, bring 3–4 cups of water to a rolling boil. Drop the sliced zucchini rounds into the water and parboil them for no more than 4 minutes. Drain the zucchini immediately, set it aside.

3. In a large frying pan, melt the butter, and add the zucchini, tossing it until it is well coated with the butter. Place the zucchini in a large bowl. Add the eggs, ricotta, mozzarella, and Parmigiano, and season with the salt and pepper.

4. Pour the zucchini filling into the prepared pie plate, roll out the small ball of pasta salata into a rectangle, cut into ¼-inch-wide strips, and form a lattice on top of the zucchini mixture.

5. Place the tart in a preheated 350°F oven and cook for 30 minutes.

Torta di Riso e Limone
Lemon Rice Crostata

> 2 tablespoons unsalted butter, melted
> ¼ cup fine breadcrumbs
> 2½ cups whole milk
> ¾ cup Arborio rice
> ½ cup ground almonds
> Zest of 2 lemons
> 4 eggs, separated
> ⅔ cup sugar

1. Preheat the oven to 400°F. In a springform pan, place the melted butter and lightly spread the breadcrumbs across the melted butter on the bottom of the pan.

2. In a medium-size saucepan, bring the milk to a slow boil and stir in the rice, making sure it doesn't stick. Continue to stir the rice until it has absorbed all the milk 10–15 minutes. Set the mixture aside and let it cool.

3. After the rice mixture has cooled, stir in the almonds and lemon zest. With a whisk or a tablespoon, blend the egg yolks into the rice mixture. Then stir in the sugar.

4. With a hand mixer beat the egg whites until stiff peaks form, and then fold the egg whites into the rice mixture. Pour the mixture into the springform pan, and bake for 30 minutes.

Menu 20
SERVES 8

Bruschetta alla Napoletana Bruschetta, Neapolitan style
Spaghetti ai due Pomodori Spaghetti with Two Types of Tomatoes
Baccala alla Napoletana Cod, Neapolitan style
Verdure Arrostiti di Lisa Lisa's Roasted Vegetables
Torta di Cioccolato e Mandorle Chocolate Almond Cake

What is more southern Italian than baccala? We even have a cheesy Italian-American song written about this fish! In this menu, the baccala is prepared in typical Neapolitan fashion, with salty olives and capers, and juicy, ripe tomatoes. Melts in your mouth!

As many of you may know, it is traditional for Italians to eat seven different fish, each representing the seven sacraments of the Holy Roman Catholic Church, on Christmas Eve. It is a southern Italian tradition, however, and one that is not practiced in northern Italy. Baccala—dried and salted cod—is a very popular fish in the Naples region. Preserving it in salt makes it last a long time, and you need only soak it overnight in freshwater for the fish to be ready for cooking the next day. While it is a Christmas tradition, I make baccala all year long.

I can remember, as if it were yesterday, holding my father's hand, as we walked along the streets of Italy and passed by huge wooden crates, stacked with large fillets of baccala, outside of small grocery stores, just waiting to be purchased. If you cannot find the dried, salted cod used in the recipe for Baccala alla Napolitana in your area, feel free to use fresh or frozen cod fillets. It will be equally delicious!

Flourless cakes are very popular for dessert in Italy, because Italians prefer a dense, thick torte, rather than the airy, fluffy cakes that are preferred in the United States. The flourless cake in this menu, typical of the region of Naples, has a distinctive flavor due to the limoncello liqueur, which is added to the batter and gives the cake a lovely kick.

Tutti a tavola! (Everyone to table!)

Bruschetta alla Napoletana
Bruschetta, Neapolitan style

- 1 loaf of dense, country-style Italian bread, cut into 8 slices (page 186)
- 4 teaspoons extra virgin olive oil
- 8 slices mozzarella, sliced ½ inch thick
- 24 cherry tomatoes, halved
- 8 anchovies
- 1 teaspoon dried oregano
- 1 teaspoon freshly ground black pepper

1. With a pastry brush, brush the bread on one side with the olive oil and arrange the slices on a baking sheet. Top each slice of bread with a slice of mozzarella, leaving ¼ inch around the edges. Arrange a few halves of tomatoes on each slice of cheese; drape 1 or 2 anchovy fillets on top, and sprinkle with oregano. Drizzle with the olive oil.

2. Place the bread under a broiler until the cheese melts, but do not allow it to brown. Serve.

Spaghetti ai due Pomodori
Spaghetti with Two Types of Tomatoes

For the Due Pomodori Pesto
- 1½ cups sun-dried tomatoes, drained
- 1 cup extra virgin olive oil
- 3 teaspoons capers, preferably salt-packed, rinsed, and drained
- 4 cups cherry tomatoes, halved
- ½ cup Parmigiano Reggiano, grated
- 2 pounds spaghetti

1. In a blender or a food processor, puree the sundried tomatoes, olive oil, and capers. Add the cherry tomatoes, pureeing until smooth. If the mixture is too thick, add 2–3 tablespoons of hot water.

2. Transfer the tomato pesto to a large pasta bowl and stir in the cheese.

3. Cook the spaghetti according to the directions on the package and mix it into the sauce in the pasta bowl.

Baccala alla Napoletana
Cod, Neapolitan style

½ cup extra virgin olive oil

6 garlic cloves, chopped

2 pounds very ripe tomatoes, chopped

12 ounces black olives, pitted, cut in half (excellent quality, preferably imported from Italy)

3 ounces salted capers, rinsed and patted dry with a paper towel

2 teaspoons Sicilian sea salt, fine, plus more for seasoning the flour

1 teaspoon freshly ground black pepper, plus more for seasoning the flour

1½ cups unbleached flour, for dredging

8 cod fillets

1 cup Italian flat leaf parsley, chopped

LISA'S TIP

When buying pasta, think of the sauce you will be making for the dish. Pasta cuts in Italy are made specifically for different sauces, so that they'll adhere to the pasta. For example, when making pesto, use corkscrew pasta (rotini), as all the chunky pesto adheres to the turns of the pasta and you taste your sauce in every bite! Watch my "How to Select the Perfect Pasta" video at lisacaponigri.com!

1. Preheat the oven to 300°F.

2. In a large frying pan, heat half the olive oil and sauté the garlic for 2 minutes. Using a slotted spoon remove the garlic and set it aside. Add the tomatoes, olives, and capers to the olive oil in the pan. Season the mixture with 1 teaspoon of salt and a ½ teaspoon of pepper. Cook for 15 minutes until the tomatoes are very soft. Take the pan off the heat and set it aside.

3. In a medium-size shallow dish, such as a pie plate, place the flour and season with salt and pepper. Dredge each cod fillet until it is coated on all sides with the flour mixture.

4. In another large frying pan, heat the remaining olive oil to medium-high and fry the cod until it is golden on all sides, approximately 3 minutes on each side. Place the 8 cod fillets into the frying pan with the tomato mixture. (You may have to leave 4 of the cod fillets in the frying pan, in which they were fried, and then add half the tomato mixture to that frying pan so you do not crowd all the cod fillets in one pan.)

5. Cook the cod for 10 more minutes in the tomato mixture. Garnish with parsley and serve.

The famous Piccolo Bar on Capri, where my parents had their coffee in 1950, and I have my coffee now.

Verdure Arrostiti di Lisa
Lisa's Roasted Vegetables

- 2 pounds small red potatoes, quartered
- 2 pounds Roma tomatoes, quartered
- 1 pound black pitted olives, preferably imported, halved
- 6 garlic cloves, sliced lengthwise
- ½ cup extra virgin olive oil
- 1 tablespoon dried rosemary
- 1 teaspoon Sicilian sea salt, fine
- ½ teaspoon ground black pepper
- ½ cup Parmigiano Reggiano, grated

1. Put the potatoes, tomatoes, olives, and garlic in a large bowl and toss with the olive oil, rosemary, salt, and pepper. Spread the mixture on a large jelly-roll pan and roast the vegetables in a preheated 450°F oven for 20 minutes.

2. Transfer the veggies to a serving platter and top with the cheese.

Torta di Cioccolato e Mandorle
Chocolate Almond Cake

- 2 sticks unsalted butter
- 6 eggs, separated
- 1 cup sugar
- ½ cup limoncello liqueur
- 2 cups sliced, chopped almonds
- 12 ounces excellent-quality dark chocolate, roughly chopped
- ¼ cup confectioners' sugar

1. Preheat the oven to 350°F.

2. Melt the butter in a double boiler (or, if you don't have a double boiler, place a heatproof glass bowl over a medium saucepan of boiling water, making sure that the bowl does not touch the boiling water). Allow the butter to cool.

3. In a large bowl, beat the egg yolks with the sugar and the limoncello until creamy.

4. In a separate bowl, whisk the eggs whites (with a whisk or a hand beater) until peaks form, and fold them into the egg yolk mixture. Then fold the butter into the egg mixture. Add the almonds and chocolate and fold them in gently, being careful not to break down the egg whites.

5. Line a 10-inch round cake pan with parchment paper, pour in the batter, and bake it in the preheated oven for approximately 45 minutes, or until a toothpick comes out clean. Sprinkle the top of the cake with confectioners' sugar and serve.

Menu 21

SERVES 8

This is another of my favorite Neapolitan menus that conjures memories of my childhood! Of course, Naples is the birthplace of pizza. The classic Margherita (tomato sauce, mozzarella, and fresh basil) is the city's signature pizza. But another, far less well known Neapolitan specialty is *Pizza in Bianco*—White Pizza, which is made without tomato sauce. The ricotta gives the pizza a creamy, decadent topping!

The island of Capri is off the coast of Naples and forms part of the Region of Campania. I grew up eating *Penne alla Caprese,* which literally means "Penne Capri Style," on the beaches of Italy—and it is what I would prepare for my children when they were little and we would eat seaside. This pasta is great to eat warm or at room temperature. We do not eat cold pastas in Italy as it diminishes the flavor.

The cake in this menu is from the town of Amalfi, and it is just as delicious as the *Penne alla Caprese.* Typical of our southern Italian desserts, the cake is simple, fresh, easy to prepare, and utterly delicious!

This is another Sunday dinner menu full of wonderful dishes for you and your family and wonderful family memories for me.

Auguri! (Enjoy!)

Pizza in Bianco
White Pizza

2 balls of pizza dough, enough
for 2 (12-inch-diameter) pizzas,
homemade (recipe below)
or store-bought

Oil, for greasing the pans
(approximately 4 tablespoons)

4 cups white button mushrooms, sliced

1 cup onion, chopped

½ cup extra virgin olive oil

6 garlic cloves, chopped

½ cup fresh basil, chopped

2 cups whole milk mozzarella,
shredded

2 cups whole milk ricotta

1 cup Pecorino Romano, grated

¼ cup Italian flat leaf parsley, chopped

1. Roll out the 2 balls of pizza dough into
either two rectangles or two ¼-inch circles and
then place the dough on baking sheets or pizza
pans that have been lightly oiled.

2. In a large skillet, sauté the mushrooms and
onion in 4 tablespoons of the olive oil for 5
minutes. Add the garlic and cook for 2 more
minutes. Stir in the fresh basil.

3. In a medium-size bowl, mix the mozzarella,
ricotta, pecorino romano, and parsley. Spread
the cheese mixture over the pizza dough.
Sprinkle the mushroom and onion mixture on
top. Bake the pizzas in a preheated 400°F oven
for 40 minutes.

Pizza! Pizza! Pizza! The hallmark
of Naples, birthplace of this
thin, crunchy delectable dish! At
the famous Pizzeria da Franco,
I roll out the dough with the
masters, pop the pizza in a 500
degree oven, and "eccola"!
Here it is! Perfect Pizza!

Pizza Dough

makes enough for one 12-inch pizza

- 1 envelope dried yeast
  (2½ tablespoons)
- 1 cup warm water
- 4 cups unbleached flour
- 1 tablespoon Sicilian Sea Salt, fine
- ½ cup warm water

1. Dissolve yeast in 1 cup warm water. Stir in ½ cup of the flour, cover with a kitchen cloth, and let stand until it doubles, about 30-45 minutes.

2. In a separate bowl, combine the rest of the flour with the yeast mixture, the salt, and the remaining ½ cup of water. Mix well with your hands.

3. Spread some flour on a surface and turn out the ball of dough. Knead for approximately 10 minutes, adding a little bit of flour at a time if the dough is too sticky.

4. The dough is finished when it does not stick to the surface of your work area.

5. Place the ball of dough back in the bowl, cover with the cloth, and let rise for one hour. It will again double in size.

6. Roll out to desired size.

Penne alla Caprese
Penne, Capri Stlye

- ½ cup extra virgin olive oil
- 1 (32-ounce can) crushed San Marzano tomatoes
- Sicilian sea salt, ½ teaspoon, fine
- Freshly ground black pepper, ¼ teaspoon
- 2 (8-ounce) glass jars of tuna in oil, imported from Italy*
- ½ cup black olives, pitted and halved
- 1 cup fresh mozzarella, diced
- 2 pounds penne rigate

1. In a large frying pan, heat 3 tablespoons of the olive oil and add the tomatoes. Simmer the tomatoes for 15 minutes, or until they have reduced and thickened. Season with salt and pepper to taste. Set the pan aside.

2. In another large frying pan, heat 3 tablespoons of the olive oil and add the tuna. With a fork, flake the tuna in the pan. Add the olives and stir.

3. Meanwhile, add the mozzarella to the warm tomato sauce in the other frying pan.

4. Cook the penne, according to the directions on the package, and then drain it. Toss the penne in a large pasta bowl with the tomato sauce. Pour the tuna sauce into the bowl, mix it in thoroughly with the pasta and tomato sauce, and serve.

★ Substitute with good-quality canned albacore (not light) tuna, if jarred tuna is not available

Spezzatino alla Napoletana
Beef Stew, Neapolitan Style

½ cup unsalted butter

½ cup extra virgin olive oil

2 white onions, chopped

4 pounds chuck roast, cubed
and cleaned, fat removed

4 cups green peas

6 cups beef bouillon

1 cup tomato passata, imported from
Italy (if passata is not available use an
16-ounce can of crushed tomatoes)

1 tablespoon rosemary

2 teaspoons Sicilian sea salt, fine

1 teaspoon freshly ground black
pepper

1. Heat the butter and olive oil in a large
frying pan and sauté the onions for 5 minutes
until they're soft and translucent. Add the
meat and brown it on all sides, about 12
minutes.

2. Transfer all the ingredients to a slow cooker
or a Dutch oven. Add the peas, bouillon, and
tomato passata. Sprinkle in the rosemary, salt,
and pepper. If you are using a slow cooker,
cook the stew for 4 hours. If you're using a
Dutch oven, cook the stew in a 350°F oven
for 2–3 hours.

Stufato al Forno di Peperone Rosso
Baked Red Pepper Casserole

8 red bell peppers

4 whole salted anchovies (or one
3-ounce can anchovy fillets)

12 large black olives, pitted and
chopped

2 tablespoons capers, rinsed and
chopped coarsely

8 tablespoons extra virgin olive oil

2 teaspoons dried oregano

4 cloves garlic, chopped

1 cup breadcrumbs

1. *To make the roasted peppers:* Line a jelly-roll
pan with aluminum foil. Place the peppers
on the aluminum foil. Place the pan directly
under a broiler set on high. Broil the peppers
until the skins turn black and bubble. Turn
the peppers over, until each side is black and
bubbly. This can also be done on a grill. Set
the peppers aside until they cool thoroughly.
Peel off the black charred skin, rinse each
pepper under cold water, and remove the stem,
seeds, and pith. Slice the roasted peppers into
1-inch-wide slices.

2. Preheat the oven to 400°F. In a large mixing
bowl, combine the sliced roasted peppers (see
pages 186 and 187), anchovies, olives, capers,
olive oil, oregano, garlic, and breadcrumbs.
Mix well.

3. Transfer the mixture to a casserole dish,
bake for 10 minutes, and serve.

This Is Sunday Dinner

Torta di Amalfi
Amalfi Cake

2 excellent-quality, store-bought
pound cakes, such as Entenmann's
or Sara Lee

For the Filling

1 cup heavy cream

2 cups whole milk ricotta

1 cup granulated sugar

1 teaspoon pure vanilla extract

For the Pears

2 large pears (Bosc or d'Anjou), peeled
and chopped

½ cup sugar

1 cup pear liqueur, such as William
Pear Liqueur

½ cup pear juice

1. *To make the filling:* Whip the cream in a bowl. Set it aside. In a large bowl, whip the ricotta, sugar, and vanilla, and then gently fold in the whipped cream. Set the bowl aside.

2. *To make the pears:* Place the pears and sugar in a large frying pan. Sauté the pears until the sugar has melted and has thoroughly coated the chopped pears. Add the pear liqueur, simmer the pears, and allow the liqueur to evaporate. Set the pears aside to cool.

3. *To assemble the cake:* Slice the pound cakes into ¼-inch-thick slices and then cut each in half to form a triangle. Place a layer of the triangles on the bottom of 2 loaf pans. Brush the cake triangles with the pear juice, using a kitchen pastry brush.

4. Fold the cooled pears and sugar into the ricotta and whipped cream mixture. Place a layer of the ricotta-and-pear mixture on top of the cake triangles, and smooth with the back of a rubber spatula. Repeat the process until all the cake triangles and pear mixture have been used. Sprinkle the top layer with confectioners' sugar.

5. Refrigerate the cake for approximately 30 minutes. It is delicious served chilled or at room temperature.

LISA'S TIP

Since a pound cake comes in a rectangle, I like to cut the pieces approximately ¼ inch thick and then slice each piece on the diagonal, forming a triangle.

Menu 22

SERVES 8

Fagioli con Gamberi Caldi Warm Shrimp with Green Beans

Fusilli con Ragù di Aragosta Fusilli with Lobster Ragù

Scaloppine di Vitello di Montagna Veal Scaloppine, Mountain Style

Pomodori Napoletani al Forno Baked Tomatoes, Neapolitan Style

Torta Napoletana di Aranci con Glassa di Arance
Neapolitan Orange Cake with Orange Glaze

What a decadent Neapolitan menu! The best kind!

This Lobster Ragù will become your go-to elegant sauce for special occasions, like every Sunday for Sunday dinner! It does not get more special than that! In southern Italy we combine lobster with tomatoes, which I love. The flavor of the tomatoes with the meaty lobster is an ideal pairing.

The veal dish in this menu is typical of the ones found in the countryside outside the city of Naples, where veal is raised. The saltiness of the prosciutto and the delicate flavor of the veal are reminiscent of saltimbocca, a Roman dish. Here, we combine mushrooms and tomatoes to give the sauce an earthy flavor, which explains why the dish is called *Scaloppine di Vitello di Montagna*—Veal Scaloppine of the Mountains. Delicious!

The dessert in this menu is another that highlights the amazing citrus fruit that grows in such abundance in Campania. You will fall in love with this orange cake and glaze. Make a double portion of the orange glaze and use it to top sugar cookies—out of this world!

Buon cibo, buoni amici! (Good food, good friends!)

Fagioli con Gamberi Caldi
Warm Shrimp with Green Beans

   2 pounds fresh green beans, trimmed

   ½ cup extra virgin olive oil

   2 tablespoons lemon juice

   1 teaspoon Sicilian sea salt, fine

   ½ teaspoon freshly ground black pepper

   2 pounds medium-size to large shrimp, shelled and deveined

   Lemon slices for garnish

1. Snip each end of the green beans and cook them in a large, 4–6-quart pot of water for only 4 minutes, or until they turn bright green, but are still crisp. Using a slotted spoon, remove the green beans and place them in a large bowl—do not discard the water. Bring the water back up to a boil.

2. In a small bowl, mix the olive oil, lemon juice, ½ teaspoon of the salt, and the pepper. Toss the green beans with half the dressing.

3. Add the shrimp and the remainder of the salt to the pot of boiling water. Cook the shrimp for 2–3 minutes. Drain. Toss the shrimp with the remaining dressing.

4. On 8 small plates, make a bed of the green beans and place a generous tablespoon of the shrimp on top. Garnish with lemon slices and serve.

Fusilli con Ragù di Aragosta
Fusilli with Lobster Ragù

   8 tablespoons extra virgin olive oil

   4 pounds lobster meat, chopped into approximately 1-inch pieces

   1 teaspoon garlic, chopped

   2 onions, diced

   1 celery stalk, diced

   12 plum tomatoes

   1 tablespoon tomato paste (preferably, concentrato di pomodoro, imported from Italy)

   Handful of Sicilian sea salt, coarse, for salting the pasta water

   2 pounds fusilli

   ½ cup dry white wine

   2 tablespoons Italian flat leaf parsley, chopped

   1½ teaspoons Sicilian sea salt, fine

   1 teaspoon freshly ground black pepper

1. In a large frying pan, heat 4 tablespoons of the olive oil and sauté the lobster, just until the lobster is warmed through. Do not overcook the meat. If your frying pan is over medium heat, do not cook the lobster for more than 2–3 minutes.

2. In a separate, large frying pan melt the remaining 4 tablespoons of oil and add the garlic, onions, celery, and tomatoes. Cook the mixture for 20 minutes, or until the fresh tomatoes are very soft and the garlic and onions are translucent. Add the tomato paste and stir in well to slightly thicken the sauce. Add the salt and pepper.

3. Meanwhile, bring a 6- to 8-quart pot of water to a rolling boil. Add a handful of coarse Sicilian sea salt to the water and cook the fusilli for 2 minutes less than the cooking instructions on the package.

4. While the pasta is cooking, add the wine to the tomato mixture. The wine should evaporate slightly. Gently add the sautéed pieces of lobster to the tomato sauce. Drain the fusilli and in a large pasta bowl, add the tomato and lobster sauce and mix thoroughly.

LISA'S TIP

In Italy we very rarely put cheese on a pasta dish that contains seafood, particularly lobster, because the cheese will overwhelm the seafood's delicate flavor. So cheese is not recommended for this dish or any dish like it.

Scaloppine di Vitello di Montagna
Veal Scaloppine, Mountain Style

- 1 cup unbleached flour, for dredging
- 1 teaspoon Sicilian sea salt, fine, plus more for seasoning the casserole
- ½ teaspoon freshly ground black pepper, plus more for seasoning the casserole
- ½ cup extra virgin olive oil, plus more for greasing the casserole dish and drizzling over the casserole
- 4 pounds veal scaloppine (scaloppine means "sliced very thin")
- 12 ounces mushrooms, sliced
- 6 ounces prosciutto crudo, such as San Daniele or Prosciutto di Parma
- 2 pounds ripe tomatoes, sliced
- 8 teaspoons capers packed in salt, rinsed
- Salt and pepper, to taste
- 4 teaspoons oregano
- 4 teaspoons Italian flat leaf parsley, chopped
- 4 tablespoons fresh basil, chopped

1. Preheat the oven to 350°F.

2. Place the flour in a shallow plate, such as a pie plate, and season with the salt and pepper.

3. Place ¼ cup of the olive oil in a large frying pan over medium to high heat. Dredge the veal in the flour on each side. Sear the veal for no more than 2 minutes on each side in the frying pan.

4. Lightly oil a 13 × 9-inch casserole dish, and, as you remove the veal from the frying pan, place it in the oiled casserole. After you have arranged all the veal on the bottom of the casserole, cover it with aluminum foil and set it aside.

5. In the same large frying pan used to cook the veal, add the remaining ¼ cup of olive oil and sauté the mushrooms until they are soft, approximately 5 minutes. Drain the mushrooms in a colander, removing all the liquid from the mushrooms.

6. Remove the foil from the casserole and place the slices of prosciutto crudo on top of the veal, followed by the slices of tomato, the capers, and the sautéed mushrooms. Season with a little more salt and pepper. Sprinkle with the oregano, parsley, and basil, and drizzle with some more olive oil. Place the casserole in the oven and bake for 12 minutes.

Pomodori Napoletani al Forno
Baked Tomatoes, Neapolitan Style

8 tomatoes, either beefsteak or Campari, ripe but firm

8 tablespoons extra virgin olive oil, plus more for greasing the casserole dish

¼ cup Italian flat leaf parsley

6 cloves garlic, chopped

1 cup breadcrumbs, half fine, half panko, plus more for sprinkling on tomatoes

3 small to medium-size zucchini, chopped

1 white onion, chopped

1 teaspoon oregano

12 ounces fresh mozzarella, cubed

1 teaspoon Sicilian sea salt, fine

½ teaspoon freshly ground black pepper

1. Preheat the oven to 350°F.

2. Cut off the top of each tomato (the stem top). Using a small spoon, hollow out the tomatoes. Put all the pulp in a colander in the kitchen sink. With your fingers, remove the seeds from the pulp. Place only the pulp of the tomato in a small bowl. Chop the pulp finely and set it aside.

3. Lightly oil the bottom of a 13 × 9-inch casserole dish and place the tomatoes in the casserole standing up.

4. In a large bowl, mix together the diced tomato pulp, 4 tablespoons of the extra virgin olive oil, 2 teaspoons of the parsley, 2 cloves of the chopped garlic, salt and pepper, and the breadcrumbs. Stir until well combined with the oil, and all the breadcrumbs are very moist.

5. In a large frying pan, heat the remaining olive oil over medium heat. Add the zucchini, the remaining chopped garlic, and the onion to the pan and cook for 5 minutes, until the zucchini is tender but not brown. Stir in the oregano and cook for another 2 minutes.

6. Transfer the zucchini mixture to the bowl with the tomato pulp. Allow the vegetables to cool. Stir in the mozzarella.

7. Spoon the mixture into the 8 tomatoes, and then sprinkle extra breadcrumbs on top of the tomatoes. Bake for 30 minutes. Garnish with the remaining parsley and serve.

1. Preheat the oven to 350°F and butter a 9-inch cake pan.

2. Melt the butter in a double boiler or in a heatproof bowl over a saucepan of boiling water. Set the melted butter aside.

3. In a medium bowl, mix together the eggs, sugar, and 1 cup of the confectioners' sugar until light and fluffy. Stir in the melted butter and slowly stir in the flour, baking powder, orange zest, and ½ cup of the orange juice. Pour the mixture into the prepared pan and bake for 25 minutes.

4. *To prepare the glaze:* In a separate bowl, combine the remaining ½ cup of orange juice and the remaining 1 cup of confectioners' sugar. When cake has cooled, place it on a cake platter and drizzle the orange glaze on top of the cake.

Torta Napoletana di Aranci con Glassa di Arance
Neapolitan Orange Cake with Orange Glaze

½ cup unsalted butter, plus extra for greasing the cake pan

2 eggs

½ cup granulated sugar

2 cups confectioners' sugar

1 cup unbleached flour

½ teaspoon baking powder

Juice of 2 oranges (approximately 1 cup)

Zest of 2 oranges

LISA'S TIP
I like to poke holes in the cake with a toothpick before I glaze it, so that some of the glaze goes into the cake as well.

Polpette di Carciofi & Ricotta Artichoke and Ricotta Balls

I Famosi Gamberi di Lisa Lisa's Famous Shrimp Scampi

Pollo di Napoli Chicken Napoli

Pomodori Cigligini Arrostiti Roasted Cherry Tomatoes

La Torta di Ricotta di Ricigliano Ricigliano's Ricotta Cake

My father's family, the Caponigris, hail from Ricigliano, a small hilltop town in the mountains behind Naples, in the beautiful region of Campania. Ricigliano is isolated, rustic, and its natural beauty is unadulterated. But to arrive there is quite an expedition! There is only one road to the village, and when my son Guido was little, and we were going round and round the mountain, he would ask me if I was sure I was on the right road! I always responded: "This is the only road!" But the trip is worth it. When you arrive in Ricigliano, the views are breathtaking, and the homemade provolone cheese, typical of that region, is beyond delicious.

I instantly fell in love with the dessert in this menu—Ricotta Cake—and it has become one of my staples. In Ricigliano, the ricotta used to make the cake is homemade and fresh, as are all their cheeses, but I have made it countless times with store-bought ricotta here in the States and the cake tastes equally delicious. Make sure you buy whole milk ricotta, though, as that makes all the difference!

I have been making shrimp scampi since I began cooking, and it is one of my favorite dishes. Typical of southwest Sicily, where my

Nana was born and raised, you find shrimp scampi in every trattoria in the region, and, as with most regional dishes in Italy, every cook has a different version. After perfecting mine for years, the recipe in this menu is my favorite way to make shrimp scampi.

We return to Naples, on our culinary adventure in this menu, for Chicken Napoli! Utilizing the scrumptious provolone cheese that is native to this region, this is a dish your children will love—breaded chicken breasts topped with gooey cheese and sun-dried tomatoes! And they can assemble it, too, while helping you to prepare Sunday dinner!

Tutti a tavola! (Everyone to table!)

Polpette di Carciofi & Ricotta
Artichoke and Ricotta Balls

½ cup extra virgin olive oil

1 white onion, chopped

1 teaspoon Sicilian sea salt, fine

½ teaspoon freshly ground black pepper

2 (12-ounce) bags frozen artichoke hearts, thawed

1 or 2 slices Italian bread, 1 inch thick each, crusts removed

1 cup fresh whole milk ricotta

½ cup Parmigiano Reggiano, grated

2 egg yolks

2 tablespoons Italian flat leaf parsley, chopped

2 eggs

1 cup unbleached flour, for dredging

1 cup breadcrumbs, for dredging

2 cups canola oil, for frying

1. In a large frying pan, heat the extra virgin olive oil over medium heat and sauté the onion with the salt and pepper for 5 minutes. Reduce to low. Add the artichoke hearts and cook for 5 more minutes until the artichokes are tender. If there is a lot of liquid in the pan, increase the heat to medium-high and simmer until it has reduced.

2. In a blender, place 1 slice of the bread, the ricotta, Parmigiano, egg yolks, and parsley. The mixture should be thick. If it is too runny, add a second slice of bread. Transfer the bread-and-ricotta mixture to a large bowl, add the artichokes, and combine well. Set the mixture aside and allow it to cool.

3. Line up 3 shallow bowls. In the first, place the cup of flour. In the second, whisk the two eggs. In the third, place the cup of breadcrumbs. With a tablespoon, make a golf ball–size ball of the artichoke-and-ricotta mixture. Place it first in the flour, then in the beaten egg, and then in the breadcrumbs.

4. Fill a large, deep frying pan with approximately 1 inch of canola oil and heat it until tiny bubbles form around the edge of the frying pan. Cook the artichoke balls in the oil until they are golden on all sides. Remove and drain on paper towels.

Strolling on the beautiful beach at Positano.

I Famosi Gamberi di Lisa

Lisa's Famous Shrimp Scampi

    6 tablespoons unsalted butter
    6 large cloves garlic, chopped
    ½ cup Italian flat leaf parsley, chopped
    ¼ cup lemon zest
    4 pounds extra large shrimp (usually 15–20 shrimp per pound), peeled and cleaned (deveined and tails removed)
    1 cup dry white wine
    ¼ cup fresh lemon juice
    1 teaspoon crushed red pepper flakes
    2 ribs celery, chopped
    2 pounds linguine

1. In a large frying pan, melt 4 tablespoons of the butter over medium heat. Add the garlic, parsley, and lemon zest and cook for 2 minutes, until the garlic is translucent. Do not allow the garlic to brown.

2. Turn the heat to high and add the shrimp. Cook until the shrimp turn bright pink, 1–2 minutes. Add the wine and cook an additional 2 minutes, until reduced by about a third. Add the lemon juice and crushed red pepper flakes, and stir well. Add the remaining 2 tablespoons of butter until melted. Coat the shrimp well in the wine sauce. Reduce the heat to low and cover the pan to keep the mixture warm.

3. Fill a large 6- to 8-quart pot with water and bring it to a rolling boil. Cook the linguine according to the directions on the package. Drain the linguine in a large pasta bowl. Pour the shrimp scampi over the linguine and serve.

Pollo di Napoli

Chicken Napoli

    1½ cups breadcrumbs
    1 teaspoon Sicilian sea salt, fine
    ½ teaspoon freshly ground black pepper
    1 cup extra virgin olive oil
    8 chicken breasts, boneless, skinless, and pounded to ¼-inch thickness
    4 cups arugula
    8 slices provolone, preferably imported from Italy
    8 teaspoons sun-dried tomatoes
    ¼ cup Italian flat leaf parsley, chopped

1. In a shallow bowl, such as a pie plate, place the breadcrumbs and season with salt and pepper.

2. In a large frying pan, place ½ cup of the olive oil. Dredge the chicken breasts in the breadcrumbs and fry in the oil on each side until golden, approximately 4 minutes.

3. In a medium-size bowl, toss the arugula with the remaining ½ cup olive oil.

4. Arrange the arugula on a platter. Place the breaded chicken breasts on top of the arugula. Top each one with 1 slice of provolone cheese and a teaspoon of the sun-dried tomatoes.

5. Garnish with the parsley and serve.

Pomodori Cigligini Arrostiti
Roasted Cherry Tomatoes

2 pounds cherry tomatoes, halved

1 teaspoon Sicilian sea salt, fine

½ teaspoon freshly ground black pepper

1 cup Parmigiano Reggiano, grated

1 tablespoon dried thyme

¼ cup extra virgin olive oil

1. Preheat the oven to 350°F.

2. Line a jelly-roll pan with parchment paper or a silpat. Arrange the tomatoes on the pan and season with the salt and pepper. Sprinkle the Parmigiano Reggiano and thyme over the tomato mixture and drizzle with the olive oil.

3. Bake for 12 minutes. Serve.

This Is Sunday Dinner

La Torta di Ricotta di Ricigliano
Ricigliano's Ricotta Cake

Lisa's Pasta Frolla (Pastry Dough)

1¼ cups flour

¼ teaspoon baking powder

Pinch salt

⅓ cup sugar

1 stick, plus 1 tablespoon unsalted
butter, cold and sliced

1 egg yolk

Combine the flour, baking powder, salt, and
sugar. Make a well in the center of the flour
mixture, and add the sliced butter and egg yolk.
Knead the mixture into soft dough, adding a
few drops of ice water. Work the ingredients
together by hand or with a pastry blender. (This
can be done in a stand mixer by simply placing
all the ingredients in the mixing bowl and using
a paddle to mix the dough on medium speed.)
Separate the dough into 2 balls, 1 large and
1 small. Roll out the large ball of dough and
place it in a 9 or 9½-inch fluted, loose-bottomed
tart or quiche mold. Prick the dough with a
fork. Chill the pastry for 30 minutes.

For the Filling

2 pounds whole milk ricotta

1 cup sugar

4 tablespoons Strega liqueur*

8 tablespoons candied orange peel,
finely chopped

3 eggs, beaten

8 ounces bittersweet chocolate, grated

2 tablespoons unsalted butter

1. In a large mixing bowl, beat the ricotta,
sugar, Strega, orange peel, and eggs.

2. Preheat the oven to 350°F. Spoon half the
ricotta filling mixture into Lisa's Pasta Frolla
(Pastry Dough), rolled out into the chilled
dough in the tart pan or quiche mold.

3. Sprinkle the grated chocolate over the
filling and pour the remaining ricotta mixture
over the chocolate.

4. Roll out the second ball of dough. Cut the
dough into ½-inch-wide strips and place them
over the ricotta filling to form a lattice design.
Bake for 45 minutes and serve.

★ If Strega is unavailable, use Benedictine or Drambuie instead.

Menu 24

SERVES 8

Antipasto di Peperoni Arrostiti e Mozzarella
Antipasto of Roasted Peppers & Mozzarella

Spaghettoni al Settaccio Garbage Pail Spaghetti

Braciola alla Napoletana Braciole, Neapolitan Style

Torta Farcita di Formaggio alla Napoletana Neapolitan Cheese Gattó

Tiramisù con Frutta di Bosco Tiramisù with Wild Berries

What a fun Sunday menu! If you have young children in the family, they will delight in Garbage Pail Spaghetti! You will find that's because you'll find everything in this hearty, robust dish.

Those of you who own my first cookbook, *Whatever Happened to Sunday Dinner?*, are familiar with the recipe for my Sicilian Nana's classic *braciole*, made with beef. The recipe in this book, by contrast, comes from my great-grandmother, who was from Amorosi, a beautiful town with a romantic name as well (amorosi means "lovers"!), in Provincia di Benevento, outside of Naples. For this reason, the recipe for braciole utilizes pork, which is more common in Campania than beef. It is absolutely delicious and tender!

Tiramisù is a pudding, not a cake and therefore should be eaten with a spoon as it is soft and whipped. Loving it as I do, I have made various versions, among them Limoncello Tiramisù (see page 92). The recipe for tiramisù in this menu includes mixed berries, which are prevalent in Campania, and it's so easy to make, the younger cooks in your family can help assemble this luscious dessert!

Benvenuti alla mia tavola! (Welcome to my table!)

Antipasto di Peperoni Arrostiti e Mozzarella
Antipasto of Roasted Peppers & Mozzarella

 8 red, green and yellow bell peppers

 4 cloves garlic, chopped

 2 teaspoons oregano

 1 teaspoon Sicilian sea salt, fine

 ½ teaspoon freshly ground black pepper

 ½ cup extra virgin olive oil

 12 ounces fresh mozzarella, sliced

1. Roast the peppers according to the directions on page 128. Remove the peppers from the oven or the grill, and set them aside to cool completely. When they have cooled completely, peel the black, charred skin off the peppers and discard it. Rinse each pepper under cold water, removing the stem and the seeds, and pat it dry with a paper towel. Slice each pepper into quarters. (Depending on whether you have a 3-point bell pepper or a 4-point bell pepper, there should be either 4 or 6 natural strips to the pepper, lengthwise.) Set the peppers aside.

2. *To make the dressing*: Combine the garlic, oregano, salt, pepper, and olive oil in a medium bowl.

3. Transfer the roasted peppers to a platter, place the sliced mozzarella pieces on top of the peppers, pour the dressing on top, and serve.

Spaghettoni al Settaccio
Garbage Pail Spaghetti

 ½ cup extra virgin olive oil

 ¼ cup walnuts, chopped

 2 tablespoons pine nuts

 1 cup cherry or grape tomatoes, halved

 ¼ cup golden raisins

 2 tablespoons capers, rinsed and chopped

 1 teaspoon dried oregano

 ¼ cup Italian flat leaf parsley, chopped

 ½ cup good-quality black olives, chopped, preferably imported from Italy

 ½ cup good-quality green olives, chopped, preferably imported from Italy

 1 teaspoon Sicilian sea salt, fine

 ½ teaspoon freshly ground black pepper

 2 pounds spaghettoni (thick spaghetti, or, if you cannot find this product, you can use regular spaghetti)

 1 cup Pecorino Romano cheese, grated

1. In a large frying pan, heat the oil and add the walnuts and pine nuts. Sauté the nuts over medium heat for 2–3 minutes, or until they are golden brown, being very careful not to burn them. Add the tomatoes, raisins, and capers, and cook for an additional 7 minutes. Add the oregano, parsley, olives, salt, and pepper and cook 3 minutes longer. Pour the sauce into a large pasta bowl.

2. Fill a large 6- to 8-quart pasta pot with water and bring it to a rolling boil. Cook the spaghettoni according to the directions on the package. Drain the pasta well, toss it with the sauce, and scatter the grated Pecorino on top.

Braciola alla Napoletana
Braciole, Neapolitan Style

1 (4-pound) pork loin

12 ounces ground pork (can be ground pork with Italian seasonings already added, if it's available at your grocery store)

12 ounces prosciutto crudo, chopped

½ cup Parmigiano Reggiano, grated

¼ cup golden raisins

¼ cup pine nuts

3 garlic cloves, chopped

¼ cup flat leaf Italian parsley, chopped

½ cup breadcrumbs

1 teaspoon Sicilian sea salt, fine

½ teaspoon freshly ground black pepper

¼ cup extra virgin olive oil

1 white onion, chopped

4 cups good-quality red wine, preferably imported from Italy, such as Chianti, Sangiovese, or Nero d'Avola

2 pounds ripe tomatoes (can be Roma or beefsteak), chopped

1 tablespoon sugar

1. Cut the pork loin into thin slices (about ¼ inch thick). Place a piece of wax paper or plastic wrap over the slices of pork and, using a kitchen hammer, pound the pork until it is very thin.

2. *To prepare the stuffing*: Combine well the ground pork, prosciutto, Parmigiano, raisins, pine nuts, garlic, parsley, breadcrumbs, salt, and pepper in a medium-size bowl.

3. *To assemble the braciole*: Spread ½–¾ teaspoon of the stuffing over each slice of the pork loin. Roll up each slice of the pork to form a log, and either tie it together with butcher's twine or use 2 toothpicks, 1 on either side of the log, to secure it.

4. In a large frying pan, heat the olive oil over medium heat and sauté the onion. While the onion is sautéing, place the braciole in the oil and brown it on all sides. After the pork is browned, pour in the red wine and cook for 15 minutes, allowing the wine to reduce by one-third. Add the tomatoes and the sugar. Cook for another 10 to 15 minutes.

5. To serve, place the pork braciole on a large platter and top it with the tomato sauce.

Torta Farcita di Formaggio alla Napoletana
Neapolitan Cheese Gattó

Handful Sicilian sea salt, coarse

4 pounds potatoes, such as Yukon gold, peeled and cut into 1-inch cubes

1 cup Parmigiano Reggiano, grated

1 cup whole milk

1 stick unsalted butter, cut into ½-inch pieces

3 eggs beaten

¼ cup extra virgin olive oil

4 garlic cloves, chopped

½ teaspoon crushed red pepper flakes

3 bunches broccoli rabe, chopped

16 ounces smoked mozzarella or scamorza cheese, cut into ½-inch cubes

1 teaspoon Sicilian sea salt, fine

½ teaspoon freshly ground black pepper

1. Bring a large pot of water to a rolling boil and add a handful of coarse Sicilian sea salt. Place the potatoes in the boiling water and cook until tender. Drain the potatoes and place them in a large bowl. With the back of a fork, smash the potatoes, and, while they are still hot, add the Parmigiano, milk, butter, salt, peppers, and eggs. Set the mixture aside.

2. In a large frying pan, pour the olive oil, garlic, and crushed red pepper flakes. Sauté the mixture until the garlic is translucent, being careful not to burn the garlic. This takes approximately 2 minutes. Add the broccoli rabe and cook for approximately 8 more minutes. Remove the broccoli rabe from the frying pan with a slotted spoon and place it in a medium-size bowl.

3. Use a wooden spoon to break up the broccoli rabe until it is small and crumbly. Spoon half the potato mixture into the bottom of a 13 × 9-inch baking dish or casserole, and then top it with all the broccoli rabe. Then, top it with half the cubed cheese. Spoon the remaining half of the potato mixture over the broccoli rabe and scatter the remaining cheese cubes on top.

4. Bake the mixture for 30 minutes in a preheated 350°F oven.

Tiramisù con Frutta di Bosco
Tiramisù with Wild Berries

16 ounces mascarpone cheese
(approximately 2 cups)

6 tablespoons sugar

3 tablespoons pure vanilla extract

3 eggs, separated

¾ cup crème de cassis liqueur,
excellent quality

24 savoiardi (ladyfinger cookies,
imported from Italy)

1 pint raspberries

1 pint blackberries

1. With a hand mixer, beat the mascarpone, sugar, vanilla, and egg yolks in a bowl.

2. In a separate, medium-size bowl, beat the egg whites until stiff. Fold the egg whites into the mascarpone mixture very gently, until they are evenly incorporated.

3. Coat the bottom of a medium-size serving bowl or trifle bowl with 4 tablespoons of the mascarpone mixture.

4. In a shallow dish, such as a pie plate, pour the crème de cassis. Dip the ladyfingers, one by one, into the crème de cassis until they are saturated, but do not fall apart. Place them on top of the mascarpone mixture. Top the ladyfingers with 4 more tablespoons of the mascarpone mixture. Scatter the raspberries and blackberries on top. Repeat with another layer of ladyfingers, then the mascarpone mixture, and then the fresh berries, filling the bowl to the top. Finish the tiramisù with a layer of the mascarpone mixture and the rest of the berries on top. Serve.

Menu 25

SERVES 8

Frittata di Ricotta Salata con Pomodori Secchi
Ricotta Salata Frittata with Sun-Dried Tomatoes

Ditalini con Peperoni Arrostiti Ditalini with Roasted Peppers

Agnello Arrostito con Olive Olive Roasted Lamb

Torta di Pomodoro Tomato Pie

Coviglia al Caffe Coffee Parfait

My memories of Naples, Italy, harken back to childhood. My parents moved to Naples in the 1950s, before I was born, and lived there for many years with my older sister. Later, after I was born, we would return to Naples for months at a time, as my father's research for many of his academic projects was based there. I formed wonderful friendships in Naples with the children of my parents' very close friends and colleagues. Fortunately, some of these friendships have lasted my entire life, and now my children are friends with their children. As a result, I have gone back to Naples with my own children, and we have spent countless hours eating our favorite desserts in Naples' famous pasticcerie (pastry shops).

Coviglia al Caffe, the dessert in this menu, is not only a historic Neapolitan dessert, but it is also one of my absolute favorites. I love the history of food, and *coviglia al caffe* evokes the history of Naples, as well as incorporating one of my favorite drinks in the world: Italian espresso! The word *coviglia* is only used in Naples, and it means the little cup in which semifreddo (a chilled, but not a frozen dessert) is

served. When I was growing up and went to Naples with my parents, you'd see the small silver cups lined up behind the glass display case in every coffee bar and pasticcerie. Today, you only see them in elegant, old-fashioned bars. But, for me, the silver cups represent an important time in my childhood, and conjure up memories of my father, a dessert lover like me, indulging in a *coviglia al caffe*.

Frittata di Ricotta Salata con Pomodori Secchi
Ricotta Salata Frittata with Sun-Dried Tomato

2 tablespoons extra virgin olive oil

2 cloves garlic, chopped

½ cup sun-dried tomatoes, chopped

1 tablespoon fresh basil leaves, chopped

¼ teaspoon oregano, dried

½ cup pitted black olives, halved

½ teaspoon freshly ground black pepper

8 large eggs, beaten

½ cup ricotta salata, grated

1. Place the olive oil in a medium-size (about 10-inch) frying pan and cook the garlic until it turns golden, being careful not to burn it. This should take approximately 2 minutes. Stir the sun-dried tomatoes, basil, oregano, olives, and black pepper into the olive oil in the pan.

2. In a large bowl, beat the eggs with a fork and beat in the ricotta salata. Pour the egg mixture into the skillet and allow it to set. Do not touch the eggs until you see the eggs cooking around the edge of the pan. Very gently, with the back of a wooden spoon or spatula, lift the corners of the frittata, allowing the liquid egg from the center of the frittata to spill down into the pan and cook. Continue until all the liquid egg has practically solidified.

3. Place a dinner plate upside down on top of the frying pan. Flip the frittata onto the plate and then slide it back into the pan to cook the other side.

4. Allow the frittata to cook for 1 more minute, until there is no runny egg, and then slide it onto a serving platter.

5. Slice the frittata and serve.

Ditalini con Peperoni Arrostiti
Ditalini with Roasted Peppers

8 large red bell peppers

½ cup extra virgin olive oil, plus more for greasing the pan

½ cup capers

3 cloves garlic, chopped

2 cups Roma tomatoes, chopped

½ cup Italian flat leaf parsley, chopped

1 tablespoon dried oregano

½ teaspoon crushed red pepper flakes

2 pounds ditalini (if ditalini pastina is not available, substitute stelline or alphabet pastina)

1 cup Pecorino Romano cheese, grated

1. Cut the peppers in half lengthwise. Remove the stem, all the seeds, and any white pith. Lightly oil a 13 × 9-inch heatproof glass casserole (you may require 2 of these, depending on the size of your peppers).

2. In a large bowl, mix all the ingredients except the pasta and the cheese.

3. Place a large pot of water on the stove and bring it to a rolling boil. Cook the ditalini for 3 minutes less than the cooking instructions on the package, and then drain the pasta.

This Is Sunday Dinner

4. Add the ditalini to the other ingredients in the bowl. Fill each half of the peppers with the mixture, top them with cheese, and bake them in a preheated 350°F oven for 30–40 minutes, until the peppers are soft.

Agnello Arrostito con Olive
Olive Roasted Lamb

1 (5-pound) leg of lamb, preferably from New Zealand

½ cup extra virgin olive oil

1 tablespoon Sicilian sea salt, coarse

1 tablespoon freshly ground black pepper

1 tablespoon dried oregano

1 tablespoon dried thyme

8 cloves garlic, peeled but left whole

1 cup dry white wine

1 cup excellent-quality black olives, pitted, preferably imported from Italy

1. Preheat the oven to 450°F.

2. Place the leg of lamb on a rack (either a flat or an inverted V rack) in the center of a large casserole dish. Cover the lamb well with olive oil, coarse sea salt, freshly ground black pepper, oregano, and thyme. With the point of a sharp knife (such as a paring knife), cut small, ½-inch-long slits into the leg of lamb and stuff the cloves of garlic into the slits.

3. Roast the leg of lamb for 20 minutes. Remove the casserole from the oven. Spoon any juices from the bottom of the casserole over the lamb and then pour the white wine over the meat. Return the casserole to the oven and roast

the lamb for an additional 20 minutes. Remove the casserole from the oven and add the olives. Roast the lamb for 10 more minutes.

4. Remove the lamb from the oven and let it rest on a cutting board for another 10 minutes, before slicing and serving the meat.

Torta di Pomodoro
Tomato Pie

For the Pasta Salata (Pastry Dough)

2⅓ cups all-purpose flour

1 cup unsalted butter

1 teaspoon salt

3 cloves garlic, minced

8 tablespoons cold water

½ cup grated Fontina cheese

For the Tomato Filling

4 tablespoons unsalted butter

1 white onion, chopped

4 cloves garlic, chopped

1 teaspoon Sicilian sea salt, fine

1 teaspoon freshly ground black pepper

4 cups Roma tomatoes, chopped

3 tablespoons unbleached flour

1 cup Parmigiano Reggiano, grated

1. *To make the dough:* Place flour, butter, salt, and garlic into a large bowl, and mix together until it forms a coarse dough. Drizzle in some of the cold water and stir the dough gently with a fork until it comes together. (Add a bit more water, if needed; it's better to have dough that is slightly wet than too dry.) (The dough may also be made in an electric mixer or a stand mixer.) Separate the dough into 2 balls, one that is approximately ¾ of the dough and one that is about ¼ of the dough. Cover the dough in plastic wrap and let it rest for 15–30 minutes at room temperature.

2. In a large frying pan, melt the butter, Add the onion, garlic, salt, and pepper. Cook the onion and garlic until they are translucent, about 7 minutes. Add the tomatoes and the flour, stirring the mixture to thoroughly incorporate the flour. Remove the pan from the heat and set it aside.

3. Roll out the larger ball of dough and line a 9–9½-inch pie pan with the dough. Pour the filling into the pan. Roll out the second ball of dough into a rectangle, and then cut it into ¼-inch strips to form a lattice on top of the tomato filling. Bake the pie in a preheated 350° oven for 30 minutes.

Coviglia al Caffe
Coffee Parfait

6 whole, large eggs, separated

1 cup sugar

½ cup very strong espresso

1 cup heavy cream

1. In a medium-size bowl, beat the egg yolks with a hand mixer and add ½ cup of the sugar.

2. In another medium-size bowl, dissolve the remaining sugar into the espresso.

3. Combine the mixtures in the two bowls in a large bowl, thoroughly mixing the egg yolks into the coffee and sugar.

4. In a clean medium-size bowl, beat the heavy cream with a hand mixer until it forms soft peaks. Then very gently, fold the cream into the coffee and egg mixture.

5. In another clean bowl, beat the egg whites with the hand mixer until it forms stiff peaks. Fold the egg whites into the egg, coffee, and cream mixture, and then pour it into individual cups, such as espresso cups or ramekins. Place the cups or ramekins in the freezer for a minimum of 3 hours, until the mixture is firm but not frozen. Serve.

Menu 26

SERVES 8

This is one of my favorite Campania menus. I love the Artichoke Sauce—the delicate flavor and texture of this vegetable, paired with the saltiness of the pancetta, makes for a unique, satisfying combination.

Baked Shrimp in Breadcrumbs is one of my favorite dishes from childhood. My mother has beautiful plates shaped like shells, which she bought many, many years ago in Italy. She would fill them with flavorful shrimp, coated in garlic and seasonings, top them with breadcrumbs, and pop them in the oven. They were pure heaven. In case you don't have shell-shaped dishes, a casserole is fine!

Everyone will be delighted with the many cheeses and yellow potatoes in the Gattó Napoletano (gattó is Italian for "casserole"). It is creamy and delicious and a wonderful complement to the shrimp dish.

This menu ends with an amazing, rustic Torta di Limone, a lemon cake from the Sorrento region of Campania, known for its giant lemons and incredible limoncello.

Buonissimo! (Delicious!)

Bruschetta alle Erbe
Bruschetta with Fresh Herbs

- ½ cup extra virgin olive oil
- 2 tablespoons Italian flat leaf parsley, chopped
- 2 tablespoons fresh basil, chopped
- 1 teaspoon marjoram
- 1 teaspoon Sicilian sea salt, fine
- 1 teaspoon freshly ground black pepper
- 4 garlic cloves, peeled and left whole
- 8 slices, ½ inch thick, good, rustic Italian bread

1. Preheat the broiler (or the grill).

2. Combine the oil, parsley, basil, marjoram, salt, and pepper in a small bowl.

3. Toast the bread until golden on both sides.

4. Slice the garlic cloves in half. With the flat side of a garlic clove, rub each slice of Italian bread. Brush the olive oil mixture on the toast with a pastry brush and serve.

Rigatoni con Salsa di Carciofi
Rigatoni with Artichoke Sauce

- ½ cup extra virgin olive oil
- 8 ounces pancetta (substitute with good-quality American bacon, cut into 1-inch pieces)
- 1 teaspoon Sicilian sea salt, fine
- 2 (12-ounce) bags frozen artichoke hearts
- 3 garlic cloves, chopped
- ¼ cup Italian flat leaf parsley, chopped
- 1 teaspoon freshly ground black pepper
- 2 pounds rigatoni
- 1 cup Parmigiano Reggiano, grated

1. Place ¼ cup of the olive oil, the pancetta, ½ cup water, and the salt in a large frying pan with the artichoke hearts. Cook until the pancetta is cooked through, 15–20 minutes. Allow the mixture to cool. Remove the pancetta from the mixture and set it aside.

2. In a blender, puree the artichoke heart mixture. Add the garlic, parsley, and pepper. Pour the artichoke puree into a large frying pan and warm it over low heat for a few minutes. Add the remaining ¼ cup of olive oil.

3. Fill a large 6- to 8-quart pasta pot with water and bring it to a rolling boil. Add the rigatoni and cook it al dente, according to the instructions on the package. Reserve ½ cup of the pasta cooking water.

4. In a large pasta bowl, toss the rigatoni with the artichoke puree. Add the pancetta. If the sauce is very thick, add a little bit of the pasta water. Toss well and top with the Parmigiano Reggiano.

Gamberi al Forno in Pangrattato
Baked Shrimp in Breadcrumbs

1 cup breadcrumbs (if not homemade, use excellent-quality, store-bought breadcrumbs), plus more for sprinkling

1½ teaspoons Sicilian sea salt, fine

2 teaspoons dried oregano

3 garlic cloves, chopped

1 teaspoon hot paprika

¼ cup extra virgin olive oil

3 pounds large shrimp (16–20 to the pound), cleaned

10 to 12 lemon wedges

1. Preheat the oven to 400°F.

2. In a large bowl, combine the breadcrumbs, salt, oregano, garlic, paprika, and oil. Stir well. Add the shrimp to the bowl and toss until all the shrimp are well coated.

3. In a 13 × 9-inch casserole (you may need two of them), place the shrimp in a single layer and sprinkle with additional breadcrumbs.

4. Bake the shrimp for 15 minutes and serve with lemon wedges.

Gattó Napoletano
Potato Casserole

4 eggs

¾ cup whole milk

½ cup whole milk ricotta

4 pounds yellow potatoes, such as Yukon gold

2 cups Parmigiano Reggiano, grated

1 cup Pecorino Romano, grated

½ cup flat leaf Italian parsley, chopped

2 teaspoons Sicilian sea salt, fine

8 tablespoons unsalted butter

¾ cup breadcrumbs

1 pound fresh mozzarella, cubed

1. Preheat the oven to 400°F.

2. Beat the eggs in a bowl. Add the milk and ricotta to the eggs and blend well. Set the bowl aside.

3. Peel and dice the potatoes into 1-inch cubes. Cook the potatoes in boiling water until they're tender, about 30 minutes (dicing the potatoes will make them cook quickly), and drain them in colander. Place the potatoes in the bowl of a stand mixer, or a large bowl, if you are using a hand mixer, and beat them. Continue to beat the potatoes while adding the Parmigiano and Pecorino. Stir in the parsley and salt and mix well. Gently stir in the egg mixture.

4. Butter a 12-inch springform pan with 2 tablespoons of the butter and dust the bottom of the pan with some of the breadcrumbs. Divide the potato mixture into 2 portions and smooth half the mixture onto the bottom of the springform pan. Sprinkle the mozzarella over the potato mixture. Top with the remaining half of the potato mixture and smooth it flat with a rubber spatula. Sprinkle the mixture with the remaining breadcrumbs and dot with the remaining 4 tablespoons of butter.

5. Bake for 30 minutes. Remove the *gattó* from the oven. Let it rest for 5 minutes, and then slice it into wedges, like a pie, and serve.

Torta di Limone
Lemon Cake

For the Cake

 2 sticks unsalted butter

 1 cup sugar

 4 eggs

 2 tablespoons lemon zest

 3 cups unbleached flour

 ½ teaspoon Sicilian sea salt, fine

 2 teaspoons baking powder

 ½ cup whole milk

For the Syrup

 ¼ cup water

 ½ cup sugar

 ½ cup freshly squeezed lemon juice

For the Garnish

 Sliced almonds

1. Preheat the oven to 350°F.

2. *To make the cake:* Butter and flour a 9-inch bundt pan. In a stand mixer or using a hand mixer, mix the butter and sugar together for 5 minutes, until light and fluffy. Add eggs and beat well. Stir in the lemon zest. Add the flour, salt, and baking powder and mix well. Stir in the milk. Pour the mixture into the bundt pan and bake for 40 minutes.

3. *To make the syrup:* Combine the water and sugar in a small saucepan. Bring the mixture to a boil and stir until the sugar is dissolved. Let the syrup cool, and then add the lemon juice.

4. Let the cake cool for 15 minutes. Flip the cake onto a platter and poke holes in it with a toothpick, then slowly pour the lemon syrup over the cake, letting it drip down through the holes. Top with the sliced almonds. After you cut the cake, you can pour more of the syrup on each slice, if desired.

Summer in Sicily

$\mathcal{A}$nd now we enter full summer, and there is no more splendid place to be than Sicily with its verdant hills, grapes, and fruits of all types. Sicily is alive in summer like no other place!

The philosopher Goethe said, "Sicily is the key to everything." His words ring true even today. Invasions by Phoenicians and Greeks; Carthaginians and Romans; Goths and Byzantines; Arabs and Normans; Germans, Spaniards, and French—all have left their mark on this mysterious, melancholy, and beautiful island, including on its exotic cuisine. Sicily holds the key to beauty, too, with its rustic, pristine landscape—from fiery, explosive Mt. Etna to exquisite, calm beaches.

I frequently spend time in Sicily, renting a seaside cottage in my grandmother's birthplace. Sicily is like taking a trip back in time—back to a much more rustic place, where the pace of life is slower and the food is genuine and fresh—like nothing you have ever eaten before.

I love Sicily for myriad reasons. For me, it represents my grandmother, Nana, who was born and raised in Castelvetrano. Nana taught me so many of the Sicilian dishes I make on a regular basis, and she was the greatest inspiration for my love for cooking and my family. Sicily also represents for me an island full of mystery and beauty. Every time I visit, I discover another hidden gem of the island, and another creative use of a vegetable or seafood. Sicilians are imaginative cooks. Sicily's strategic location at the heart of the breathtaking Mediterranean and the island's amazing harvests make it the "fruit and vegetable basket" of Italy. Golden raisins, pine nuts, honey, and cinnamon are just a few of the ingredients that set Sicilian cuisine apart from that in the rest of Italy, and make it exotic and exciting. The use of the famous agrodolce sauce—a sweet and savory combination of honey and vinegar—for example, gives everything from cheese to vegetables to dessert an exotic tang.

Benvenuti alla mia Sicilia! (Welcome to my Sicily!)

Lisa's Favorite Wines from Sicily

Just like everything else about my beloved island of Sicily, the wines are exciting, fiery, and vigorous! In the northeast corner of the island, where Mt. Etna explodes, the soil is very rich in minerals and one of the resulting grapes, the Nerello, has been compared to some of the greatest reds of Tuscany and Piemonte—at a fraction of the price. Known as the "Etna reds" (*Etna rosso*), these wines are ruby red with a fruity bouquet. They are delicious with everything and ridiculously inexpensive!

In the southeast corner of the island, near the historic and fascinating city of Siracusa, you find my favorite red from the island—Nero d'Avola. I have spent many summers in Sicily, specifically in the area where my grandmother was born, and when I first began drinking Nero d'Avola it was virtually unavailable in the States. It has since become very highly regarded as a red from Sicily—I like to say I discovered it first!

Most wineries in Sicily dot the beautiful coastline of the island, where the vineyards hug the hills that lead down to the sea. *Nero d'Avola* means "black from Avola." Avola is the small town, where this grape was first harvested, and *nero* refers to the dark, ruby red color of the wine. An excellent bottle of Nero d'Avola, with its robust flavor, can be purchased in the United States for as little as $12! So enjoy a good Etna rosso or Nero d'Avola with each of these Sicilian Sunday dinners!

Buon cibo, buon vino e sempre famiglia! (Good food, good wine, and family first!)

My favorite wine store in Castelvetrano.

Menu 27

SERSES 8

Crostini con Olive Nere Fritti di Lisa Lisa's Fried Black Olive Crostini

Bucatini con Cavolfiore Bucatini with Cauliflower

Pesce Grilliata con Salsa Verde Siciliana Grilled Swordfish with Sicilian Green Sauce

Verdure Grilliata con Muddica Grilled Vegetables with Breadcrumbs

Torta di Olio di Oliva Olive Oil Cake

This menu brings back many memories! My great-grandmother, Grandma Franco, was known for her use of cauliflower with pasta, as in this menu (both recipes are in my first cookbook, *Whatever Happened to Sunday Dinner?*) It's an earthy, satisfying primo!

Salsa Verde Siciliana is delicious on everything: fish, chicken, and vegetables. Being a traditionalist myself when it comes to Italian food, I do not add any green herbs to my salsa verde, other than the parsley, just as my Nana did. Feel free to double this recipe and keep it in a jar in the refrigerator.

When my children were little, and I wanted them to eat their vegetables, I sautéed breadcrumbs in olive oil, scattered them over the vegetables, and watched those vegetables disappear. My children are grown now and still ask for this! The breadcrumbs are fabulous on grilled vegetables.

Olive Oil Cake—one of my favorite Sicilian desserts—is the crowning glory of this menu. Food in Sicily is very simple, rustic, and delicious—and my recipe for Olive Oil Cake is just that! In Sicily, we use Extra Virgin Olive Oil in many of our desserts, instead of butter, and the result is a moist, satisfying cake.

Buon Appetito a tutti! (Good appetite to all!)

Crostini con Olive Nere Fritti di Lisa

Lisa's Fried Black Olive Crostini

½ cup extra virgin olive oil

4 cloves garlic

1 pound black olives (preferably Sicilian), pitted

1 tablespoon fennel seeds

¼ teaspoon Sicilian sea salt, fine

¼ teaspoon ground black pepper

1. Pour the olive oil into a large frying pan. Slice the garlic lengthwise and sauté it in the olive oil until it is golden and translucent, but not burned. Add the olives, fennel seeds, salt, and pepper to the pan, and stir until the olives are well coated. Sauté the mixture over medium heat for 3 minutes.

2. Transfer the olives to a medium-size serving bowl. Use the back of a large fork to crush approximately one-third of the olives. Stir the crushed olives into the whole olives until you have a good mixture.

3. Serve with crunchy toasted Italian bread.

LISA'S TIP

Visit www.lisacaponigri.com for a "How-to" video on how to properly devein garlic.

Bucatini con Cavolfiore

Bucatini with Cauliflower

6 cups cauliflower florets

1 cup extra virgin olive oil

2 teaspoons Sicilian sea salt, fine

1 teaspoon pepper

2 pounds bucatini pasta

Handful Sicilian sea salt for pasta water, coarse

2 tablespoons lemon zest

3 tablespoons fresh lemon juice

1 cup fresh Parmigiano Reggiano, grated

1. Fill a large pasta pot with water and bring it to a boil.

2. While you are waiting for the water to boil, place the cauliflower florets on a jelly-roll pan (a cookie sheet with a rim), and drizzle with ½ cup of the olive oil. Sprinkle the cauliflower with the salt and pepper. Roast the cauliflower in the oven, at 375°F, for 20 minutes, until the cauliflower begins to turn golden around the edges.

3. Cook the bucatini pasta in the boiling water, according to the directions on the package—and don't forget to salt the pasta water with coarse Sicilian sea salt (visit www. lisacaponigri.com to watch my 3-minute video on salting pasta water!).

4. Remove roasted cauliflower from the oven. Transfer it to a large serving bowl.

5. Toss the bucatini with the roasted cauliflower, lemon zest, lemon juice, and the remaining ½ cup olive oil. Toss until all the bucatini and cauliflower are well coated.

6. Sprinkle Parmigiano Peggiano on top and serve.

Pesce Grilliata con Salsa Verde Siciliana
Grilled Swordfish with Sicilian Green Sauce

- 2 tablespoons white wine vinegar
- 2 slices Italian bread (preferably Italian country bread or ciabatta, crust removed)
- 2 cups flat Italian parsley, finely chopped
- 6 anchovy fillets
- 1 cup capers, preferably imported from Sicily
- 4 cloves garlic
- 1 cup green olives, preferably Castelvetrano olives from Sicily
- 1 teaspoon Sicilian sea salt, fine
- 8 thick swordfish steaks
- 2 teaspoons Sicilian sea salt, fine, for seasoning the fish
- 1 teaspoon freshly ground pepper, for seasoning the fish

1. *To prepare the Sicilian green sauce:* Place the wine vinegar in a small bowl. Remove the *mollica* (the Italian word for the white part of the bread) and soak it in the vinegar. With your hands squeeze the bread until the wine vinegar is absorbed and the rest drains out.

2. Combine the parsley, anchovy fillets, capers, garlic, olives, and 1 teaspoon salt in a blender. Add the *mollica*. Process the mixture until it is thick enough to cover the back of a spoon.

3. *To prepare the fish:* Wash the swordfish steaks well and pat them dry with a paper towel. Season the fish with plenty of salt and pepper. Grill or broil the swordfish steaks for 3 minutes on each side. Place the steaks on a platter, and pour a generous amount of Sicilian green sauce on top.

Verdure Grilliata con Muddica
Grilled Vegetables with Breadcrumbs

- 3 large red bell peppers
- 4 medium eggplants
  - Sicilian sea salt, coarse, for draining eggplant ground
- 4 green zucchini
- 2 yellow zucchini
- 1 cup extra virgin olive oil
- 1 cup breadcrumbs (fresh or a good brand of store-bought breadcrumbs, preferably with Italian seasoning added)
- 4 garlic cloves, finely chopped
- ½ cup fresh Italian flat leaf parsley, chopped
- 1 teaspoon crushed red pepper
- 4 tablespoons red wine vinegar
- 2 tablespoons oregano

1. Core, seed, and quarter the red bell peppers. Rinse them under cold water to be sure that all seeds have been removed. Pat the peppers dry with a paper towel. Set them aside.

2. Cut the eggplant lengthwise into ¼-inch slices. Place the slices in a colander and generously sprinkle the sea salt over each layer. (Visit www.lisacaponigri.com to watch my video on how to drain an eggplant!) Allow the eggplant to drain for 30 minutes in the kitchen sink.

3. Rinse the green and yellow zucchini; remove the stems, and cut the zucchini lengthwise into ¼-inch slices. Set them aside.

4. Thoroughly rinse each eggplant slice under cold, running water, ensuring that you have removed all the sea salt from each slice (this is very important). Dry each eggplant slice with a paper towel.

5. Place the bell peppers, zucchini, and eggplant on a large platter. Sprinkle ½ cup olive oil over the vegetables, making sure that they are well coated with the oil on all sides. Grill the vegetables on each side for 3–4 minutes. (If you are using the oven to cook the vegetables, place the vegetable on a cookie sheet and roast them for 20 minutes at 375°F.)

6. Meanwhile, mix together the remaining ½ cup olive oil, breadcrumbs, garlic, parsley, crushed red pepper, vinegar, and oregano in a medium-size bowl until well combined.

7. Remove all the vegetables from the grill (or the oven) and place them on a large platter. Generously top each vegetable slice with the breadcrumb mixture and serve.

Torta di Olio di Oliva
Olive Oil Cake

1½ cups extra virgin olive oil, plus
    2 tablespoons for greasing the pans

1 cup freshly squeezed orange juice

3 large eggs

1¼ cups whole milk

2 cups sugar

¼ cup Grand Marnier orange liqueur

1 tablespoon lemon zest

1 teaspoon fresh rosemary, chopped

2 cups unbleached flour

½ teaspoon baking soda

½ teaspoon baking powder

1 jar imported Sicilian orange
    marmalade

1. Preheat the oven to 350°F.

2. Oil two 9-inch round cake pans with 2 tablespoons of olive oil.

3. Heat the orange juice over medium heat until it reduces to ¼ cup. Let it cool.

4. In a large bowl, beat together the eggs, milk, sugar, Grand Manier, 1½ cups olive oil, orange juice reduction, lemon zest, and rosemary with a whisk. Mix until well blended. Add the flour, baking soda, and baking powder, and mix until the batter is smooth. Pour half the batter into each pan. Bake for 1 hour. Flip each of the cakes onto a separate plate or platter (this is not a recipe for a stacked cake). To serve, top each slice of cake with a tablespoon of Sicilian orange marmalade.

Mazzara del Vallo, Sicily, is well known for its fishing traditions: from the huge fish market to the early morning fish auction. Here I fish with a local fisherman, Pasquale, for the day's catch!

Menu 28

SERSE 8

Palline di Ricotta Ricotta Cheese Balls

Fusilli al Ragù Siciliano Fusilli with Sicilian Ragù

Vitello alla Griglia Grilled Veal, Sicilian Style

Carote Arostiti con Miele Honey-Roasted Carrots

I Cucidata della mia Nonna My Nana's Fig Cookies

This warm, comforting menu starts with classic ricotta cheese balls. Ricotta is native to the island of Sicily, and the word ri-cotta means "cooked again." It has this name because ricotta is made from the whey left over after the cheese is made and therefore the cheese is literally cooked twice.

Sicilian ragù is rustic Italian cooking at its best. The word ragù in Italian refers to any meat sauce that is made with ground meat. Sicilian ragù is made with ground beef, peas, and velvety tomato puree. It is always used to fill arancini, classic Sicilian rice balls. (The recipe for arancini is in my first cookbook, *Whatever Happened to Sunday Dinner?*)

In this menu, the Honey-Roasted Carrots are a great example of agrodolce—the savory-sweet flavor that is so prevalent on the island of Sicily, and which is reminiscent of the Arab influence on our cooking. When my daughter Felicia was little, she was diagnosed with lazy eye, and although it may be an old wives' tale, I'm convinced that the carrots she ate—only if they were roasted and served in delicious honey sauce—helped heal her eye! The recipe for Honey-Roasted Carrots is

perfect for your children to make—it's easy for them to toss the honey on the carrots, and gives them the satisfaction of contributing to the preparation of Sunday dinner.

My Nana's famous fig cookies (Cucidata, as they are called in Sicilian), round out this menu. A wonderful combination of dried fruit—figs, dates, and apricots, which are so prevalent in Sicilian cuisine, thanks to the Arab influence—these cookies are usually made at Christmastime. But they are so delicious I love to make them all year round!

Tutti a tavola! (Everyone to table!)

Palline di Ricotta
Ricotta Cheese Balls

2 pounds ricotta, well chilled

1 teaspoon Sicilian sea salt, fine

½ teaspoon freshly ground black pepper

1 red bell pepper (seeded and finely chopped)

¼ cup sesame seeds

¼ cup pistachios, chopped

1. Line a cookie sheet with plastic wrap.

2. Place the ricotta in a large bowl. Mix in the salt and pepper. With a small ice cream scoop or a teaspoon, shape the ricotta into 24 equal-size balls. Divide them into 3 groups of 8 balls. Roll 1 group of 8 balls in the chopped red bell pepper. Roll the second group of 8 balls in the sesame seeds. Roll the third group of 8 balls in the chopped pistachios. Arrange all 24 balls on the cookie sheet and refrigerate for 30 minutes. Arrange the colorful ricotta balls in rows on a platter. Serve with either toasted Italian bread slices or crackers.

Fusilli al Ragù Siciliano
Fusilli with Sicilian Ragù

4 tablespoons extra virgin olive oil

1 cup chopped white onion

1 cup finely minced carrots

1 cup finely minced celery

2 pounds ground round

1 cup good-quality Sicilian red wine, such as Nero d'Avola

4 cups crushed imported San Marzano tomatoes

3 teaspoons Sicilian sea salt, fine

1 teaspoon freshly ground black pepper

2 cups frozen green peas

Handful Sicilian sea salt, coarse

2 pounds fusilli pasta

1. Heat the olive oil in a large 3- to 4-quart saucepan. Sauté the onion, carrots, and celery for 20 minutes, stirring frequently until the vegetables are very tender. Add the ground round to the saucepan, coating it very well with the vegetables and breaking up the meat with a wooden spoon. Cook until all the red is gone from the meat. Add the Sicilian wine to the pan, and allow it to cook for approximately 5 minutes. Add the San Marzano crushed tomatoes, salt, and pepper. Simmer the ragù on medium to low heat for 30 minutes. Add the peas. Stir well and cook for 10 more minutes, until the peas are cooked through.

2. Fill a 6-quart pot with water and bring it to a boil. When the water comes to a rolling boil, add a handful of coarse Sicilian sea salt (visit www.lisacaponigri.com, and watch my "How-to" video on salting pasta water). Cook the fusilli according to the directions on the package.

3. Transfer the ragù to a large pasta bowl. Drain the fusilli and add it to the sauce in the bowl. Toss the pasta in the sauce until it is completely coated, and serve.

LISA'S TIP

It is not traditional to serve cheese with Sicilian meat ragù because it is a peasant dish, and for centuries cheese was considered a luxury in Sicily. But if you would like some grated cheese on the top, I recommend Pecorino Romano or Ricotta Salata.

Vitello alla Griglia
Grilled Veal

- 4 tablespoons extra virgin olive oil
- 1 cup white onion, finely chopped
- 4 tablespoons pignoli (pine nuts)
- 6 tablespoons golden raisins
- 8 cups breadcrumbs (if buying store-bought breadcrumbs, use a good brand, preferably with Italian seasoning)
- 4 tablespoons chopped Italian flat leaf parsley
- 3 tablespoons chopped garlic
- 3 cups grated cacciocavallo cheese, preferably imported from Sicily, or Pecorino Romano
- 1 teaspoon Sicilian sea salt, fine
- 1 tablespoon freshly ground black pepper
- 3 pounds veal scaloppine (sliced very thin)

1. Place 2 tablespoons of olive oil in a large frying pan over medium heat. Add the onions and cook them until they're soft and translucent. Add the pine nuts, raisins, and breadcrumbs, and cook approximately 3 minutes over low heat, until the breadcrumbs begin to turn golden. Stir in parsley, garlic, cheese, and the remaining olive oil. Season with salt and pepper.

2. Lay each piece of veal scallopine on a clean work surface. Place 2 tablespoons of the breadcrumb filling on 1 end of each piece of veal. Roll the veal scallopine, making sure that none of the filling falls out of the sides, and stick a toothpick through each end of the roll to secure it. Brush each roll up with some of the remaining olive oil.

3. If you're using a grill, cook the veal over medium heat for 6 minutes, or, if you're using an oven, bake the veal in a preheated 350°F oven for 20 minutes. Serve the roll-ups on a platter.

Carote Arrostiti con Miele
Honey-Roasted Carrots

2 pounds carrots, peeled and sliced in ¼-inch rounds

4 tablespoons extra virgin olive oil

3 tablespoons excellent-quality honey

2 tablespoons balsamic vinegar, imported from Italy

1 teaspoon Sicilian sea salt, fine

½ teaspoon freshly ground black pepper

1. Preheat the oven to 350°F.

2. Place all the carrot rounds in a single layer on a jelly-roll pan.

3. In a small bowl or measuring cup, mix together the olive oil, honey, balsamic vinegar, salt, and pepper. Pour the mixture over the carrots, coating them well, and roast for 20 minutes in the preheated oven. Transfer the carrots to a platter or bowl and serve.

I Cucidata della mia Nonna
My Nana's Sicilian Fig Cookies

Makes at least 24 cookies

For the Dough

2½ cups unbleached flour

½ cup sugar

1 teaspoon baking powder

½ teaspoon salt

6 tablespoons unsalted butter

2 large eggs

⅓ cup whole milk

For the Filling

12 ounces dried figs, preferably imported from Sicily

1½ cup each chopped pine nuts, chopped walnuts.

4 tablespoons granulated sugar

4 tablespoons whiskey

4 tablespoons orange marmalade, preferably imported from Italy

2 teaspoons ground cinnamon

1 egg lightly beaten (for egg wash)

For the Glaze

1 cup confectioners' sugar

5 teaspoons whole milk

1 teaspoon almond extract

1 one-ounce jar multicolored sprinkles

1. *To make the cookie dough:* In a food processor combine the flour, sugar, baking powder, and salt. Add the butter, eggs and milk until smooth. Form the dough into a ball, wrap it in plastic wrap, and refrigerate it for a minimum of 2 hours.

2. *To make the filling:* Combine the figs, pine nuts, walnuts, sugar, whiskey, marmalade, and cinnamon in a food processor or mixer, until well blended. These ingredients will remain slightly chunky.

3. Preheat the oven to 350°F.

4. *To assemble the cookies:* Roll out the dough on a floured surface. Use either a 5-inch-diameter round cookie cutter (or a 5-inch-diameter round glass or mug) to form about 24 cookie rounds. Place 1 teaspoon of the filling in the center of each cookie-dough round. Gently lift the dough to form a pouch around the filling. Pinch the dough together with your fingers at the top. Use a pastry brush to lightly coat each cookie with the egg wash. Repeat this process until all the dough has been used.

5. Line a baking sheet with parchment paper (or a silicone baking sheet). Place the cookies on the sheet, spacing them 1½ inches apart. Bake the cookies for 12–15 minutes, or until they've turned lightly golden.

6. *To make the glaze:* Combine the sugar, milk, and almond extract in a small bowl. Before the cookies have cooled completely, dip each one upside down into the glaze. Place the glazed cookies on a platter, sprinkle them immediately with the sprinkles, and serve.

Menu 29

SERVES 8T

Vongole Oreganate Clams with Oregano and Breadcrumbs
Zuppa di Lenticchie al Limone di Lisa Lisa's Lemony Lentil Soup
Pesce in Salsa di Menta Fish in Mint Sauce
Zuppa di Zucchini Zucchini Stew
Crostata di Pistacchio Pistachio Tart

Whenever I think of traditional Sicilian food, I think of this menu. I don't know any Sicilian-Americans (certainly no one in my family!) who don't have stuffed clams on their Sunday dinner table on a regular basis. With a crunchy breadcrumb topping, they are the perfect way to start Sunday dinner.

I grew up on lentil soup—it's hearty, full of fiber, and delicious. But while I was raising my own children, I discovered that my daughter Felicia simply didn't like the dark brown lentils that are used in the traditional recipe. So I tried a new approach and used orange lentils in the soup, instead of the brown ones, as they are lighter and the skin is much thinner, making the lentils easier to digest, as well as requiring less cooking time. Fresh vegetables and a touch of lemon make this version of lentil soup light, refreshing, and perfect for the summer table. It is excellent served at room temperature as well!

Fish in Mint Sauce is another example of Sicilian creativity and the impact of other cultures on the way we cook. The combination of meaty, white fish with the delicate mint sauce in this recipe is delicious on a hot summer afternoon, served either warm or at room temperature.

Double the recipe for Zucchini Stew in this menu because you will want to have it on Monday and Tuesday, as well as for Sunday dinner! During the summer months, how often have you asked yourself, "What am I going to do with all this zucchini?" I live in the Midwest, where zucchini is as plentiful as it is in Italy, but by the end of the season I am tired of making the same zucchini recipes. This zucchini stew is wonderful warm or cold, as a side dish (as in this menu), or as an appetizer on crunchy toasted Italian bread. It is equally delicious on top of a frittata for breakfast or brunch, or as a healthy, delicious after-school snack. It is so versatile and tasty!

Although we love pine nuts on the island of Sicily, the nut we use most often, in our cooking, is the pistachio. Being the creative cooks that we are, Sicilians bring the pistachio, with its rich, buttery flavor, into almost everything we make—from pesto to pasta to the exotic and decadent Pistachio Tart in this menu (another example of the influence of Arab cuisine in our kitchens). This delicious tart is the perfect ending for any Sunday dinner!

Buon appetito!

Vongole Oreganate
Clams with Oregano and Breadcrumbs

24 fresh clams, scrubbed clean

4 cups Sicilian sea salt, coarse

8 tablespoons extra virgin olive oil

1 large red onion, chopped

8 garlic cloves, chopped

2 cups breadcrumbs (either homemade or excellent-quality store-bought breadcrumbs)

1 teaspoon Sicilian sea salt, fine

½ teaspoon freshly ground black pepper

4 tablespoons oregano, preferably imported from Italy

1. Scrub the clamshells. Carefully open the clams and discard the top shell. Drain all the clam juice from each of the clams. With a fork, or the end of a paring knife, loosen the clams from the bottom of the shell. Pour the coarse Sicilian sea salt on a large jelly-roll pan (a cookie sheet with a rim) so it is at least ½–¾-inch deep. Arrange the clams in their shells on the salt.

2. In a large frying pan, heat the olive oil. Add the onion and garlic and cook over medium heat until the onion is translucent, being careful not to burn the garlic. Add the breadcrumbs to the pan and sauté until they are golden brown. (At this point you can add a little extra olive oil to keep the breadcrumbs moist and extra flavorful.) Add the salt and pepper, and stir in the oregano.

3. Preheat the broiler.

4. Using a teaspoon or your fingers, completely cover each clam with some of the breadcrumb mixture. Place the clams under the broiler until they're heated through, about 2 minutes, or until the breadcrumbs are golden brown. Serve immediately.

Zuppa di Lenticchie al Limone di Lisa
Lisa's Lemony Lentil Soup

2 cups orange lentils

8 tablespoons extra virgin olive oil, plus a little more for garnishing the soup

1 large white onion, chopped

3 garlic cloves, chopped

1 teaspoon Sicilian sea salt, fine

½ teaspoon freshly ground black pepper

8 cups vegetable broth (either homemade or very good quality store-bought broth)

Juice of 2 lemons

1. Wash the lentils and drain them in a colander. Pat the lentils dry with paper towels while they are still in the colander.

2. Pour the olive oil into a large frying pan over medium heat. Add the onion, garlic, and lentils, and dry-sauté them (that is, do not add any liquid other than the olive oil to the pan). Cook the mixture until the onions are translucent, approximately 5 minutes, being careful not to burn the garlic. Add the salt and pepper directly to the mixture, and sauté for 2 more minutes.

3. Transfer the lentil mixture to a 4- to 6-quart soup pan. Add the vegetable broth and lemon juice. Simmer the soup for 15–20 minutes (orange lentils are thin and cook quickly). Garnish the soup with a drizzle of extra virgin olive oil on top.

LISA'S TIP

When making soup, I always dry-sauté the legumes in olive oil before I add any broth or water to the pan, as I find this helps the legumes to absorb all the flavor of the garlic, onions, and herbs, and also helps them retain their texture and consistency.

Pesce in Salsa di Menta
Fish in Mint Sauce

- 4 tablespoons almonds, sliced
- 1 cup extra virgin olive oil
- 2 pounds any meaty white fish, such as flounder or sea bass, cut into 6- to 8-ounce fillets
- 4 ounces white wine
- 3 teaspoons sugar
- 4 cups peas (fresh or frozen)
- 4 garlic cloves, thinly sliced
- Mint leaves
- 1 teaspoon Sicilian sea salt, fine
- ½ teaspoon freshly ground black pepper

1. Preheat the oven to 350°F.

2. In a large frying pan over medium heat, toast the almonds until they're golden, approximately 2–3 minutes. Remove the almonds from the pan. Set them aside to cool.

3. Pour the olive oil into the frying pan. Place the fish fillets in the pan and brown them, about 4 minutes on each side over medium heat (you may need to cook the fish in 2 batches). When the fillets are browned on both sides, transfer them to a platter and cover it with aluminum foil. Leave the pan on the burner.

4. Add the white wine, sugar, peas, garlic, and mint leaves to the remaining oil in the frying pan. Add the salt and pepper. Cook the mixture for 5–7 minutes, until it is slightly reduced and the peas are cooked through.

5. Pour the mint-and-pea sauce over the fish fillets, top with the toasted almonds, and serve.

Zuppa di Zucchini
Zucchini Stew

- 1 cup extra virgin olive oil
- 2 white onions, chopped
- 4 garlic cloves, chopped
- 6 celery stalks, chopped
- 1 teaspoon Sicilian sea salt, fine
- ½ teaspoon freshly ground black pepper
- ½ teaspoon crushed red pepper flakes
- 4 –5 pounds small zucchini, sliced into ¼-inch rounds
- 2 cups crushed San Marzano tomatoes, imported from Italy
- 1 cup freshly grated Pecorino Romano cheese

1. In a large frying pan, heat the olive oil and sauté the onions, garlic, and celery, until the onion is translucent. Add the salt, black pepper, and crushed red pepper flakes. Add the zucchini. Cook for 5–7 minutes.

2. Transfer the vegetable mixture to a large, 6- to 10-quart soup pot. Add the San Marzano tomatoes to the mixture and cook for 30 minutes over low to medium heat. Pour the stew into a serving bowl and top with the Pecorino Romano.

Crostata di Pistacchio
Pistachio Tart

For the Dough

- 1¼ cups unbleached flour
- ¼ teaspoon baking powder
- ⅛ teaspoon Sicilian sea salt, fine
- ⅓ cup sugar
- 1 stick, plus 1 tablespoon unsalted butter, cold
- 1 egg yolk
- ⅛ cup ice cold water

For the Filling

- 6 cups pistachios, finely chopped
- 1¼ cups sugar
- 2 teaspoons pure vanilla extract
- Zest of 4 oranges
- 2 eggs
- 3 cups mascarpone cheese

1. *To make the dough:* Combine flour, baking powder, salt, and sugar. Add the butter and egg yolk. Knead into a soft mixture, either in a stand mixer or with a hand mixer. Add the ice water a few drops at a time. Separate the dough into 2 balls—1 large and 1 small. Roll out the large ball of dough into a 10- to 12-inch circle. Line a 9- to 9½-inch pie dish with the dough. Chill in the refrigerator for 30 minutes. Wrap the small ball of dough in plastic wrap and refrigerate it for 30 minutes as well.

2. Preheat the oven to 350°F.

3. *To make the filling:* Mix the pistachios, sugar, vanilla extract, orange zest, eggs, and mascarpone together in a stand mixer or with a hand mixer.

4. To assemble the tart: Spoon the filling into the chilled dough in the pie pan. Roll out the small ball of dough into a rectangle. Cut the dough into ½-inch wide strips. Place the strips over the filling in a crisscross, lattice pattern. Bake the tart in the oven for 30 minutes.

Castelvetrano, Sicily, is the birthplace of my maternal grandmother. Sicilian women live a tradition-filled life: here I partake in one of them, making a donation to our corner shrine of the Madonna after a morning of vegetable shopping from one of my favorite vendors, Antonio, and before going home to prepare pranzo for the family.

Crostata di Peperoni Dolci Sweet Pepper Tart

Pasta alla Carrettiera Cart Driver's Pasta

Pollo con Arance e Olive Chicken with Oranges and Olives

Scarola con Pignoli Escarola with Pine Nuts

Torta di Polenta al Arancio Orange Polenta Cake

This menu reflects the history of Sicilian cuisine. Sicily is the largest island in the Mediterranean and the largest producer of citrus fruits—oranges, lemons, and the famous Sicilian blood orange. As a result, the use of lemons and oranges is prevalent in our cooking. Sicily is hot eight months of the year, and citrus fruit is delicious and refreshing. In this menu, typical of the coast, oranges are used in the main course, Chicken with Oranges and Olives, as well as in the dessert, Orange Polenta Cake.

The pasta in this menu is characteristic of both the creativity and the practicality of the Sicilian people. It is called Cart Driver's Pasta, named after the drivers of the most iconic symbol of our island—the colorful, hand-painted Sicilian carelli, which were brought to Sicily by the Greeks. These carts were commonly used all over the island from the 1920s through the 1960s. Today, unfortunately, the colorful carts have been replaced by three-wheeled *Apes*, and have been relegated to museums of history on the island. I have, however, included a photo of the carelli here, for those of you who have never seen one. They are all hand-painted and beautiful to behold! Since the cart drivers were always out peddling their wares—fruits, vegetables, and herbs—they not only had to be creative

but also efficient with the ingredients they used to make a satisfying and filling pasta sauce to eat for pranzo ("lunch"). The result is a pasta dish that has been popular on the island of Sicily for generations.

The secondo—the main course—in this menu reminds me of one of my favorite aunts, who loved chicken with oranges, and who also inspired my now-famous orange, fennel, and red onion salad (featured in my first cookbook, *Whatever Happened to Sunday Dinner?*). Chicken with Oranges and Olives is perfect for a warm summer Sunday dinner, as it tastes great hot or cold.

The contorno is another tribute to my Sicilian grandmother, whose favorite vegetable was scarola (escarole), and is also a tribute to her island, where pignoli—pine nuts—are added to just about everything.

Finally, to round out this menu, we have a refreshing, satisfying, orange polenta cake—another inspired Sicilian concoction that makes use of the island's beautiful citrus, while never skimping on the sweetness and richness of dessert! In short, this is a menu full of Sicilian and personal history.

Crostata di Peperoni Dolci
Sweet Pepper Tart

    4 tablespoons extra virgin olive oil,
      plus 1 teaspoon for greasing the
      cookie sheet

    1 cup white onions, thinly sliced

    2 red bell peppers, cored, seeded,
      and cut into ¼-inch slices

    2 yellow bell peppers cored, seeded,
      and sliced into ¼-inch slices

    3 cloves garlic, chopped

    1 tablespoon chopped fresh rosemary

    3 tablespoons chopped fresh basil leaves

    1 tablespoon chopped fresh thyme

    1 teaspoon Sicilian sea salt, fine

    ½ teaspoon freshly ground black pepper

    1 sheet frozen puff pastry, thawed

    18 pitted black olives, preferably
      imported from Italy

1. In a large frying pan, heat the olive oil over medium heat. Add the onions and bell peppers and cook for 30 minutes. Stir occasionally so nothing sticks to the pan. After 30 minutes, add the garlic, rosemary, basil, thyme, salt, and pepper. Cook for 15 more minutes until the vegetables are very soft and wilted. Set the mixture aside to cool.

2. Preheat the oven to 375°F.

3. Spread 1 teaspoon of olive oil on a rimless cookie sheet. Place the puff pastry on the cookie sheet. It should form a rectangle, approximately 9 × 12 inches. Spread the cooled bell pepper mixture on the pastry. Leave at least 1 inch of puff pastry uncovered, all around the edge

of the vegetable mixture (it will spread as it bakes). Arrange the olives on top of the pepper mixture. Bake the pastry in the oven for 20 minutes. Remove the tart from the oven and let it rest for 15 minutes before slicing and serving.

Pasta alla Carrettiere
Cart Driver's Pasta

    6 cups chopped fresh grape tomatoes
      or cherry tomatoes

    4 tablespoons extra virgin olive oil

    6 cloves garlic, chopped

    20 basil leaves, chopped

    12 mint leaves, chopped

    2 teaspoons Sicilian sea salt, fine

    1 teaspoon freshly ground black pepper

    2 pounds spaghettoni (if you cannot
      find this thick spaghetti, use bucatini)

    Handful of coarse Sicilian sea salt for
      the pasta water

    2 cups Pecorino Romano cheese, grated

1. In a pasta bowl, large enough to hold 2 pounds of spaghetti, place the chopped tomatoes, olive oil, garlic, basil, mint, and salt and pepper. Let the mixture sit for a minimum of 1–2 hours.

2. Bring a large pasta pot, filled with water, to a boil, and add a handful of coarse Sicilian sea salt. Cook the pasta according to the directions on the package. Drain the pasta and place it in the big bowl with the tomato mixture. Toss the pasta in the sauce very well, and then top it with the cheese.

Pollo con Arance e Olive
Chicken with Oranges and Olives

6 tablespoons extra virgin olive oil

4 tablespoons unsalted butter

2 cups unbleached flour

½ teaspoon Sicilian sea salt, fine

¼ teaspoon freshly ground black pepper

4 pounds boneless, skinless chicken breasts, thinly sliced

3 large navel oranges, sliced

1 cup freshly squeezed orange juice

2 teaspoons orange zest

1 cup white wine, preferably Italian, such as Pinot Grigio

1 teaspoon fennel seeds

2 cups pitted black olives, preferably imported from Sicily

1. In a large frying pan, heat the olive oil and butter over medium heat.

2. Place the flour in a wide, shallow dish, such as a pie pan. Add the salt and pepper and mix well. Dredge each of the thin chicken slices in the flour mixture. Place the chicken in the frying pan and cook the slices for about 15 minutes on each side until they're golden brown. Remove the chicken from the pan and place it on a platter.

3. Cover the platter and set it aside.

4. Place the orange slices, orange juice, orange zest, wine, and fennel seeds in the pan, and simmer for 5 minutes (the wine will evaporate and the sauce will thicken). Add the black olives to the sauce and stir. Pour the orange sauce over the chicken cutlets and serve.

Scarola con Pignoli
Escarole with Pine Nuts

   3 heads escarole (approximately
      3 pounds)
   6 tablespoons extra virgin olive oil
   6 cloves garlic, chopped
   6 tablespoons pine nuts
   1 teaspoon crushed red pepper flakes

1. Wash the escarole well, remove the outer leaves, and core. Chop the escarole leaves roughly into large pieces.

2. Place 4 tablespoons of olive oil in a large frying pan over medium heat and cook the escarole until it is wilted, approximately 5 minutes. Do not overcook the escarole; you do not want it to look withered and limp. If you do not overcook the escarole it will not lose its slightly tangy bite.

3. In a small frying pan over medium heat, place 2 tablespoons of the olive oil. Cook the garlic in the oil until it is translucent, but not brown, approximately 2 minutes. Add the pine nuts. Cook the mixture for about 1 minute and then add the crushed red pepper flakes. Stir the mixture and then add it to the escarole, tossing it well. Transfer to a serving bowl and serve.

Torta di Polenta al Arancio
Orange Polenta Cake

For the Cake

   1 cup cake flour
   ¾ cup polenta (preferably imported
      from Italy) or use cornmeal
   1 teaspoon baking powder
   ½ teaspoon Sicilian sea salt, fine
   2 sticks unsalted butter, softened, plus
      more for greasing the cake pans
   1½ cups sugar
   4 large eggs
   1 cup freshly squeezed orange juice
   4 tablespoons orange zest

For the Topping

   1 cup orange marmalade, preferably blood
      orange marmalade imported from Italy

1. Preheat the oven to 350°F.

2. Butter 2 round 9-inch cake pans.

3. Combine the flour, polenta or cornmeal, baking powder, and salt, and set the mixture aside.

4. Using a stand mixer or a hand mixer, cream the butter and sugar, adding the eggs one at a time. Then add the orange juice and orange zest.

5. Slowly add the flour mixture to the wet ingredients and mix until well blended. Fill the 2 cake pans. Bake for 30 minutes. Transfer the cakes to 2 cake stands or platters (the cakes are not meant to be layered).

6. To serve, cut the cake into slices and dollop 1 teaspoon of orange marmalade on top of each slice.

Menu 31

SERVES 8

Torta di Bietola Swiss Chard Pie

Peperoni Arrostiti con Uova in Carozza
Egg in a Basket with Roasted Peppers

Salsiccia Grilliata, Finocchio e Erbe Fresche
Grilled Sausage, Fennel, and Fresh Herbs

Insalata di Pomodori Piccanti Spicy Tomato Salad

Granita di Limone e Menta Lemon and Mint Italian Ice

The appetizer in this menu is a sformato. The word sformato means "without a shape," and it is basically a vegetable quiche without the crust. In Italy, we make sformati with every type of vegetable imaginable. It is a great way to use fresh vegetables that are, perhaps, a day or two old and have lost their luster. With the added cheese and seasonings, the vegetables take on new flavor and life.

I love this family-oriented menu! In southern Italy we eat eggs as a second course very frequently, and since my parents both loved eggs, they were plentiful in our house. How much fun is uova in carozza ("egg in a basket")? It's the perfect dish for your children to help you make! Be as creative as you like—as long as the hole in the carozza is large enough for the egg!

There's nothing that says summer more than the taste—and the smoky scent!—of grilled sausages, like the ones in this menu, which are prepared with fennel and fresh herbs.

To end the meal on a perfect note, enjoy two of the most popular flavors in Sicily—lemon and mint—which come together beautifully in a refreshing, cool, granita (Italian ice).

Torta di Bietola
Swiss Chard Pie

3 tablespoons extra virgin olive oil

1½ pounds Swiss chard, cut into 3-inch pieces

16 ounces ricotta

2 large eggs, beaten

1 teaspoon Sicilian sea salt, fine

½ teaspoon freshly ground black pepper

1. Preheat the oven to 350°F.

2. Spread 1 tablespoon of the olive oil in a round casserole dish or a deep-dish pie pan.

3. Place the remaining olive oil in a large frying pan. Add the Swiss chard to the pan and sauté until the chard is tender, 5–7 minutes.

4. In a large bowl, beat the ricotta with a fork, breaking up all the bumps to make the texture smooth. Beat in the eggs. Add salt and pepper to the ricotta-egg mixture. Drain the Swiss chard from the frying pan to eliminate any excess water and extra olive oil. Add the chard to the ricotta mixture and transfer it to the prepared baking dish. Bake the mixture for 10 minutes in the preheated oven.

Peperoni Arrostiti con Uova in Carozza
Egg in a Basket with Roasted Peppers

8 slices rustic Italian bread, at least 4 inches in diameter, cut into 1-inch-thick slices (if you wish to make it yourself, see Lisa's Rustic Italian bread recipe, below)

8 tablespoons extra virgin olive oil

4 tablespoons unsalted butter, cut into 4 pads

8 eggs

2 teaspoons Sicilian sea salt, fine

1 teaspoon freshly ground black pepper

6 roasted peppers (page 128)

1. Cut a hole in the center of each slice of bread with a cookie cutter or a glass that is approximately 3 inches in diameter. Discard the cut-out pieces of bread (or save them for another use).

2. Place 2 tablespoons of the olive oil and 1 pad of the butter in a large frying pan over medium heat. Allow the butter to melt. Put 2 slices of bread in the frying pan at a time, and brown them on both sides until they're crispy and golden. When you are browning the second side of the bread, gently crack an egg into the hole in the middle of the slice. Keep browning the bread until the white of the egg is hard, but the yoke is still runny. With a wide spatula, remove the egg in its "basket" of bread to a platter. Repeat this process with each of the eggs. When all the eggs in a basket are on the platter, sprinkle each of the yolks with the salt and pepper.

3. Slice each roasted pepper in 4 pieces lengthwise. Place 3–4 slices of roasted pepper on top of each egg in the basket. To keep any leftover peppers, place them in a small casserole, and cover them completely with the rest of the extra virgin olive oil. The roasted peppers keep for up to 5 days in the refrigerator.

Lisa's Rustic Italian Bread

    3 cups bread flour

    2 teaspoons sugar

    ½ teaspoon salt

    1 package active dry yeast

    1 cup water, heated to 120°F–130°F

    2 tablespoons extra virgin olive oil

    ¼ cup polenta or cornmeal

    1 egg white, beaten

1. In a large bowl, combine the flour, sugar, salt, and yeast, and mix well. Add the warm water and olive oil and mix well. Turn the dough out on a lightly floured surface. Knead the dough for 10 minutes or until the dough is smooth. Place the dough in a lightly greased bowl, and cover it with plastic wrap or a cloth towel. Let the dough rise in a warm place for 30–40 minutes.

2. Sprinkle an ungreased cookie sheet with the polenta or cornmeal. Punch down the dough with your fist on a floured surface. Cover the dough with an inverted bowl and let it rest for 15 minutes on your kitchen table or counter. Shape the dough into a loaf, approximately 12 inches long. Place the loaf on the cornmeal- or polenta-coated cookie sheet. Cover the loaf with a cotton dish towel and let it rise in a warm place for 35–40 minutes, or until the loaf has doubled in size.

3. Preheat the oven to 375°F.

4. With a sharp knife, make a deep slash lengthwise in the top of the loaf. Brush the surface of the loaf with the egg white. Bake the loaf for 25–35 minutes.

This Is Sunday Dinner

Salsiccia Grilliata, Finocchio e Erbe Fresche

Grilled Sausage, Fennel, and Fresh Herbs

6 bulbs fresh fennel, quartered

1 cup extra virgin olive oil

1 teaspoon fresh rosemary

1 teaspoon fresh basil

1 teaspoon Sicilian sea salt, fine

½ teaspoon freshly ground black pepper

1 teaspoon crushed red pepper flakes

1 teaspoon fresh (or dried) oregano

2 pounds sweet Italian sausage (in the casing, not loose)

2 pounds hot Italian sausage (in the casing, not loose)

1. In a large bowl, combine the fennel, olive oil, rosemary, basil, salt, pepper, crushed red pepper flakes, and oregano, and toss well. Set the mixture aside.

2. Cook the sausages on a grill, over a medium flame, for 30 minutes.

3. Remove the fennel from the bowl and cook it on the grill over direct medium heat for 12–15 minutes. Place the sausages on a platter and arrange the fennel around the sausages.

Insalata di Pomodori Piccanti
Spicy Tomato Salad

- 8 anchovies, finely chopped
- 4 large ripe tomatoes, chopped
- 3 large garlic cloves, chopped
- 2 tablespoons crushed red pepper
- 1 red onion, chopped
- 1 cup chopped Italian flat leaf parsley
- 1 tablespoon chopped fresh oregano or 1 teaspoon dried oregano
- ¾ cup extra virgin olive oil
- 6 tablespoons red wine vinegar, excellent quality, preferably imported from Italy

Combine all the ingredients in a large salad bowl. Do not refrigerate the salad—serve it at room temperature.

Granita di Limone e Menta
Lemon and Mint Italian Ice

- 7 cups bottled water (still, not mineral or carbonated water)
- 2 ounces fresh mint leaves, plus more for garnish
- 1¼ cups granulated white sugar
- 1 cup freshly squeezed lemon juice

1. Fill a large soup pot with the water. Add the mint leaves to the pot and bring the water to a boil. Add the sugar to the boiling water and stir until the sugar dissolves. Take the pot off the stove. Remove the mint leaves from the water and discard them. Stir the lemon juice into the mixture in the pot and allow it to cool.

2. Pour the mint and lemon water into a 9 × 12-inch, cold-resistant, glass casserole dish. Place the casserole dish in the freezer. Every 10 minutes, take the casserole dish out of the freezer and stir the ice crystals with a kitchen fork, repeating this process every 10 minutes for 2 hours. Keep the granita in the freezer until you're ready to use it. Serve the granita in small bowls or wineglasses and garnish with a fresh mint leaf.

Menu 32

SERSES 8

Caciocavallo al Pomodoro Caciocavallo in Tomato Sauce
Lasagne Siciliana d'Estate Sicilian Summer Lasagne
Pollo Grilliata alla Siciliana di Lisa Lisa's Sicilian Grilled Chicken
Insalata Siciliana Estiva Sicilian Summer Salad
Budino al Espresso Espresso Pudding

---

*C*aciocavallo cheese is very popular in southern Italy, and has an amusing name. The literal meaning of caciocavallo is "horse cheese," although it has absolutely nothing to do with horses. Rather, the name originated in the regions of Sicily, Campania, and Basilicata, where the cheese is made into its distinctive shape: a dumbbell with two lobes, one smaller than the other, with a rope wrapped around the cylindrical area between the two lobes. The rope used to wrap the cheese is tied onto the two "heads" of the caciocavallo, and the rope is then draped over a piece of wood, allowing the cheese to dry a cavallo, which means "horseback-style"—hence the name. The smooth texture of caciocavallo is similar to provolone, but it has a little less bite. You can find the most popular dish in Italy that utilizes caciocavallo cheese—Spaghetti Cacio e Pepe—in my cookbook *Whatever Happened to Sunday Dinner?*

In Sicily we love our lasagne. And all Sicilian cooks are very creative, which means that, depending on the season, we use a variety of ingredients to make it. In this menu, which focuses on summer in Sicily, the light and refreshing lasagne features delicious eggplant and fresh tomatoes.

It is excellent, eaten warm or served at room temperature, and is just as good the next day. Make two pans—one for Sunday dinner and one for dinner later in the week. (Children love to assemble lasagne—it's easy to do, and they can see exactly what they'll be eating!)

The tomato paste in my Grilled Chicken reminds me of the concentrato used in Sicily. Because tomatoes are so prevalent there, all home cooks make their own tomato concentrato (the Italian word for "paste") at the end of the season. The concentrato is stored in glass jars and lasts all winter long. In this menu, it gives the grilled chicken a sweet caramelized flavor.

And Espresso Pudding for dessert? Decadent!

A tavola! (To table!)

Caciocavallo al Pomodoro
Caciocavallo in Tomato Sauce

1 pound fresh tomatoes, chopped (you can use large tomatoes on the vine or cherry or grape tomatoes)

16 green olives pitted, preferably Castelvetrano from Sicily

2 teaspoons capers, not in salt, preferably imported from Sicily

2 cloves garlic, chopped

1 tablespoon red wine vinegar, very good quality

1 teaspoon Sicilian sea salt, fine

½ teaspoon ground black pepper

1 pound caciocavallo, sliced into eight pieces

To make the sauce, stir together the tomatoes, olives, capers, garlic, red wine vinegar, salt, and pepper in a large bowl. Spoon the sauce into 8 small bowls. Place 1 slice of the caciocavallo in the center of the sauce. If desired, serve with sliced, crunchy Italian bread.

Lasagne Siciliana d'Estate
Sicilian Summer Lasagne

4 large eggplants

2 tablespoons Sicilian sea salt, coarse

1 cup extra virgin olive oil

2 white onions, sliced

2 (1-pound) boxes imported Italian lasagne (such as De Cecco or Del Verde)

12 large, firm tomatoes (such as roma), sliced in ¼-inch rounds

1 bunch fresh basil, chopped

8 tablespoons Parmigiano Reggiano, grated

1 pound fresh goat cheese

4 tablespoons unsalted butter, sliced in 4 pieces

1 teaspoon Sicilian sea salt, fine

½ teaspoon freshly ground black pepper

1. Peel the eggplants and slice them lengthwise. Layer the slices in a colander, alternating layers with coarse Sicilian sea salt to drain the eggplant of its bitter juices. (Watch my video on how to drain eggplant at www.lisacaponigri. com.) Allow the eggplant slices to drain for a minimum of 30 minutes, and then rinse each slice under cold water to remove all the coarse sea salt, as well as any brown, bitter juices that have drained from the eggplant. Pat the eggplant dry with paper towels.

2. Pour ¼ cup of the olive oil into a large frying pan over medium heat. Fry each slice of eggplant in the olive oil until it is golden brown on both sides. Because eggplant is a very porous vegetable, it absorbs oil very quickly, so you may need to keep adding olive oil, as you cook the eggplant, to keep it from sticking to the pan. Drain the cooked eggplant on paper towels.

3. Add ¼ cup of the olive oil to the same frying pan in which you fried the eggplant. Place the onions in the frying pan and sauté them until they are translucent, but not brown.

4. Cook the lasagne according to the directions on the package.

5. Preheat the oven to 400°F.

6. Grease the bottom of a 9 × 13-inch lasagne pan with 2 tablespoons of the olive oil and cover the bottom of the pan with a layer of the noodles. Place a layer of the eggplant slices over the noodles, followed by a layer of the tomatoes, and then a layer of the onions. Sprinkle some of the basil and Parmigiano Reggiano over the vegetables, and then place 4 teaspoon-size dollops of the goat cheese on top. Repeat this process until the lasagne pan is full. Finish the top layer with fresh tomatoes, Parmigiano Reggiano, and dollops of goat cheese. Sprinkle a little more fresh basil on top and bake the lasagne for 15 minutes.

LISA'S TIP

Since this lasagne uses fresh tomatoes instead of tomato sauce, it is delicious eaten hot or at room temperature.

Sunday dinner *al fresco*.

Pollo Grilliata alla Siciliana di Lisa
Lisa's Sicilian Grilled Chicken

- 1 cup almonds, chopped
- 3 tablespoons garlic paste, preferably imported from Italy (comes in a tube)
- 3 tablespoons Italian tomato paste, concentrato di pomodoro, preferably imported, in a tube
- 1 cup fresh basil leaves, chopped
- 2 teaspoons Sicilian sea salt, fine
- 1 teaspoon freshly ground black pepper
- 1 cup extra virgin olive oil, plus an additional ½ cup if you're cooking on the stovetop
- 8 boneless, skinless chicken breasts
- 1½ cups Parmigiano Reggiano, grated

1. In a blender or food processor (or using a mortar and pestle) combine the almonds, garlic paste, tomato paste, basil, salt, and pepper. Add 1 cup of the olive oil to the mixture and blend it in. Divide this mixture into 2 portions and set them aside.

2. Place the chicken breasts on a platter. With a kitchen brush, brush the almond, garlic, and tomato paste onto both sides of each chicken breast, using only half of the paste.

3. Cook the chicken breasts on a grill, over medium heat, for 5–6 minutes on each side. (If you are making the chicken on the stovetop, pour ½ cup of olive oil into a frying pan and cook the chicken for 5–6 minutes on each side.) Remove the chicken from the grill (or the frying pan) and place it on a clean platter. Top each chicken breast with the remaining almond, garlic, and tomato paste. Sprinkle the Parmigiano Reggiano on the chicken and serve.

Insalata Siciliana Estiva
Sicilian Summer Salad

- 6 roasted peppers (page 128)
- 1 pound fresh mozzarella, cut into 1-inch cubes
- 6 large on-the-vine tomatoes, cut into 1-inch cubes
- 2 tablespoons capers (not packed in salt), preferably imported
- ½ cup chopped fresh basil
- ½ cup extra virgin olive oil
- 2 teaspoons Sicilian sea salt, fine
- 1 teaspoon freshly ground black pepper

Combine all the ingredients in a large salad bowl and serve.

Budino al Espresso
Espresso Pudding

- 4 cups whole milk
- 3 large eggs
- 1 cup sugar
- 1 cup cocoa powder, unsweetened
- ½ cup espresso

Pour the milk into a medium saucepan, and heat over medium heat for 3–4 minutes, while whisking in one egg at a time. Whisk in the sugar, stirring it until it dissolves, followed by the cocoa powder and the espresso. Pour the mixture into 8 small ramekins or pretty wineglasses. Cover each ramekin or wineglass with plastic wrap and refrigerate for a minimum of 2 hours before serving the pudding.

San Domenico, the church in Castelvetrano, where my Nana was baptized and made her First Holy Communion, is a perfect example of the Baroque style that is so prevalent in Sicily. Here I lay a rose, and say a prayer, for my grandmother.

Menu 33

SERVES 8

Fagioli Bianchi Siciliani con Tonno Sicilian White Beans with Tuna

Risotto con Mandorle e Broccolini Risotto with Almonds and Broccolini

Salmone Grilliata con Puree di Peperoni Gialli
Grilled Salmon with Yellow Pepper Puree

Patate al Forno con Erbe Roasted Herb Potatoes

Crostata di Limone Lemon Pie

The flavors of the island of Sicily are wide and varied, because of the gorgeous sea and wonderful climate. So the legumes—cannellini beans—in this menu, blend beautifully with tuna to give the antipasto a salty yet smooth taste. Topped with extra virgin olive oil and a little salt and pepper, Sicilian White Beans with Tuna is wholly satisfying. I love this antipasto, with a piece of crunchy Italian bread or crackers, as a quick lunch during the week!

In Sicily, nuts are frequently found in primos (first courses), in pasta sauces and risotto. So the risotto dish in this menu, which includes almonds and broccolini, is another nod to the influence of Arabs and Greeks in our cuisine.

And what could be more heavenly than the yellow pepper puree—so sweet from cooking down in extra virgin olive oil—which perfectly complements the salmon in the main course?

I have been making Crostata di Limone since I was young, and it is one of my very favorite desserts. Refreshing and light, it is the ideal ending to this summery Sicilian menu.

Fagioli Bianchi Siciliani con Tonno
Sicilian White Beans with Tuna

- 2 (15½ ounce) cans cannellini white beans, preferably imported from Italy
- 2 (6- or 7-ounce) glass jars imported Sicilian or Italian tuna
- 6 tablespoons extra virgin olive oil
- 6 tablespoons red wine vinegar, excellent quality, preferably imported
- 4 cloves garlic, chopped
- 1 red onion, chopped
- 1 teaspoon Sicilian sea salt, fine
- ½ teaspoon freshly ground black pepper
- ¼ teaspoon crushed red pepper flakes
- Handful Italian flat leaf parsley, chopped

In a medium-size deep bowl, combine the beans, tuna, olive oil, vinegar, garlic, onion, salt, black pepper, and red pepper flakes. Mix well. Top the mixture with the fresh parsley, and serve with toasted Italian bread.

LISA'S TIP

I purchase imported Sicilian tuna (it's available at most major supermarkets now) in glass jars, rather than buying it in cans, because the jars contain fillets. Not only do they make for a much better presentation, you can also slice the fillets for nice, bite-sized pieces of tuna.

LISA'S TIP

Always have a chilled bottle of Prosecco on hand in your refrigerator. Prosecco, a light, bubbly, white wine from the Veneto region of Italy, literally goes with every type of food—whether it's pastries or cookies for unexpected guests who drop by in mid afternoon or antipasti for a spontaneous cocktail or toast. It is also wonderful with a Saturday or Sunday morning brunch. Prosecco makes every day a party! It rarely costs more than $20 a bottle—and it is available everywhere.

Risotto con Mandorle e Broccolini
Risotto with Almonds and Broccolini

½ cup extra virgin olive oil

1 small white onion, chopped fine

2 cloves garlic, chopped

1 pound fresh broccolini, chopped
  into about six 1-inch pieces

1 cup sliced almonds

2½ cups Arborio rice

4 cups vegetable broth

1 cup white wine

½ stick unsalted butter, sliced

1 cup Parmigiano Reggiano, grated

1. In a 6-quart pasta pot, place the olive oil, onion, garlic, broccolini, and almonds. Add the Arborio rice. Stir and sauté the rice and vegetables for 5–7 minutes, until the rice looks slightly toasted and golden. Add the broth, one ladle-full at a time, while maintaining a medium heat under the pot. Do not add a second ladle-full of vegetable broth until the first ladle is fully absorbed by the rice. Continue this process until you have used all the vegetable broth and the risotto has a slightly creamy texture.

2. After all the vegetable broth has been absorbed, add the white wine. Stir the risotto until it has absorbed all the white wine. This should take about 20 minutes. Drop the slices of butter into the risotto and stir the mixture until the butter has melted.

3. Remove the pot from heat. Place the risotto in a serving bowl and top it with the Parmigiano Reggiano.

LISA'S TIP
Risotto should never be too creamy and absolutely never mushy. It should remain al dente—meaning slightly chewy—just as pasta should be cooked.

Salmone Grilliata con Puree di Peperoni Gialli
Grilled Salmon with Yellow Pepper Puree

- 1 cup extra virgin olive oil
- 3 garlic cloves, chopped
- 6 sweet yellow bell peppers, seeded and sliced
- 2 teaspoons Sicilian sea salt, fine, plus more for seasoning the fish
- 1 teaspoon ground black pepper, plus more for seasoning the fish
- 8 salmon fillets, preferably center cuts, skinned

1. Pour ½ cup of the olive oil into a large frying pan. Add the garlic and bell peppers. Cook the mixture over low heat for about 7 minutes, or until the peppers are wilted. Set the mixture aside and allow it to cool. Add the salt and pepper. Transfer the bell pepper mixture to a blender and puree it. Set the mixture aside.

2. To prepare the salmon fillets, coat them on both sides with the remaining olive oil and season with some additional salt and pepper. Cook the fillets on a grill for 4 minutes on each side, or in a 325°F oven for 8 minutes. If you bake the fish in the oven, turn it over after 4 minutes so that it bakes evenly on both sides.

3. Pour the yellow pepper puree from the blender into a small saucepan. Heat the mixture over low heat just until it is warm, not boiling. Plate the salmon fillets, top them with the yellow pepper puree, and serve.

LISA'S TIP

Here's how to core, seed, and quarter a bell pepper: With a paring knife, slice off the stem at the top of the pepper. To cut the pepper into segments, use the knife to follow the natural indentations (segments) of the pepper. With the side of the paring knife, gently remove the seeds and white pith from each section of the pepper.

Patate al Forno con Erbe
Roasted Herb Potatoes

- 2 pounds red and gold potatoes, about 2 inches in diameter, mixed, and quartered
- ¼ teaspoon dried thyme
- ¼ teaspoon dried rosemary
- ¼ teaspoon dried sage
- ¼ teaspoon dried oregano
- ¼ teaspoon dried basil
- 1 teaspoon Sicilian sea salt, fine
- ½ cup extra virgin olive oil

Toss the potatoes with the thyme, rosemary, sage, oregano, basil, salt, and olive oil. Place the potato mixture in a large casserole dish in a preheated 350°F oven for 30 minutes or until the potatoes are golden and crispy.

Crostata di Limone
Lemon Pie

For Lisa's Crostata Dough

1¼ cups flour

¼ teaspoon baking powder

⅛ teaspoon Sicilian sea salt, fine

⅓ cup granulated sugar

1 stick plus 1 tablespoon unsalted butter, cold

1 egg yolk

⅛ cup ice cold water

For the Filling

16 ounces mascarpone cheese

2 large eggs

¾ cup granulated sugar

1 teaspoon pure vanilla extract

3 tablespoons fresh lemon juice

Zest of 1 lemon

Confectioners' sugar, for garnish

1. *To make the dough:* Combine the flour, baking powder, salt, and sugar. Add the butter and egg yolk. Knead the mixture into a soft dough—either in a stand mixer or with a hand mixer. Add the ice water a few drops at a time. Separate the pastry into 2 balls—1 large and 1 small. Roll out large ball of dough to 10 to 12 inches. Line a 9- or 9½-inch pie plate with the dough. Chill the dough in the pie plate for 30 minutes. Wrap the small ball of dough in plastic wrap and refrigerate it for 30 minutes as well.

2. Preheat the oven to 350°F.

3. *To make the filling and assemble the crostata:* In a medium-size bowl, combine the mascarpone, eggs, sugar, vanilla, lemon juice, and lemon zest with a mixer. Mix until fluffy. Pour the filling into the prepared pie plate. Roll out the small ball of dough into a rectangle and cut it into ¾-inch strips. Place the strips on top of the crostata to form a lattice across the filling. Bake the crostata for 30 minutes. Garnish with a sprinkle of confectioners' sugar and serve.

Sicilian Sea Salt is considered the best in the world. This is due to perfect climactic conditions: clear Mediterranean water, hot North African winds, and constant sun. The process is simple. Pans or dividers are built in the water by the shore (photo 1). Since the water close to shore is more shallow, the windmills direct the hot winds toward the pans, causing the water to evaporate and allowing the sea salt to be raked from the pan easily. Mounds of sea salt (photo 2) are gathered. The result is a delicious, wholly natural product that seasons your food perfectly!

Menu 34

SERVES 8

Panini di Melanzane Eggplant Sandwiches
Sugo Siciliano di Pomodoro di Lisa Lisa's Sicilian Tomato Sauce
Filetto Siciliano Ripieno di Manzo Stuffed Sicilian Beef Roll
Pomodori Ripieni alla Marsala Stuffed Tomatoes, Marsala Style
Tartufo Bianco di Cioccolato e Pistacchio White Chocolate-Pistachio Truffle

I always joke that eggplant is the national vegetable of the island of Sicily. The melted mozzarella make these eggplant sandwiches a hit!

Lisa's Sicilian Tomato Sauce is another of my inventions that goes back to a day when my children were little and we were on the beach in Sicily. Everyone was hungry and wanted pasta for lunch. So we ran back up to the house and, using what I had in the kitchen, Lisa's Sicilian Tomato Sauce was born!

Falsomagro is a traditional Sicilian method of preparing meat that literally means "false thin," because, although the cut of the meat may be lean, everything that goes in it is not! The Sicilians love to stuff everything—rice balls, meatballs, beef, pork, and vegetables!

My grandmother was from Castelvetrano, in the province of Trapani, which is right next to the beautiful town of Marsala. Marsala, of course, is famous for its sweet, delicious cooking wine. I learned how to make the amazing stuffed tomatoes in this menu from a little trattoria, where I stopped to eat with my children after touring the cathedral of Marsala.

The recipe for White Chocolate–Pistachio Truffle that completes this menu is delicious and fun to make. Let the young members of your dinner party roll the gelato in the yummy toppings!

Panini di Melanzane
Eggplant Sandwiches

2 medium eggplants, peeled and cut into 16 round slices (8 slices from each eggplant)

Handful Sicilian sea salt, coarse

½ cup extra virgin olive oil

1 (3-ounce can) anchovy fillets, preferably imported from Italy, drained and chopped

½ cup Italian flat leaf parsley, chopped

4 tablespoons capers, NOT packed in salt, drained and chopped

2 teaspoons Sicilian sea salt, fine

½ teaspoon freshly ground black pepper

8 slices mozzarella (same diameter as the eggplant slices)

1. Layer the slices of eggplant in a colander, alternating with coarse Sicilian sea salt, and drain for 30 minutes. (Watch the video on how to let your eggplant "cry" on www.lisacaponigri.com). Rinse each slice of eggplant and pat it dry with paper towels.

2. Preheat the oven to 400°F.

3. Cover the bottom of a jelly-roll pan (a cookie sheet with a rim) with 3 tablespoons of olive oil, until the pan has a thin coating of olive oil. Arrange the 16 eggplant slices in a single layer on the pan and bake them for 15 minutes, turning the slices over once. After 15 minutes, the eggplant slices should be fork-tender, and slightly golden.

4. In a small bowl, combine the anchovies, parsley, capers, salt, pepper, and the rest of the olive oil. Remove the eggplant from the oven. Put a tablespoon of the anchovy mixture on 8 of the eggplant slices and top each one with a slice of mozzarella. Place the remaining 8 slices of eggplant on top of the mozzarella to form 8 eggplant sandwiches. Place the sandwiches back in the oven until the mozzarella is melted. Serve immediately.

Sugo Siciliano di Pomodoro di Lisa
Lisa's Sicilian Tomato Sauce

1 cup extra virgin olive oil

1 cup white onion, chopped

6 garlic cloves, chopped

1 cup red bell pepper, chopped

1 cup green bell pepper, chopped

2 carrots, peeled and chopped

4 celery stalks, chopped

2 tablespoons capers, not packed in salt and drained

2 (26-ounce) cans imported crushed San Marzano tomatoes

1 cup good-quality, imported red wine from Sicily (such as Nero d'Avola)

1 cup green olives, sliced in half

1 cup black olives, sliced in half

1 tablespoon dried basil

1 tablespoon dried oregano

2 teaspoons Sicilian sea salt, fine

1 teaspoon ground black pepper

Pour the olive oil into a large 6- to 8-quart pasta pot. Sauté the onion, garlic, red pepper, green pepper, carrots, and celery for 10 minutes or until soft. Add the capers to the mixture, smashing them slightly with the back of a fork or a wooden spoon. Add the crushed tomatoes and stir them into the mixture for a minute. Add the wine, and let the sauce simmer over medium heat for 15–20 minutes. Add the green olives, the black olives, basil, oregano, salt, and pepper. Let the sauce simmer for 10 more minutes over low to medium heat.

To serve with pasta: Cook 2 pounds rigatoni, according to the instructions on the package. Drain, toss with Lisa's Sicilian Tomato Sauce, and place in a large pasta bowl. Top with a generous amount of grated ricotta salata cheese and serve.

Filetto Siciliano Ripieno di Manzo
Stuffed Sicilian Beef Roll

3 pounds round steak, 2 inches thick, butterflied

½ pound prosciutto, sliced very thin

½ cup caciocavallo or Pecorino Romano cheese, grated

8 ounces sharp provolone, grated

1 tablespoon Italian flat leaf parsley, chopped

1 teaspoon Sicilian sea salt, fine

½ teaspoon freshly ground black pepper

5 tablespoons extra virgin olive oil

1 medium onion, chopped

1 cup red wine

4 cups crushed San Marzano tomatoes

1 cup breadcrumbs

1. Lay the steak on a work surface or cutting board with the butterflied part of the meat facing up. Place the sliced prosciutto, the caciocavallo or pecorino and provolone, the parsley, salt, and pepper on 1 side of the butterflied meat. Close the butterflied meat and roll it from the bottom up. Tie the meat every 2 to 3 inches with butcher's twine.

2. Preheat the oven to 300°F.

3. In a large casserole dish, place 2 tablespoons of olive oil. Set the casserole dish aside.

4. *To make the sauce:* In a large frying pan, place 3 tablespoons of olive oil. Heat the oil over medium to high heat and brown the roast, turning it around so it is evenly browned on all sides. When the roast is browned, approximately 3 minutes on each side, remove it from the frying pan and place it in the well-oiled casserole dish.

5. Add the onion to the frying pan, and cook it in the oil for 5 minutes, until it is translucent, but not brown. Pour in the wine, reduce the heat, and scrape any brown drippings from the bottom of the pan. Reduce the wine by about half, for roughly 7–8 minutes. Add the tomatoes to the sauce and stir well. Pour the sauce over the roast.

6. Cover the roast with aluminum foil, place it in the oven, and cook for 90 minutes. Remove the roast from the oven. Let it rest for 15 minutes before cutting off the strings and carving the meat. Ladle the tomato sauce onto the sliced beef and serve.

Pomodori Ripieni alla Marsalese
Stuffed Tomatoes, Marsala Style

- 1 pound cooked shrimp
- 8 medium-size, on-the-vine tomatoes (such as Campari tomatoes)
- 6 ounces green olives, preferably Castelvetrano
- 8 tablespoons extra virgin olive oil
- 2 teaspoons Sicilian sea salt, fine
- 1 teaspoon ground black pepper

1. Cut the cooked shrimp into ¼-inch pieces. Slice off the top of the tomatoes and remove the pulp.

2. In a separate bowl, mix the shrimp, olives, olive oil, salt, and pepper. Stuff the tomatoes with this mixture. Place the tomatoes in an oiled baking dish and bake in a preheated 350°F oven for 20 minutes. These tomatoes are delicious served warm or at room temperature.

Tartufo Bianco di Cioccolato e Pistacchio
White Chocolate–Pistachio Truffle

1½ gallons chocolate ice cream, very good quality and slightly softened

1 cup white chocolate chips

2 cups pistachios, chopped

Line a baking sheet with parchment paper. Using a 2-inch ice cream scoop, form 8 ice cream balls. On a large piece of wax paper, mix the white chocolate chips and pistachios. Roll the balls of ice cream in the chopped mixture and place them on the baking sheet. Immediately place the baking sheet in the freezer until you are ready to serve the ice cream.

Menu 35

SERES 8

Torta di Ricotta e Salsiccie Sausage and Ricotta Pie
Farfalle con Zucchini Fritti Pasta with Fried Zucchini
Peperoni Siciliani Ripieni Sicilian Stuffed Peppers
Caponata d'Estate Summer Caponata
Fichi Gratinati Baked Figs

This menu is a classic Sicilian Sunday dinner. Sausage and Ricotta Pie is a staple in Sicily—you will see it sold by the slice in pizzerias. All cooks in Sicily have their own recipe for this classic pie, with one or two ingredients that are different—I've perfected mine after years of making it for my family. It is delicious and satisfying and makes a great weekday lunch or after-school snack!

Sicilians use zucchini in so many recipes—because we have so much of it! My Sicilian grandmother loved Pasta with Fried Zucchini, made with sweet, end-of-summer zucchini tossed with tangy Castelvetrano olives from her hometown. (You can now find Castelvetrano olives in most delicatessens and Italian grocery stores across the United States.) Making this pasta dish is a creative, healthy, and delicious way to use up the summer's bounty, but make sure you choose small zucchini— they're sweeter than the larger vegetables.

My Nana and my mother could stuff peppers with anything! I grew up on my mother's version of the classic Italian dish, which she made with rice and tomato sauce. The recipe for stuffed peppers in this menu has a Sicilian twist—the bite of provolone is delicious!

Of all the well-known vegetable-based delicacies from Sicily, caponata is definitely the island's signature dish. In my first cookbook, *Whatever Happened to Sunday Dinner?*, I gave you my recipe for Classic Caponata. Here, I share my recipe for what I call Summer Caponata, because it features all the fresh vegetables of the season. Caponata is excellent served warm or cold, and is perfect, spread on a piece of toasted Italian bread, as a snack.

Figs are abundant in Sicily and, lately, you can find them everywhere in the United States, especially since stores featuring organic foods have become so popular. My Nana had the most beautiful fig tree outside her kitchen windows—it grew from two fig saplings that my grandfather planted, without knowing that one was for green figs and the other for purple! The result: He and my Nana had a huge strong fig tree with both types of figs! Throughout our youth, and well into adulthood, all of us took turns climbing on a step stool to pick the figs. I can still close my eyes and see my Nana standing at the base of the tree instructing my daughter Felicia on which fig to pick next!

Beautiful Sicilian produce—*che bontá!*

Torta di Ricotta e Salsiccie
Sausage and Ricotta Pie

For Lisa's Savory Pie Crust

    1 cup unsalted butter

    2⅓ cups flour, unbleached

    1 teaspoon Sicilian sea salt, fine

    3 cloves garlic, chopped

    8 tablespoons cold water

For the Filling

    1 pound Italian sausage, loose (without
      the casing)

    1 teaspoon Sicilian sea salt, fine

    ½ teaspoon ground black pepper

    ⅛ cup fennel seeds

    2 pounds ricotta

    ½ cup Pecorino Romano, grated

    ¼ cup Italian flat leaf parsley, chopped

1. *To make the crust:* Place the butter, flour, salt, and garlic in a stand mixer, and mix all the ingredients together. Drizzle the cold water into the dough until all the dough comes together. Cover the dough in plastic wrap and let it rest for 15–30 minutes at room temperature.

2. Preheat the oven to 350°F.

3. *To make the filling:* In a large frying pan, cook the Italian sausage over medium heat, until all the pink is gone. Add the salt, pepper, and fennel seeds. Cook until the sausage is brown. Drain all grease out of the pan.

4. In a medium bowl, mix the ricotta,

Pecorino Romano, parsley, and the sausage.

5. Break the pie dough into 2 balls. Roll out 1 ball into a 10- to 12-inch circle and place it in a 9- to 9½-inch pie plate. Spoon the cheese and sausage mixture into the pie plate. Roll out the second ball of dough and cover the pie with it.

6. Bake the pie for 1 hour. Let it rest for 15 minutes before cutting and serving.

Farfalle con Zucchini Fritti
Pasta with Fried Zucchini

    ½ cup extra virgin olive oil

    6 small zucchini or 5 medium
      (approximately 2 pounds), sliced into
      ¼-inch rounds

    4 cloves garlic, chopped

    ½ teaspoon crushed red pepper flakes

    1 cup sliced, pitted Castelvetrano
      olives (or any good-quality green
      olives)

    Handful Sicilian sea salt, coarse,
      for pasta water

    2 pounds farfalle pasta

    4 tablespoons fresh lemon juice

    1 cup ricotta salata, grated

    10 large fresh mint leaves, chopped

1. Pour the olive oil into a large skillet and place it on the stove over medium heat. Add the zucchini slices and cook them until they're golden brown on both sides, 4–6 minutes. Add the garlic, red pepper flakes, and olives—and cook the mixture for 1 minute more.

2. Fill a large 10-quart pasta pot with water. When the water comes to a rolling boil, drop a handful of coarse sea salt into the water. Add the pasta to the water and cook it according to the directions on the package. Drain the pasta.

3. In a large bowl, toss the pasta with the zucchini mixture, top it with the ricotta salata and fresh mint, and serve.

Peperoni Siciliani Ripieni
Sicilian Stuffed Peppers

8 large bell peppers (green, red, yellow, and orange—2 of each)

½ cup extra virgin olive oil, plus more for drizzling over the peppers

4 cups breadcrumbs

2 teaspoons Sicilian sea salt, fine

1 teaspoon grated fresh black pepper

6 fresh basil leaves, chopped

4 ounces sharp provolone, grated

5 tablespoons capers, not packed in salt

6 tomatoes, preferably Roma

6 anchovies, chopped

1. Preheat the oven to 400°F.

2. Cut off the top of each pepper and remove the seeds and pith from the inside with a paring knife.

3. Pour the olive oil into a large skillet over medium heat. Brown the breadcrumbs in the skillet, while seasoning them with the salt, pepper, and basil. Add the cheese, capers, tomatoes, and anchovies. Mix well.

4. Stuff the peppers with the mixture.

5. Oil a large casserole dish. Place the peppers in the casserole dish and drizzle a little extra olive oil on top. Cover the casserole with aluminum foil and bake for 20 minutes. Serve the peppers warm or at room temperature.

Caponata d'Estate
Summer Caponata

Note: Prepare Lisa's Classic Tomato Sauce (recipe below) before making the caponata.

2 large eggplants, peeled and cubed

Handful Sicilian sea salt, coarse

1 cup extra virgin olive oil

2 white onions, chopped

4 celery stalks, chopped

1 cup black olives, pitted

3 tablespoons sugar

1½ cups red wine vinegar, excellent quality, preferably imported

4 zucchini, cut into ½-inch slices

2 fennel bulbs, cut into cubes

2 cups Lisa's Classic Italian Tomato Sauce (recipe below)

1 cup pine nuts

½ cup golden raisins

8–10 fresh basil leaves, chopped

2 teaspoons Sicilian sea salt, fine

1 teaspoon freshly ground black pepper

1 loaf Italian bread, cut into 2- to 3-inch chunks

1. Place the eggplant, sprinkled with the coarse sea salt, in a colander in the kitchen sink and let it drain for a minimum of 30 minutes. Rinse the chunks of eggplant thoroughly to remove all the salt and any brown liquid that may have been drawn out by the salt. Pat the eggplant dry with paper towels.

2. Pour the olive oil into a large 8-quart saucepan. Sauté the onion, celery, and olives for approximately 5 minutes over medium heat. Add the sugar and vinegar to the mixture in the pan and continue to cook over medium heat, until the sugar is dissolved, 3–4 minutes. Add the zucchini and fennel. Sauté for 10 minutes. Add the eggplant and sauté for 10 more minutes until the eggplant is golden and brown on most of its edges. Add the tomato sauce, keeping the heat on low to medium, and simmer the mixture, covered, for 25 more minutes. Occasionally stir the mixture so it does not stick to the bottom of the pan.

3. While the vegetables are cooking, place the pine nuts in a small frying pan and toast them until they're golden, but not burned, 2–3 minutes. (Keep an eye on the pine nuts— they can burn very quickly.)

4. Add the golden raisins, pine nuts, chopped basil leaves, salt, and pepper to the vegetables and mix well. Pour the caponata into a bowl and serve it at room temperature with chunks of Italian bread.

LISA'S TIP

Pine nuts are very high in oil and, therefore, burn very quickly. Whenever you toast pine nuts, to bring out their buttery flavor, make sure the flame is low, and keep a watchful eye on them, so they don't burn.

Lisa's Classic Italian Tomato Sauce

- 1 cup extra virgin olive oil
- 12 cloves garlic, cut in half, and green vein removed
- 8 (26-ounce) cans San Marzano tomatoes, crushed (see Lisa's Note below)
- 1 tablespoon imported Italian oregano
- 1 tablespoon fresh basil leaves, chopped
- 1 teaspoon Sicilian sea salt, fine
- 1 teaspoon freshly ground black pepper
- 3 tablespoons sugar

Pour the olive oil into a large saucepan and sauté the garlic for 3 minutes over a low flame. Do not allow the garlic to brown. Pour the tomatoes into the saucepan and add the oregano, basil, salt, pepper, and sugar. Allow the mixture to simmer for at least 3 hours over a very low flame.

LISA'S TIP

I make a large batch of this sauce because it goes with so many different dishes. Don't hesitate to freeze any of the tomato sauce that you do not use in this recipe. It will definitely come in handy for other dishes!

Fichi Gratinati
Baked Figs

- 16 ripe figs, cut in half
- 1 cup fig jam, preferably imported from Italy
- 8 tablespoons grappa
- 4 tablespoons sugar
- 2 tablespoons honey, excellent quality
- 1 cup sliced almonds

1. Preheat the oven to 350°F.

2. Place the figs in a 9 × 9-inch casserole dish, cut side up.

3. Place the fig jam, grappa, sugar, and honey in a medium-size saucepan, over low heat, until the sugar has melted. Distribute the mixture evenly over the figs. Bake the figs for 8 minutes. Remove the pan from the oven. Cover the figs with foil to keep them warm.

4. Place a single layer of sliced almonds on a small cookie sheet and toast them in the oven for 5 minutes. Allow the almonds to cool. Serve the figs with the toasted almonds sprinkled on top.

Menu 36

SERSE 8

Fior di Zucchini Ripieni Stuffed Zucchini Blossoms
Cavatappi al Pesto di Pistacchi Cavatappi with Pistachio Pesto
Filetto di Tuna Agrodolce Sweet and Savory Tuna Steaks
Stufato di Patate, Peperoni e Cipolle Potato, Pepper, and Onion Casserole
Torta ai Cannoli Cannoli Cake

Nothing says summer in southern Italy like zucchini blossoms! Available for only a few weeks of the year, they are light as air and melt in your mouth. In my family, our favorite way to prepare zucchini blossoms is stuffed with creamy ricotta.

Pistachio Pesto is a hidden gem of the island of Sicily: rich, creamy and decadent, it transforms your pasta! Sweet and Savory Tuna Steak, the main course in this menu, highlights agrodolce sauce, one of the strongest influences of the Arabs on our Sicilian cuisine.

I have been making Potato, Pepper, and Onion Casserole for my children since they were little. It is a simple, fresh way to give children their vegetables, and perfect for summer, as it is delicious at room temperature.

In my first cookbook, *Whatever Happened to Sunday Dinner?*, I shared my Nana's famous recipe for her cannoli—they are the best in the world! In my house we never tire of cannoli, but sometimes, as a change, this cannoli cake just hits the spot! And it is so much fun to make with the little ones in your crowd, as they can break the cannoli shells, make their own design on the cake, and then eat away!

Ogni bella cosa! (I wish you every beautiful thing!)

Fior di Zucchini Ripieni
Stuffed Zucchini Blossoms

> 30 ounces fresh whole milk ricotta cheese
> 1 cup golden raisins
> 1 cup pine nuts
> 2 teaspoons Sicilian sea salt, fine
> 1 teaspoon freshly ground black pepper
> 4 eggs
> 1 cup unbleached flour
> 20 large zucchini blossoms
> 1 cup extra virgin olive oil

1. In a medium bowl, mix the ricotta, raisins, pine nuts, 1 teaspoon salt, and ½ teaspoon pepper. Set the bowl aside.

2. In a flat, wide bowl (such as a pie plate) beat the eggs.

3. Pour the flour into a similar type of bowl and add 1 teaspoon salt and ½ teaspoon pepper to the flour.

4. One at a time, very gently spread the petals of each zucchini blossom, just slightly, so that you can fill the cavity ½ to ¾ of the way full with the ricotta mixture. Use a teaspoon to carefully fill each blossom. Close the petals. Dip each zucchini blossom into the egg, and then into the flour.

5. Pour the olive oil into a large frying pan over low heat, until tiny bubbles begin to form around the edge of the pan. Place 3 or 4 stuffed zucchini blossoms into the oil and cook for 2 minutes on each side.

6. Plate and serve the blossoms immediately.

Cavatappi al Pesto di Pistacchi
Cavatappi with Pistachio Pesto

> 1½ cups pistachios, shelled
> 4 cloves garlic
> 2 cups fresh basil leaves
> 2 cups extra virgin olive oil
> 1 teaspoon Sicilian sea salt, fine
> 1 teaspoon freshly ground black pepper
> Handful Sicilian sea salt, coarse, for the pasta water
> 2 pounds cavatappi
> 1 cup Pecorino Romano cheese, grated

1. Preheat the oven to 350°F.

2. Place the pistachios in a single layer on a large baking sheet and roast them for 6 minutes. When they are cool, roughly chop the pistachios, using a sharp knife or a mortar and pestle. Place the chopped pistachios, garlic, and basil in a blender, and slowly add the olive oil, with the blender speed on low. Season the mixture with the salt and pepper.

3. Fill a large 6- to 8-quart pot with water. Toss in a handful of coarse sea salt and bring the water to a boil. Cook the pasta for 2 minutes less than the directions on the package.

4. Place the pesto in a large frying pan. Drain the pasta, pour it into the frying pan, and mix it into the pesto, allowing the pasta to *saltare* (or as we would say in English, "blend") with the pesto for approximately 2 minutes.

5. Serve the pasta with a generous topping of Pecorino Romano cheese.

Filetto di Tuna Agrodolce
Sweet and Savory Tuna Steaks

- 8 tablespoons extra virgin olive oil
- 8 tuna steaks, approximately 6 ounces each
- 1 cup unbleached flour
- 4 cups sliced onion (approximately 4 medium-size onions)
- 4 tablespoons sugar
- 2 teaspoons salt
- ¾ cup white wine vinegar, excellent quality
- 1 cup fresh Italian flat leaf parsley, chopped

1. Heat the olive oil in a large frying pan until it is very hot. Dredge the tuna steaks in the flour and sear them in the hot oil for 2 minutes on each side. Place the steaks in a large casserole dish.

2. Sauté the onions in the same oil in which you seared the tuna, for approximately 5 minutes, until the onions are translucent and wilted. Add the sugar, salt, and vinegar to the onions and cook for a minimum of 5 to 10 minutes, or until the onions begin to caramelize. Using a wooden spoon, stir any caramelized bits at the bottom of the pan with the onions. Simmer the mixture for 2 minutes. Pour the onion mixture over the tuna steaks, sprinkle the parsley on top, and serve.

Stufato di Patate, Peperoni e Cipolle
Potato, Pepper, and Onion Casserole

- 1 cup extra virgin olive oil
- 8 Yukon gold potatoes
- 4 yellow bell peppers, seeded and cut into strips
- 4 large onions, sliced
- 1 teaspoon Sicilian sea salt, fine
- ½ teaspoon black pepper
- 1 tablespoon dried oregano

1. Preheat the oven to 350°F.

2. Place approximately 2 tablespoons of olive oil in the bottom of a 9 × 12-inch casserole dish. Cut the potatoes into approximately ¼-inch-thick wedges and place them in the casserole dish. Add the peppers and onions to the casserole.

3. In a small bowl, mix the rest of the olive oil, salt, pepper, and oregano and pour this over the vegetable mixture. Bake for 1 hour until the vegetables are golden.

Torta ai Cannoli
Cannoli Cake

For the Cake
1½ cups unbleached flour, plus more for preparing the cake pans

1½ cups cake flour

1 tablespoon baking powder

½ teaspoon Sicilian sea salt, fine

2 sticks unsalted butter, softened, plus more for greasing the cake pans

2 cups granulated sugar

6 large eggs

1½ cups heavy whipping cream

1 cup chocolate chips

1 cup shelled, chopped pistachios

4 cannoli shells, broken into large pieces

For the Frosting
4 cups whole milk ricotta

2 tablespoons orange zest

2 tablespoons lemon zest

1 teaspoon cinnamon

1 cup confectioners' sugar

1 cup heavy whipping cream

1. *To make the cake:* Heat the oven to 350°F. Grease two 9-inch cake pans with butter and dust them with some of the unbleached flour. Shake any excess flour out of the pans.

2. In a large bowl, mix the unbleached flour, cake flour, baking powder, and salt. Set the bowl aside.

3. Using a stand mixer or a handheld mixer, beat the 2 sticks of softened butter and sugar in a large bowl until light and fluffy, then beat in the eggs. On low speed, gradually add the flour mixture, as well as the heavy whipping cream, until well mixed. Fold in half the chocolate chips and half the chopped pistachios. Divide the batter between the prepared pans and bake for about 30 minutes until a toothpick comes out clean from the center of the cake. Let the cakes cool for about 20 minutes.

4. *To make the frosting:* Using an electric mixer, a stand mixer, or a hand mixer, beat the ricotta until smooth.

5. Beat in the orange zest, lemon zest, and cinnamon. Mix in the confectioners' sugar. Add the heavy cream, and beat for 4–5 minutes, until the frosting is very thick.

6. *To assemble the cake:* Frost one 9-inch cake. Place the other 9-inch cake on top, and frost that one as well. Press the remaining chocolate chips and the remaining pistachios into the side of the cake and place the broken pieces of cannoli shells into the icing on top of the cake and on the sides. Keep the cake cold in the refrigerator until you're ready to serve.

This Is Sunday Dinner

Menu 37

SERVES 8

Zucchini Marinati alla Siciliana Marinated Zucchini, Sicilian Style

Cavatelli con Tonno, Pignoli, Menta e Limone
Cavatelli with Tuna, Pine Nuts, Mint, and Lemon

Spigola in Salsa di Olive e Caperi
Sea Bass in Olive and Caper Sauce

Barbabietola Arrostiti con Finocchio Affetato
Roasted Beets with Sliced Fennel

Pere Affogate in Marsala Poached Pears in Marsala

I love this delicious, refreshing, summer Sicilian menu because it showcases typical dishes that you can only find on my beloved island!

Starting with the appetizer, you have another creative, delicious way to use all those zucchini in the summertime! This dish is wonderful served at room temperature, as it makes the savory-sweet sauce pop. Pass this antipasto around while sitting at a big summer dinner table in your backyard.

Tuna and pine nuts, together with mint and lemon, are two typical Sicilian combinations. All four ingredients are prevalent on the island of Sicily, and work beautifully in the refreshing summer pasta in this menu. Make the sauce ahead of time and serve this dish at room temperature—it's perfect!

Mediterranean sea bass is very different from the sea bass we usually eat in the United States, which is from Central and South America (Chilean sea bass, for example.) While you can find Mediterranean sea

bass (which is small, thin, and delicate), in some stores in the States, Chilean sea bass will taste just as good with the olive and caper sauce in which it is served.

Marsala wine is by far one of the most versatile cooking wines. This sweet and delicious wine from the town of Marsala (which is approximately 30 minutes from my grandmother's hometown), works well in a wide range of dishes, from savory Chicken Marsala (that recipe is in my first cookbook, *Whatever Happened to Sunday Dinner?*) to the deliciously refreshing Poached Pears in this menu.

Tante belle cose! (Best wishes for many beautiful things!)

Zucchini Marinati alla Siciliana
Marinated Zucchini, Sicilian Style

2 pounds zucchini

Handful Sicilian sea salt, coarse, for prepping the zucchini

4 tablespoons extra virgin olive oil

1 cup white wine vinegar

1 cup sugar

1 teaspoon crushed red pepper flakes

2 teaspoons Sicilian sea salt, fine

6 garlic cloves, thinly sliced

8 tablespoons fresh basil leaves, chopped

8 tablespoons fresh flat leaf Italian parsley leaves, chopped

1. Cut the zucchini lengthwise into ⅓-inch-thick slices. Place the zucchini slices in a colander and sprinkle them with the coarse sea salt. Set the colander aside and allow the zucchini to drain for 2 hours.

2. In a large saucepan, heat the olive oil over medium heat. Place the drained zucchini slices in the pan and cook them gently until they're brown on both sides, 3–4 minutes per side. Do not let the zucchini slices burn. Set them aside.

3. In another large saucepan, bring the vinegar and sugar to a boil over high heat. Add the red pepper flakes and the finely ground sea salt. Let the mixture cool.

4. Place the zucchini slices flat in a shallow bowl with the garlic slices, basil, and parsley scattered throughout. Pour the vinegar mixture over the zucchini slices and let the mixture marinate, covered, for at least 2 hours before serving.

Cavatelli con Tonno, Pignoli, Menta e Limone
Cavatelli with Tuna, Pine Nuts, Mint, and Lemon

1 cup extra virgin olive oil

¾ cup chopped scallions, including the green and white parts

2 pounds cavatelli

1 cup golden raisins

4 tablespoons lemon zest

½ cup fresh-squeezed lemon juice, from two lemons

20 mint leaves, sliced very thinly

3 (8-ounce) jars or cans tuna, imported from Italy, packed in olive oil

½ cup toasted pine nuts

1 teaspoon Sicilian sea salt, fine

½ teaspoon freshly ground fine black pepper

1. Place ½ cup of the oil into a large frying pan and set it over low heat. Sauté the scallions for 3–4 minutes.

2. Cook the pasta according to the directions on the package. Place the scallions, raisins, lemon zest, lemon juice, and mint in a large pasta bowl and toss well. Drain the tuna and add it to the pasta bowl as well. Add the rest of the olive oil, the pine nuts, salt, and pepper to the pasta bowl. Drain the pasta and toss it with the tuna sauce.

This Is Sunday Dinner

Cooking Your Pasta Perfectly

Always cook your pasta in an abundant amount of water—think of the pasta as swimming! And never put olive oil in your pasta water—you are not making a salad! It is an old wives' tale in the United States that putting oil in the water prevents the pasta from sticking—a method that applies only to the wrong type of pasta, which is made with soft, white flour. Always buy pasta from Italy. It is affordable and plentiful in the United States, and is made with the right type of flour—durum wheat flour—which never falls apart while you're cooking it.

Salt Your Pasta Water
Always salt your pasta water, when it comes to a rolling boil, with a generous amount of coarse Sicilian sea salt. Remember, pasta is pretty tasteless (it's made of nothing but flour and water), so the salt gives it some flavor. Coarse Sicilian sea salt is available in all major supermarkets in the United States, and the cost is very reasonable.

Finishing the Cooking of Your Pasta
When you are making sauce in a large frying pan, drain the pasta 2–3 minutes before the recommended cooking time on the package and finish cooking it in the frying pan with the sauce. This allows the pasta to "jump" (saltare, as we say in Italian) with the sauce in the last few minutes of cooking, and really helps the sauce adhere to the pasta!

Al Dente
This means "to the tooth," and, although most Americans have heard this expression, some are not sure what it means. Al dente means pasta that is cooked to the correct point of firmness; it should not be hard, but neither should it ever be overcooked or mushy. I always recommend tasting the pasta at least 2 minutes before the recommended cooking time on the package and then finishing cooking the pasta in the sauce.

Spigola in Salsa di Olive e Caperi
Sea Bass in Olive and Caper Sauce

  1 cup extra virgin olive oil

  4 celery sticks, chopped

  24 whole green olives, pitted, preferably Castelvetrano from Sicily

  2 tablespoons capers, not in salt, rinsed

  8 ounces crushed San Marzano tomatoes

  6 tablespoons white wine vinegar

  4 tablespoons sugar

  2 pounds sea bass, filleted

  1 tablespoon Italian flat leaf parsley, chopped

1. Place ½ cup of the olive oil in a large frying pan. Sauté the celery until it's soft, approximately 3 minutes. Add the olives and the capers. Sauté the mixture for 2 more minutes, and then add the tomatoes, vinegar, and sugar until it is bubbly. Let the sauce simmer for 5–10 minutes until it thickens slightly.

2. Pour the remaining ½ cup of olive oil into the bottom of a large casserole dish. Place the sea bass fillets in the casserole and top them with the sweet and sour caper sauce.

3. Bake the fish for 12 minutes at 300°F and serve, sprinkling the parsley on top.

Barbabietola Arrostiti con Finocchio Affetato
Roasted Beets with Sliced Fennel

6 red beets, cleaned and peeled

6 golden beets, cleaned

½ cup extra virgin olive oil

1 teaspoon Sicilian sea salt, fine

½ teaspoon freshly ground black pepper

6 tablespoons balsamic vinegar

4 tablespoons white wine vinegar

2 fennel bulbs, thinly sliced

1. Preheat the oven to 350°F.

2. Place the beets in a large bowl. Toss them with the olive oil, salt, and pepper.

3. Place the beets on a jelly-roll pan (a cookie sheet with a rim) and roast them for 1 hour. Let the beets cool for 10 minutes.

4. When the beets are cool enough to handle, slice them thinly, place them in a large bowl, and toss with the balsamic vinegar and white wine vinegar. Add the sliced fennel, toss well, and serve.

Pere Affogate in Marsala
Poached Pears in Marsala

8 firm pears, such as Bosc or d'Anjou

½ cup sugar

½ cup light brown sugar

4 cinnamon sticks

1 teaspoon ground cloves

1 cup Marsala wine, preferably imported (my favorite brand is Florio)

1. Peel the pears, leaving the stems on top of the pears intact. Cut off the bottom of each pear so that it can stand up. Using an apple corer or a paring knife, core the pear from the bottom. Place the pears, standing up, in the bottom of a large 6- to 8-quart pot. Fill the pot with water all the way up to the stem of the pears, and add the 2 kinds of sugar, the cinnamon sticks, and the ground cloves.

2. Boil the water for 30 minutes over medium heat. Do not allow the water to come to a rolling boil, as this will make the pears lose their shape and fall apart. With a slotted serving spoon, place the pears on a platter. Boil the remaining liquid until it reduces and becomes thick, 5–8 minutes. Stir in the Marsala wine and cook for another 2 minutes. Pour this mixture over the pears. These are excellent served warm or at room temperature.

Torta di Caponata d'Estate Summer Caponata Torte
Sugo di Pomodoro Siciliano di Felicia Felicia's Sicilian Tomato Sauce
Cavolfiore con Platessa Flounder with Cauliflower
Palline di Melanzane Eggplant Balls
Semifreddo alla Vaniglia e Ciliegi Cherry Vanilla Semifreddo

Is there any experience in the world more memorable and joyous than cooking with your children? My daughter Felicia was slow to start cooking on her own (she said that was what I was for!), but little by little she has begun to make delicious dishes of her own, and her Sicilian Sauce is a perfect example. She learned to make it while studying law in Italy, and it has quickly become a family favorite. The tomatoes take on a sweet, caramelized flavor, and the sauce is delightful warm or cold.

The main course in this menu is a flaky, delicious Flounder with Cauliflower—and a fun side dish—Eggplant Balls. They're so good, and so easy to make, that even the young (or inexperienced) cooks in the family can prepare them.

I love semifreddos—a typical Italian invention, where you get all the rich features of gelato without all the work! Semifreddo means "semi-frozen," and it is just that—a cold and refreshing, yet still creamy dessert. In the summer, the fresh cherries in this dessert are spectacular!

Mangia bene! (Eat well!)

Torta di Caponata d'Estate
Summer Caponata Torte

For the Caponata Filling

- 1 large eggplant, peeled and cubed
- Handful Sicilian sea salt, coarse, for preparing the eggplant
- 1 cup extra virgin olive oil
- 1 medium onion, chopped
- 2 red bell peppers, seeded, cored, and diced
- 2 zucchini, diced
- 2 teaspoons Sicilian sea salt, fine
- 1 teaspoon freshly ground black pepper
- 2 tablespoons oregano
- 1 (12-ounce) can crushed San Marzano tomatoes
- 2 tablespoons red wine vinegar, excellent quality, preferably imported

For the Crust

- 2⅓ cups unbleached flour
- 1 cup unsalted butter
- 1 teaspoon salt
- 3 cloves garlic, minced
- 8 tablespoons cold water
- ½ cup grated Pecorino Romano cheese

1. *To make the caponata filling:* Place the eggplant in a colander in the kitchen sink. Layer the eggplant with coarse Sicilian sea salt and toss well. Allow the eggplant to drain for 30 minutes. After 30 minutes, rinse the eggplant very well to be sure that you have removed all the salt as well as the bitter brown juices from the eggplant.

2. Pour ½ cup of olive oil into a 6-quart saucepot. Sauté the onion until it is translucent. Add the drained, cleaned eggplant and continue to cook over medium-low heat for 7–8 minutes, stirring occasionally, until the eggplant softens. Add the bell peppers, zucchini, and the remaining ½ cup olive oil. Cook until all the vegetables have softened, approximately 7 minutes. Add the fine sea salt, pepper, and oregano. Stir in the tomatoes and cook the mixture until all vegetables are tender and the sauce is thick, approximately 20 minutes. Stir in the red wine vinegar. Take the mixture off the heat and allow it to cool.

3. *To make the crust and assemble the dish:* Place the flour, butter, salt, and garlic in a large bowl. Mix the ingredients together, either in a stand mixer or with a hand mixer, until a coarse dough forms. Drizzle the cold water into the dough and stir it gently with a fork until the dough comes together. Cover the dough in plastic wrap and let it rest for 15–30 minutes.

4. Preheat the oven to 350°F.

5. Roll out the dough into a 10- to 12-inch circle and place it in a 9- to 9½-inch pie plate. Spoon the caponata into the pie plate and bake for 20 minutes in the preheated oven.

Sugo di Pomodoro Siciliano di Felicia

Felicia's Sicilian Tomato Sauce

1½ cups olive oil

10 cloves garlic (1½ bulbs)

2 (10-ounce) containers grape or cherry tomatoes (grape tomatoes give the sauce a meatier and thicker consistency and taste)

2 (24-ounce) bottles San Marzano tomato passata

1 tablespoon sugar

½ teaspoon Sicilian sea salt, fine
    Handful Sicilian sea salt, coarse, for the pasta water

2 pounds bucatini

1 cup Parmigiano Reggiano, grated

1. Cover the bottom of a large, deep sauté pan with ½ cup of olive oil. Cut and devein the garlic, and then slice each clove in half. Add about ½ of the first garlic bulb (approximately 6 cloves) to the pan. Simmer the olive oil and garlic over low to medium heat for at least 20 minutes. Add the rest of the garlic cloves to the pan, occasionally stirring them in the olive oil with a flat wooden spatula. Allow the garlic to become golden, but be careful not to let it turn brown, which will make the garlic taste bitter. After adding all the garlic to the pan, stir the mixture thoroughly with a wooden spoon.

2. Cut the grape or cherry tomatoes, in the first container, in half, lengthwise, and add them to the pan. With a flat wooden spatula, compress each tomato so that it lies flat in the olive oil and garlic mixture. (The seeds of the tomatoes will be pressed out of the tomato skin and meld with the olive oil.) Pour the remaining 1 cup of olive oil into the sauté pan. Cut the tomatoes in the second container in half and add them to the pan, flattening and compressing them with the wooden spatula.

3. Allow the mixture to simmer over medium heat for 10 minutes. Add the tomato passata to the pan. Depending on the passata, there may be too much oil, so be sure to use a passata that is thick and sturdy, without any oil in the bottle. Stir the passata into the tomato, garlic, and olive oil mixture, and allow it to rest, still over medium heat, for 2–3 minutes. Stir in the sugar (this cuts the acidity of the sauce). Allow the mixture to simmer for 1 more minute. Add the sea salt and stir it into the sauce. Set the sauté pan on a back burner over low heat. Cover the pan with a lid, and simmer the sauce on low heat for 30 minutes. Stir the sauce every 7–10 minutes.

4. Fill a large pasta pot with water and bring it to a rolling boil. Toss in a handful of coarse sea salt. Add the bucatini to the boiling water and cook as directed on the package (usually about 10 minutes). Drain the pasta.

5. Pour the hot sauce into the pasta pot and then add the cooked pasta. Stir the mixture so that the sauce coats each individual piece of bucatini. Serve with grated Parmigiano Reggiano on the side.

Cavolfiore con Platessa
Flounder with Cauliflower

       Handful Sicilian sea salt, coarse

  8 cups cauliflower florets

  8 tablespoons unsalted butter

  ½ cup finely chopped shallots

3½ teaspoons Sicilian sea salt, fine

  3 cups breadcrumbs, homemade, or, if
     using store-bought, excellent quality

  ½ cup unbleached flour

       Zest of 2 oranges, finely grated

  8 flounder fillets

  ½ teaspoon salt, to be added to
     flounder before dredging

  ¼ teaspoon freshly ground pepper, to
     be added to flounder before dredging

  2 large eggs

  6 tablespoons olive oil

  ½ cup golden raisins

1. Fill a large pot with approximately 6 quarts of water and bring it to a boil. Make sure you salt the water with a handful of coarse sea salt. Place the cauliflower florets in the boiling water and cook them for 5 minutes. Drain the florets in a colander.

2. Melt the 6 tablespoons of olive oil all together in butter in a large frying pan. Add the shallots, all the cauliflower florets, and 2 teaspoons of the fine sea salt. Cook the mixture over medium heat until the cauliflower is tender, 6–7 minutes. Remove the pan from the heat.

3. In a large bowl, combine the breadcrumbs, flour, orange zest, and 1 teaspoon sea salt.

Place the flounder fillets on a large plate or platter. Sprinkle the flounder fillets with ½ teaspoon finely ground sea salt and ¼ teaspoon pepper on both sides.

4. Place the eggs in a large bowl and beat them with a whisk. One at a time, dip the flounder fillets in the beaten egg, and then in the breadcrumb and flour mixture, coating both sides.

5. In a large frying pan, heat the olive oil and 2 tablespoons of the butter over medium-high heat. Cook the fillets a few at a time, until they're golden brown on each side—about 3 minutes on each side. Plate the cauliflower on a large platter and place the flounder fillets on top of it. Sprinkle the golden raisins on top of the flounder and serve.

Palline di Melanzane
Eggplant Balls

  2 medium-size eggplant, peeled and cubed
     Handful Sicilian sea salt, coarse

  ½ cup extra virgin olive oil

  2 cups breadcrumbs

  4 cups mollica (the white part of the
     bread)

  ½ cup fresh mint leaves, chopped

  4 garlic cloves, chopped

24 black olives, pitted and chopped

  1 cup Pecorino Romano cheese, grated

  3 large eggs, beaten

  2 teaspoons Sicilian sea salt, fine

  1 teaspoon freshly ground black pepper

Canola oil for frying

4 cups Lisa's Classic Italian Tomato
Sauce (page 213) (optional)

1. Toss the cubed eggplant with the coarse salt and place it in a colander in the kitchen sink. Let the eggplant drain for 30 minutes. Rinse it well and pat it dry with paper towels.

2. Place the olive oil in a large frying pan. Sauté the eggplant over medium-high heat for roughly 12–15 minutes, until it is very soft, but not falling apart. Allow it to cool for 30 minutes. Place the cooked eggplant and 1 cup of the breadcrumbs in a large bowl, and mix them together well. Add the mint leaves, garlic, olives, black pepper, and cheese. Work the mixture well with your hands to thoroughly combine all the ingredients.

3. Place the remaining 1 cup of breadcrumbs on a flat plate. Using your hands, form the eggplant mixture into balls, about the size of a golf ball, and roll them in the breadcrumbs. With the palm of your hand, slightly flatten each ball.

4. Heat the canola oil in a 1- to 2-inch-deep large frying pan. Heat the canola oil until it bubbles around the edges of the pan. Place the eggplant balls in the pan and cook them over medium heat for approximately 2 minutes on each side, until they're golden brown. Remove the eggplant balls from the pan and drain them on paper towels. Serve them with warmed tomato sauce, if desired.

Semifreddo alla Vaniglia e Ciliegi
Cherry Vanilla Semifreddo

4 extra-large eggs

1 cup sugar

2 teaspoons pure vanilla extract

2 cups heavy cream

2 cups cherries, pitted and chopped (fresh cherries are best in the summer; if you can't find them, you can use canned cherries, but be sure to drain them very well)

1. Line a loaf pan with plastic wrap. Let some excess plastic wrap hang over the sides of the loaf pan.

2. In a double boiler,* whip the eggs and sugar with a hand whisk until the mixture is thick and light-colored. Add the vanilla. Set the egg mixture aside and allow it to cool.

3. In a large bowl, whip the heavy cream until peaks form. Mix the whipped cream with the egg mixture, and fold in the cherries. Pour the mixture into the loaf pan and place it in the freezer. Allow the mixture to freeze for a minimum of 4–6 hours. Slice and serve.

★ If you do not have a double boiler, you can simply place a heat-resistant glass mixing bowl or a stainless steel bowl over a saucepan of boiling water, making sure the bowl does not touch the water.

Menu 39

SERVES 8

Zuppa di Ravioli di Melanzane Eggplant Ravioli Soup

Pasta alle Lenticchie Sicilian Pasta and Lentils

Polpette di Vitello Agrodolce Sweet and Savory Veal Meatballs

Insalata di Carciofi Artichoke Salad

Torta di Ricotta e Limone di Lisa Lisa's Lemon Ricotta Cake

My Nana was not only an excellent cook—she was also an ingenious cook. My mother always tells me that when she was little, and times were difficult, her mother, my Nana, would stretch the pasta in creative ways to have enough to feed a family of seven! The recipe for Sicilian Pasta and Lentils in this menu is a perfect example of that economy.

Ironically, so many of the dishes our grandparents ate out of necessity have now become "fashionable," as health experts tell us how good these ingredients are for us. It makes me think of my grandparents, who lived to be 98 (Nana) and 101 (my grandfather), and who used to say that they didn't need doctors or "experts" to tell them how good the Mediterranean diet is—they ate it every day of their lives and were living proof it is good for you!

Those of you who have my first cookbook, *Whatever Happened to Sunday Dinner?*, will undoubtedly recognize how similar the dessert in this menu is to my Nana's Ricotta Cake. I took that recipe (a classic in our family), and added a lemon twist for the summer months, when lemons are so plentiful. They add a refreshing tang to this glorious cake. It is simple and delicious—another tribute to my beloved Nana!

Zuppa di Ravioli di Melanzane
Eggplant Ravioli Soup

2 medium-size eggplant, peeled and sliced lengthwise

Handful Sicilian sea salt, coarse

1 cup extra virgin olive oil

3 pounds plum tomatoes, chopped

1½ teaspoons Sicilian sea salt, fine

1 teaspoon freshly ground black pepper

2 cups fresh ricotta (approximately 12–14 ounces)

4 tablespoons Parmigiano Reggiano, grated

Zest of 1 lemon

1 teaspoon dried oregano

6 basil leaves

1. Place the slices of eggplant in a colander in the kitchen sink and toss them with the coarse sea salt. Allow the eggplant to drain for 30 minutes. Rinse it well to ensure that all the salt and any brown liquid that may have drained from the eggplant has been removed.

2. In a large frying pan, place ½ cup of olive oil, the tomatoes, 1 teaspoon fine sea salt, and ½ teaspoon pepper. Sauté the tomatoes until they're very soft, for approximately 20 minutes. Place the tomatoes in a bowl and allow them to cool.

3. In the same large frying pan in which you sautéed the tomatoes, add the remaining olive oil and sauté or fry each eggplant slice until it is golden brown on each side, about 1 minute on each side. Drain the eggplant slices on paper towels.

4. In a medium-size bowl, combine the ricotta, Parmigiano, lemon zest, ½ teaspoon fine sea salt, and ½ teaspoon pepper. Add the oregano and stir.

5. In a blender, puree the cooked tomatoes and the basil.

6. Place the eggplant slices on a flat plate. Place 1 tablespoon of the ricotta mixture at the small end of the eggplant slice and roll it up. Continue this process until all the eggplant ravioli have been made. Divide the tomato soup equally in 8 pasta or soup bowls and place 2 or 3 of the eggplant ravioli on top. Serve at room temperature.

Pasta Siciliana alle Lenticchie
Sicilian Pasta and Lentils

- 1 cup extra virgin olive oil
- 1 white onion, chopped
- 4 garlic cloves, chopped
- 4 celery ribs, chopped
- 2 carrots, peeled and chopped
- 2 tablespoons tomato paste, preferably imported in a tube (concentrato di pomodoro)
- 1 pound brown lentils
- 2 cups crushed San Marzano tomatoes
- 1½ teaspoons Sicilian sea salt, fine
- 1 teaspoon freshly ground black pepper
- ½ pound broken spaghetti

Place ½ cup of olive oil into a 6-quart pot. Add the onion, garlic, celery, carrots, and tomato paste and sauté for 15 minutes. Add the lentils to the pot and sauté the mixture for 3 or 4 minutes. Add 2 cups of water and the San Marzano tomatoes. Cook for 30 minutes, then add the salt and pepper and the remaining ½ cup of extra virgin olive oil. Add the spaghetti, broken into 1-inch pieces, to the pot. Add the remaining ½ cup of extra virgin olive oil and cook the mixture for 7 or 8 more minutes. Serve.

Polpette di Vitello Agrodolce
Sweet and Savory Veal Meatballs

For the Meatballs

- 2 pounds ground veal
- 4 cups Pecorino Romano cheese, grated
- 3 cups breadcrumbs
- 2 garlic cloves, chopped
- ½ cup flat Italian parsley, chopped
- 3 eggs, lightly beaten
- ½ teaspoon Sicilian sea salt, fine
- Canola oil for frying

For the Sauce

- 1 onion, chopped
- 1 cup green olives, chopped
- ½ cup sugar
- ½ cup red wine vinegar
- 2 cups Lisa's Classic Italian Tomato Sauce (page 213) or excellent store-bought sauce, such as Lisa's Sunday Sauces, made with imported San Marzano tomatoes

1. *To make the meatballs:* In a medium-size bowl, mix together the veal, the cheese, breadcrumbs, garlic, parsley, eggs, and salt. Using your hands, form meatballs, approximately the size of golf balls, and flatten them slightly with your palm.

2. In a large frying pan, place the canola oil to approximately the height of an inch. Add the meatballs and cook them for about 4 minutes on each side, until they are golden brown. Drain the meatballs on paper towels.

3. *To make the sauce:* Take 6 tablespoons of the canola oil from the pan in which you cooked the meatballs, and place the oil in a clean, medium-size frying pan. Add the onion and cook it over medium heat for approximately 6–8 minutes, until onions are golden brown. Add the olives and cook for 2 more minutes. Add the sugar, red wine vinegar, and tomato sauce. Stir.

4. Place the meatballs in the simmering tomato sauce and cook for another 10 minutes. Transfer the meatballs to a serving bowl and serve either warm or at room temperature.

Insalata di Carciofi
Artichoke Salad

12 fresh baby artichokes or two
     13-ounce packages of frozen
     artichoke hearts

½ cup plus one tablespoon extra virgin
     olive oil

2 cloves garlic, chopped

1 red onion, chopped

6 tablespoons fresh lemon juice

1 cup white wine

2 tablespoons red wine vinegar

1 teaspoon Sicilian sea salt, fine

½ teaspoon freshly ground black
     pepper

8 fresh basil leaves

1. If you're using fresh artichokes, remove the hard outer leaves and cut ½ inch off the top of the artichokes. Cut off stems to ⅛-inch length from artichoke. Fill a large pot with 2 quarts of water and bring it to a boil. Cook the artichokes for about 25 minutes. Drain the artichokes.

2. If you are using frozen artichokes, place them in a single layer on a cookie sheet, sprinkle them with 1 tablespoon of the olive oil, and roast the artichokes for 10 minutes at 250°F. Let them cool.

3. Place the remaining olive oil in a large frying pan and sauté the garlic and onion. Add the artichokes, lemon juice, white wine, and red wine vinegar, salt, and pepper, and cook the artichokes for 20 minutes over low heat. The liquid will thicken slightly. Pour the artichokes into a large bowl and top with the basil. This is excellent served at room temperature.

This Is Sunday Dinner

Torta di Ricotta e Limone di Lisa
Lisa's Lemon Ricotta Cake

1 yellow cake mix

8 ounces ground almonds

1¾ cups whole milk ricotta

3 eggs

¾ cup granulated sugar

1 teaspoon vanilla

¼ cup fresh-squeezed lemon juice

Zest of 3 lemons

Confectioners' sugar for dusting

1. Preheat the oven to 350°F.

2. Prepare the yellow cake according to the package directions. Add the ground almonds to the batter. Pour the batter into a buttered 13 × 9-inch heat-resistant glass baking dish, or a 10-inch round cake pan.

3. In a medium bowl, mix the ricotta with the eggs, adding them one at a time. Add the sugar and vanilla. Mix thoroughly. Add the lemon juice and lemon zest, incorporating them well, and making sure the ricotta does not separate from the lemon juice. Pour the mixture on top of the cake batter. Bake for 1 hour. Sprinkle with confectioners' sugar and serve.

Autumn in Tuscany

Tuscany will always hold a special place in my heart. For many years, when my children were in elementary school, I raised my family in the heart of Florence. Every weekend, since we lived in the historic district of Florence and had no yard, we would pile into the car and explore another part of Tuscany. Some weekends it was Chianti country, with its rolling green hills and amazing salami and cheeses, and, of course endless availability of beautiful wine bars! Other weekends it might be the Tuscan coast, with the towns of Forte dei Marmi or Viareggio, where we would walk along the beach by the Tyrrhenian Sea, and discover hidden trattorie with amazing food. We might venture up into the Apennine Mountains to the towns of Pietrasanta and Carrara to watch the slicing of the beautiful marble by the excavators or, in Pietrasanta, the actual carving of a work of art from a block of marble by a budding sculptor. My children loved to explore the city of Lucca, just 30 minutes from Florence, which we came to know quite well, because of the wall around the city that is 30 feet wide and on which my children would ride their bicycles! But the highlight was always the pranzo or cena—delicious new dishes to discover. From all the years of exploring Tuscany with my children, I grew to love Tuscan fare and learned to prepare it very well.

The two best-known soups of Tuscany are both made with day-old bread, and I feature them both in my Tuscan menus: Ribollita and Pappa al Pomodoro. I learned a wonderful expression living in Tuscany regarding food. Friends would ask friends what they were having for Sunday

dinner and the typical Tuscan response would be *Che c'e, c'e,* which literally means, "What there is, there is." This is the Tuscan philosophy toward food: You eat what you have in that season, in that region, and you make creative, delicious use of the ingredients you have. It is a wonderful, healthy philosophy.

Tuscany is beautiful all year round, but my favorite season there is autumn. The smell of burning leaves, the scent of roasted chestnuts, the excitement of the harvest—it is truly magical.

Tutti a tavola! (Everyone to table!)

Lisa's Favorite Wines from Tuscany

Tuscany is known for its wide-ranging (and affordable) red wines (I've probably tried them all!). My favorites are Brunello di Montalcino, Chianti Classico, and Montepulciano. Tuscan reds are a wonderful, pure form of wine, such as Sangiovese, which is made from just one grape, and Chianti, which is made from four different grapes.

I have a special love affair with Brunello di Montalcino, which anyone who has ever drunk it will find understandable! This red, made with the Sangiovese grape is, in my opinion, the best red produced in Tuscany. The Sangiovese is a very delicate grape and, for that reason, it thrives where it grows: in the limestone and clay-based soils of central Tuscany, specifically around Montalcino.

In this area of Tuscany, a region where I lived for many years and raised my three children, you find beautiful high elevations on hillsides for grape-growing, as well as warmer flat areas, as you descend Tuscany, toward the Tyrrhenian Sea. A Brunello is a more elegant wine than, for example, a Chianti, and will cost a little more for a bottle (between $40 and $90), so perhaps save it for a special Sunday dinner!

White wines in Tuscany are not as popular as the reds, but the Tuscans are well known for Vernaccia of San Gimignano. It is light and crisp and readily available in the United States for approximately $15 a bottle.

Crochette di Pesce Bianco e Caperi White Fish and Caper Croquettes
Zuppa di Peperoni Gialli Yellow Pepper Soup
Sogliola Toscana di Lisa Lisa's Tuscan Sole
Patate al Rosmarino Rosemary Potatoes
Torta al Ciliegio e Arancio Orange-Cherry Cake

Although Tuscan cuisine frequently utilizes simple, plain ingredients, there is an elegance in the simplicity of the food. The croquettes in this menu, for example, are made with leftover white fish and capers—light and delicious! Yellow Pepper Soup—a dish I ate on a regular basis at one of my favorite *trattorie* in Florence—is naturally sweet from the caramelization of the peppers as they cook.

I have never in my life had sole prepared as delicately as all the years I ate sole in Tuscany. It simply melts in your mouth.

Finish this simple, elegant Tuscan meal with the magnificent Orange-Cherry Cake. One of my family's favorite things to do, when we lived in Tuscany, was to go to food festivals, called *sagre*. I first had this cake at a *sagra* and instantly fell in love! It is sweet from the orange juice and tart from the cherries—perfection!

Abbondanza! (Abundance!)

Crochette di Pesce Bianco e Caperi
White Fish and Caper Croquettes

½ cup whole milk

12 ounces white fish fillets, preferably cod or haddock, skinned and boned

1 teaspoon Sicilian sea salt, fine

½ teaspoon freshly ground black pepper

4 tablespoons unsalted butter

½ cup unbleached flour

4 tablespoons capers, chopped (packed in water—not salt—and drained)

2 garlic cloves, chopped

1 tablespoon fresh lemon juice

1 tablespoon paprika

4 tablespoons chopped, fresh, Italian flat leaf parsley

2 eggs

½ cup breadcrumbs (if store-bought, preferably with Italian seasonings added)

2 cups extra virgin olive oil

2 fresh lemons, sliced in wedges

2 cups Lisa's Homemade Mayonnaise (recipe below) (optional)

1. Pour the milk into a large frying pan and place the fish fillets in the milk. Sprinkle with salt and pepper. Boil the fish for 10 minutes (see Note below). Remove the fish fillets and place them on a platter. Flake the fish fillets with a fork. Do not discard the milk used to poach the fish. Pour the milk into a heatproof, glass measuring cup.

2. Place the butter in a clean, large frying pan, and heat it over low heat. Add the flour, and stir it into the butter for 1 minute. Gradually pour in the leftover milk (here you are making a besciamella, but in this recipe, the milk is infused with the flavor of the fish). Remove the pan from the heat. Add the flaked fish to the pan and stir it into the besciamella sauce with a wooden spoon until the fish is well coated. Add the capers, garlic, lemon juice, paprika, and parsley, and mix well. Allow the mixture to cool.

3. In a pie plate or a shallow bowl, beat the 2 eggs. In a separate dish, place the breadcrumbs. Place a generous tablespoon of the fish mixture in the palm of your hand and form it into a ball the size of a golf ball. With your fingers, press the sides of the ball into an oblong shape. Dip the fish croquette in the egg, and then coat it with the breadcrumb mixture. Continue this process until all the croquettes are made. Chill the croquettes in the refrigerator for 1 hour.

4. Place the extra virgin olive oil in a deep frying pan over medium heat until small bubbles form around the edge of the pan. Cook the fish croquettes in the oil for 2 minutes on each side until golden brown. Drain the croquettes on paper towels. If desired, serve them with Lisa's Homemade Mayonnaise (recipe below) and fresh lemon wedges.

LISA'S TIP

Poaching fish in milk is a very popular method in Italy, from the north to the south, and yields a flaky, moist fish fillet.

Lisa's Homemade Mayonnaise

1 egg, plus 1 egg yolk

½ teaspoon mustard powder

1 teaspoon Sicilian sea salt, fine, plus more to taste

½ teaspoon ground white pepper, plus more to taste

1 cup extra virgin olive oil

3 tablespoons freshly squeezed lemon juice

In a food processor or blender, blend whole egg, egg yolk, and mustard powder. Add the salt and pepper. Then add ½ cup of the olive oil and half the lemon juice. Mix thoroughly, and then add the rest of the olive oil and lemon juice. Taste for seasoning and, if you like, add more salt and pepper. Serve the fish croquettes with the mayonnaise, if desired.

Zuppa di Peperoni Gialli
Yellow Pepper Soup

1 cup extra virgin olive oil

2 large carrots, peeled and chopped

2 large onions, chopped

4 ribs celery, chopped

8 yellow bell peppers, seeded and cut into large pieces

2 pounds Yukon gold potatoes, peeled and cut into wedges

2 cups vegetable broth (store-bought, excellent quality, or use very good quality bouillon cubes)

Salt and pepper, to taste

1 cup freshly grated Parmigiano Reggiano cheese

1. Pour ½ cup of the olive oil into a 6-quart pasta pot and sauté the carrots, onions, and celery until they've wilted. Add the bell peppers and potatoes and cook until they are soft, approximately 15 minutes. Add the vegetable broth and 8 cups of water. Bring the mixture to a boil and cook it over medium heat for 45 minutes, or until all vegetables are soft. Let the mixture cool.

2. When the vegetable mixture is cool, puree it in a blender and pour in the remaining extra virgin olive oil. Add salt and pepper to taste. Ladle the soup into bowls and top them with a generous amount of the Parmigiano Reggiano.

Sogliola Toscana di Lisa
Lisa's Tuscan Sole

1 cup unbleached flour

1 teaspoon Sicilian sea salt, fine

1 teaspoon freshly ground black pepper

4 pounds fillet of sole

8 tablespoons unsalted butter

1 cup extra virgin olive oil

1 tablespoon lemon juice

1 cup Italian flat leaf parsley, chopped

4 garlic cloves, chopped

Rind of 2 lemons, cut into long julienne strips

1 cup sliced almonds

1. Preheat the oven to 350°F.

2. Place the flour in a flat baking dish or shallow bowl. Add salt and pepper to the flour and mix. Dredge each fish fillet in the flour mixture and set it aside on a platter. In a large frying pan, melt the butter and ½ cup of the olive oil. Cook the sole fillets in the butter and oil mixture over medium high heat until the fillets are golden brown, approximately 2 minutes on each side. Transfer the fish to a serving platter and tent it with aluminum foil to keep it warm.

3. In the warm frying pan, add the remaining olive oil, the lemon juice, parsley, garlic, and lemon rind. Heat the mixture in the pan for 5–6 minutes over medium to high heat. The sauce will reduce slightly.

4. Meanwhile place the almonds on a baking sheet and toast them in the preheated oven for 3–4 minutes, just until golden, but not brown. Pour the sauce over the fish, top with the toasted almonds, and serve.

Patate al Rosmarino
Rosemary Potatoes

> 3–4 pounds gold potatoes (such as Yukon gold)
> 1 cup extra virgin olive oil
> 6 sprigs of fresh rosemary
> 6 garlic cloves
> 2 teaspoons Sicilian sea salt, fine
> 1 teaspoon freshly ground black pepper

1. Wash and peel the potatoes and cube them.

2. Pour the olive oil into a large bowl and add the potatoes, rosemary, garlic, salt, and pepper, making sure the potatoes are well coated with oil. Place the potato mixture into a flat baking dish or a jelly-roll pan (a baking sheet with a rim) and bake at 350°F for 40 minutes.

Torta al Ciliegio e Arancio
Orange-Cherry Cake

    Olive oil, for greasing the pan

1 cup unbleached flour, plus more for dusting the pan

1 cup sliced almonds

1 cup freshly squeezed orange juice

4 teaspoons grated orange zest

½ cup extra virgin olive oil

2 eggs, separated

1 cup sugar

1 teaspoon almond extract

1 teaspoon pure vanilla extract

1 teaspoon baking powder

½ teaspoon Sicilian sea salt, fine

2 cups pitted dried cherries

1. Preheat the oven to 350°F.

2. Oil and flour a 9-inch springform cake pan and line it with parchment paper. Brush the parchment paper with some olive oil and sprinkle the sliced almonds into the bottom of the cake pan.

3. *To make the batter:* In a stand mixer or with a handheld mixer, beat together the orange juice, orange zest, olive oil, egg yolks, sugar, almond extract, and vanilla extract. Add the 1 cup of flour, baking powder, and salt, and fold this mixture into the orange juice mixture.

4. In a separate bowl, beat the egg whites until peaks form and fold them into the batter. Add the cherries. Pour the batter into the prepared pan and bake the cake for 45 minutes, or until a toothpick in the center comes out clean. Serve.

LISA'S TIP

I live in the Midwest, and the best dried cherries I have ever purchased in the United States come from southern Michigan. If you are able to find these, use them, as they are delicious.

Menu 41

SERVES 8

Cannellini sul Pane Tostato al Aglio Cannellini Beans on Garlic Toast

Pasta con Pangrattato Piccante Pasta with Spicy Breadcrumbs

Merluzzo con Pomodoro e Cipolla Rosso
Cod with Tomato and Caramelized Red Onion

Ceci Piccanti Spicy Chickpeas

Torta di Fichi Fig Torte

Tuscan food is a perfect example of the old adage that "The simplest things are the best things."

Simple Pasta with Spicy Breadcrumbs, Cannellini Beans on Garlic Toast, delicate Cod with Tomato and Caramelized Red Onion, Spicy Chickpeas, and a rustic Fig Torte—what menu could be better for a fall Sunday dinner?

Start dinner by getting everyone involved—even the little ones—by spreading the white-bean mixture on toast. This is a great antipasto to enjoy outside on a beautiful fall Sunday, maybe around the *chiminea*, drinking a glass of Tuscan red. The beauty of this rustic, country Tuscan fare is to enjoy it calmly, together with whom you love!

Alla famiglia! (To family!)

Cannellini sul Pane Tostato al Aglio

Cannellini Beans on Garlic Toast

  6 tablespoons unsalted butter

  4 tablespoons chopped Italian flat leaf parsley

  4 cloves garlic, chopped

  ½ cup extra virgin olive oil

  8 ounces pancetta, finely chopped (if you cannot find Italian pancetta, you can use good-quality thick-sliced bacon)

  2 shallots, chopped

  2 cans imported cannellini white beans, drained

  2 cups grape tomatoes, halved

  3 tablespoons tomato paste (preferably imported concentrato di pomodoro, which comes in a tube from Italy)

  2 teaspoons freshly ground black pepper

  10 or 12 slices, ¾-inch-thick rustic Italian bread (either purchased or make Lisa's Country Rustic Bread, page 186)

1. Combine the butter, parsley, and garlic in a small bowl. With the back of a fork, mix it very well until you get a paste. Pour the oil into a large frying pan. Add the pancetta to the pan and cook it over medium heat, stirring the pancetta until it browns, 4–5 minutes.

Add the shallots and cook the mixture for another 2 minutes. Add the cannellini beans, tomatoes, tomato paste, and pepper, and simmer for approximately 10 minutes.

2. While the bean mixture is simmering, use the back of a fork to smash approximately half the cannellini beans in the pan (see Lisa's Tip). Remove the pan from the heat.

3. Meanwhile, arrange the slices of bread on a baking sheet, and place them under the broiler. Toast the bread until it is golden on both sides, turning it once and transfer it to a platter. Spread the garlic and butter mixture on 1 side of the toasted bread and top each slice with a generous slathering of the bean mixture.

LISA'S TIP

Smashing half the beans and mixing them with the whole beans is a technique I learned when I was living in Tuscany, and it really accentuates the delicate flavor of imported cannellini. The skin on these beans is so thin that they're almost skinless, and, as a result, they are very easy to digest and have a delicate, buttery flavor.

Pasta con Pangrattato Piccante
Pasta with Spicy Breadcrumbs

> Sicilian sea salt, coarse, for the pasta water
>
> 2 pounds bucatini
>
> 1 cup extra virgin olive oil
>
> 6 cups breadcrumbs, homemade (see Note) or good-quality store-bought breadcrumbs
>
> 6 cloves garlic, chopped
>
> 1 teaspoon crushed red pepper flakes
>
> Parmigiano Reggiano, freshly grated, for garnish (optional)

1. Fill a 6- to 8-quart pasta pot with water and bring it to a rolling boil. Add a handful of coarse salt to the water. Cook the bucatini *al dente*, according to the directions on the package.

2. Meanwhile, add the olive oil to a large frying pan and sauté the breadcrumbs, garlic, and pepper flakes until the mixture is golden. Drain the pasta, add the breadcrumbs, toss well, and serve. Top with a sprinkle of freshly grated Parmigiano Reggiano, if you like.

LISA'S TIP

You can make your own breadcrumbs from day-old Italian bread. Simply place it in a blender, press the chop button, and add some Italian seasonings.

Merluzzo con Pomodoro e Cipolla Rosso
Cod with Tomato and Caramelized Red Onion

> 8 cod (or halibut) fillets, each about 8 ounces, 1 inch thick
>
> 10 tablespoons extra virgin olive oil
>
> 3 tablespoons fresh rosemary
>
> 2 teaspoons Sicilian sea salt, fine
>
> 1 teaspoon freshly ground black pepper
>
> 1 pound red onions, sliced
>
> 2 tablespoons sugar
>
> 2 pounds fresh tomatoes, either Roma or on the vine, chopped

1. Place the fillets on a large platter and drizzle 2 tablespoons of the olive oil over the fish. Sprinkle the rosemary, 1 teaspoon of the salt, and the pepper on top. Repeat on both sides of the fillets.

2. Place 4 tablespoons of the olive oil in a large frying pan and cook the onions over medium heat until they're wilted and soft. Add the sugar and the remaining 1 teaspoon of salt. Reduce the heat to low and allow the onion to simmer for 15 minutes. Add the tomatoes to the onion mixture, and cook for an additional 10 minutes.

3. Place 4 tablespoons of the olive oil in a clean, large frying pan and cook the fish fillets until they are browned on each side, approximately 4 minutes. Do not remove the rosemary—it gives the fish an excellent flavor. To serve, spoon a generous portion of the tomato-onion mixture on each plate, place a fish fillet on top, and enjoy.

Ceci Piccanti
Spicy Chickpeas

1 cup extra virgin olive oil

1 white onion, finely chopped

2 carrots, peeled and finely chopped

2 stalks celery, finely chopped

4 cups ceci beans (chickpeas), preferably imported from Italy, rinsed well

1 onion, finely chopped

1 teaspoon Sicilian sea salt, fine

½ teaspoon freshly ground black pepper

1 teaspoon crushed red pepper

Place the olive oil in a large frying pan. Add the onion, carrots, and celery (the "holy trinity," as it is called in Tuscany), and cook for 5 minutes over medium heat, until the onion is soft and golden. Add the ceci beans, the salt and pepper, and the crushed red pepper. With the back of a fork, smash about one-third of the ceci beans while they are simmering in the pan, and mix well. Serve on the same plate with the fish.

Torta di Fichi
Fig Torte

For Lisa's Pasta Frolla

1¼ cups all-purpose flour

¼ teaspoon baking powder

Pinch salt

⅓ cup sugar

1 stick, plus 1 tablespoon unsalted butter, cold and sliced

1 egg yolk

For the Fig Filling

24 fresh or dried figs, cut in half

2 cups Vin Santo (or very high-quality sherry, if Vin Santo is not available)

6 tablespoons sugar

1 piece lemon rind, the size of ¼ lemon

For the Cream Filling

8 egg yolks

½ cup sugar

¾ cup Vin Santo (or very high-quality sherry, if Vin Santo is not available)

1. *To make the pasta frolla:* Combine the flour, baking powder, salt, and sugar. Make a well in the center of the flour mixture and add the butter and egg yolk. Knead the mixture into a soft dough, adding a few drops of ice water. Work the ingredients together by hand or with a pastry blender. (This can be done in a stand mixer by simply placing all the ingredients in a mixing bowl and using a paddle attachment on medium speed.)

2. Shape the pastry into a ball and roll it out to line a 9 × 9½ inch, fluted, loose-bottomed tart or quiche mold. Prick the dough with a fork. Chill the pastry for 30 minutes.

3. *To make the fig filling:* Place the figs, Vin Santo, sugar, lemon rind, and 1 cup of water in a medium-size saucepan. Cook the mixture for 30 minutes over medium heat, until it is fairly thick and reduced by about half. Let the fig mixture cool for approximately 30 minutes.

4. *To make the cream filling:* In a double boiler, or in a glass ovenproof bowl, over a medium-size saucepan of boiling water, beat the egg yolks and sugar until the mixture is pale and thick. Add the Vin Santo, beating constantly with a wire whisk. The cream mixture should triple in volume and be soft and fluffy after approximately 4–6 minutes.

5. Meanwhile, bake the *pasta frolla* crust at 300°F for 20 minutes or until golden, and remove it from the oven. Let it cool completely. Spread the cream filling mixture across the crust, and top it with the fig mixture. Place the torte in the refrigerator for 20 to 30 minutes to allow both fillings to set. Serve.

Menu 42

SERVES 8

Tortino di Peperoni Dolce e Porri Leek and Sweet Pepper Torte

Cappellini con Briccioli di Parmigiano
Cappellini with Mushrooms and Parmesan Crunch

Uove alla Coque con Asparagi e Parmigiano
Soft-Boiled Eggs with Asparagus and Parmigiano

Tortina di Spinaci e Ricotta Spinach and Ricotta Torte

Torta di Mela con Impasto al Amaretto Apple Cake with Amaretto Crust

In my first cookbook *Whatever Happened to Sunday Dinner?* I shared a recipe I had learned in Tuscany for making grilled leeks, a vegetable that I had not used much before moving to Tuscany. For the antipasto in this menu, the soft onion flavor of the leek combines with sweet bell peppers to make for a delicious and satisfying torte.

Cappellini with Mushrooms and Parmesan Crunch is one of my children's favorite baked pasta dishes! Highlighting the unique, earthy flavor of porcini mushrooms, which are native to Tuscany, this dish, with its satisfying crunchy Parmigiano cheese topping, will quickly become a favorite for your family, too. Porcini mushrooms are now available in supermarkets all over the United States, so there is no need to buy them from specialty food stores. Porcini mushrooms are sold dried here, but all you need to do, as I explain in my recipes, is to soak them for a few minutes in warm water to reconstitute them—and the texture is wonderful!

My daughter Felicia would not touch asparagus when she was a child. When Felicia was in the second grade, she was invited to eat dinner at a classmate's house in Tuscany (they went to the International

School together). She came home that evening and announced to me that she now loved asparagus because she could dip it in egg! The recipe for Soft-Boiled Eggs with Asparagus and Parmigiano, in this menu, is a fun, healthy way to enjoy eggs and vegetables!

In *Whatever Happened to Sunday Dinner?*, I included my recipe for classic Italian apple cake, and mentioned that every region of Italy has its own version. I love the amaretto cookie crust in the Tuscan interpretation of this classic cake. The sweet flavor of the almond cookie is a wonderful complement to the custard and apple filling.

Mangia bene, beve piu! (Eat well and drink more!)

Tortino di Peperoni Dolce e Porri
Leek and Sweet Pepper Torte

For Lisa's Pasta Salata

1 cup flour

½ cup butter

Pinch Sicilian sea salt, fine

3 tablespoons milk

For the Filling

8 tablespoons unsalted butter

4 tablespoons extra virgin olive oil

1 red bell pepper, seeded and diced

1 yellow bell pepper, seeded and diced

1 leek, trimmed and diced

½ teaspoon Sicilian sea salt, fine

½ teaspoon freshly ground black pepper

3 eggs

1 cup Pecorino Romano cheese, grated

½ cup Parmigiano Reggiano cheese, grated

½ cup heavy cream

1 tablespoon Italian flat leaf parsley, chopped

1. *To make the pasta salata:* Thoroughly mix together all the ingredients. Refrigerate the pastry for 1 hour. Roll out the pastry and place it in a buttered 9-inch round pie pan, 2 inches deep.

2. *To make the filling:* Melt the butter and olive oil in a large frying pan. Add the red and yellow bell peppers, the leek, and the salt and pepper. Cook the mixture over low heat for 15 minutes. Allow it to cool.

3. Preheat the oven to 375°F.

4. Beat the eggs, Pecorino, Parmigiano, cream, and parsley together with a fork in a large bowl. Add the bell pepper mixture to the egg mixture and pour it into the prepared pie pan. Bake for 30 minutes.

Cappellini con Briccioli di Parmigiano
Cappellini with Mushrooms and Parmesan Crunch

1 cup dried porcini mushrooms

1 cup boiling-hot water (to reconstitute the dried mushrooms)

4 tablespoons unsalted butter

9 tablespoons extra virgin olive oil

4 cups breadcrumbs (homemade from day-old Italian bread or, if store-bought, good-quality breadcrumbs with Italian seasonings added)

4 cloves garlic, chopped

½ cup Italian flat leaf parsley, chopped

1 teaspoon Sicilian sea salt, fine

½ teaspoon freshly ground black pepper

1 cup Parmigiano Reggiano cheese, grated

1 white or yellow onion, chopped

2 pounds fresh button mushrooms, sliced

1 teaspoon dried oregano

Handful of Sicilian sea salt, coarse, for salting pasta water

2 pounds cappellini pasta

1. Place the dried porcini mushrooms in 1 cup of boiling-hot water and allow it to sit for 30 minutes.

2. Butter a 13 × 9-inch ceramic baking dish.

3. Place 2 tablespoons of the butter, with 6 tablespoons of the olive oil, in a large frying pan over medium heat. Add the breadcrumbs, garlic, parsley, ½ teaspoon of the salt, ¼ teaspoon of the pepper, and half the Parmigiano Reggiano to the pan, and stir until the mixture is golden brown and well combined. Set the mixture aside.

4. Drain the porcini mushrooms, pat them dry with a paper towel, and finely chop them. Set the porcini mushrooms aside.

5. Heat the remaining 2 tablespoons of butter and remaining 3 tablespoons of extra virgin olive oil in a large frying pan and sauté the onion. Add the button mushrooms, oregano, and the remaining salt and pepper. Continue to cook the mixture over low heat until the mushrooms are browned, approximately 10 minutes. Drain the button mushroom mixture in a colander, making sure there is no liquid left. Mix the button mushrooms with the porcini mushrooms.

6. Meanwhile, cook the pasta in a 6- to 8-quart pot of boiling salted water until al dente. Drain the pasta.

7. In a large bowl, mix the pasta with the mushroom mixture and transfer it to the prepared baking dish. Sprinkle the breadcrumb mixture on top and bake at 400°F for 15 minutes. Sprinkle the remaining Parmigiano on top and serve.

LISA'S TIP

Parmigiano Reggiano versus Pecorino Romano—Which to Choose?

Frequently, in an Italian restaurant in the United States, you will be offered one of these two cheeses to grate on your pasta. Do you know the difference? Does choosing one over the other make a difference? Absolutely! Parmigiano Reggiano—called the "King of all Cheeses"—is a cow's milk cheese, golden yellow, creamy, with a buttery, nutty taste and a slightly salty tang. It is excellent on classic dishes such as Tomato Sauce (page 97) and Grandma Caponigri's Meat Ragù (page 168). Pecorino Romano, on the other hand, is a sheep's milk cheese, and is much sharper and saltier than Parmigiano. It is excellent on particular sauces, such as pesto and vegetable primavera sauces. In Italy, the cheese you select to adorn your pasta should complement and bring out the flavors of the sauce—not overwhelm it!

Uove Alla Coque con Asparagi e Parmigiano
Soft-Boiled Eggs with Asparagus and Parmigiano

- 1 tablespoon Sicilian sea salt, fine
- 3 pounds asparagus spears, approximately 4 inches long
- 8 eggs
- 4 tablespoons melted, unsalted butter
- ½ cup Parmigiano Reggiano cheese, grated

1. Fill a large saucepan with water. Add the salt and bring the water to a rolling boil. Drop the asparagus spears into the water and boil them for 3 minutes, until tender. Drain the asparagus immediately and set it aside.

2. Bring a medium-size saucepan of water to a rolling boil. Lower the heat until the water is simmering. Crack each egg into the simmering water and cook for 2 minutes, until the white of the soft-boiled egg is firm, but the yolk is still soft and runny.

3. Place the asparagus spears on a platter and drizzle the melted butter over the asparagus. Sprinkle the grated Parmigiano over the spears. Place the soft-boiled eggs in small cups or bowls, 1 per person. Dip the asparagus tip into the soft-boiled egg, and enjoy.

Tortina di Spinaci e Ricotta
Spinach and Ricotta Torte

- 8 tablespoons unsalted butter, plus extra for greasing the casserole
- ¾ cup onion, chopped
- 4 ounces imported prosciutto, chopped
- 2 pounds fresh spinach or 2 (10-ounce) packages frozen chopped spinach, thawed
- 1 cup Parmigiano Reggiano cheese, grated
- 1 cup heavy cream
- ½ teaspoon nutmeg
- 2 cups whole milk ricotta cheese

1. Melt the butter in a large frying pan. Add the onion and cook for 5 minutes. Add the prosciutto and cook for 1 minute more. Stir in the spinach and cook for 3 minutes.

2. Preheat the oven to 400°F. Butter a medium-size casserole and set it aside.

3. Remove the spinach mixture from the stove. Add the Parmigiano Reggiano, the heavy cream, the nutmeg, and the ricotta. Mix well.

4. Pour the mixture into the buttered casserole and bake for 30 minutes. Serve the sformato on the same plate with Soft-Boiled Eggs with Asparagus and Parmigiano (see recipe above).

Torta di Mela con Impasto al Amaretto
Apple Cake with Amaretto Crust

For the Cookie Crust

24 amaretto cookies, imported from Italy and finely ground (may be ground in a blender or with a mortar and pestle)

6 tablespoons unsalted butter, soft but not melted, plus more for greasing the pan

For the Filling

2 pounds apples (Granny Smith or red delicious both work well for this cake), peeled, cored, and cut into quarters

¾ cup sugar

½ cup raisins

For the Custard

6 large egg yolks

6 tablespoons sugar

2 cups heavy cream

Juice of ½ lemon

½ cup Vin Santo (or very high-quality sherry)

1. *To make the crust:* With a fork, mix the ground cookies with the softened butter. Press the cookie mixture into the bottom of a buttered 10-inch springform pan. The cookie mixture should cover the bottom of the pan and approximately 1 inch up the sides of the pan.

2. *To make the filling:* Place the apples in a 6-quart pot, cover them with fresh water, and add the sugar and raisins. Cook the apple mixture over medium heat for 30 minutes, and then drain the apples and raisins. Set the mixture aside for 30 minutes.

3. *To make the custard:* Place the egg yolks in a glass bowl and add the 6 tablespoons of sugar. Stir the mixture with a wooden spoon until it turns a light yellow. Add the heavy cream and lemon juice, and mix together. Put the glass bowl over a medium-sized sauce pan of boiling water over medium heat, and stir the mixture with a wooden spoon until it thickens enough to coat the back of the spoon. Do not allow the mixture to boil. Allow the custard to rest for approximately 1 hour and cool at room temperature.

4. *To assemble the cake:* Mash the cooked apples and raisins with a fork. Add the Vin Santo to the apple mixture and mix very well. Pour the apple mixture into the cookie crust. Top the apple mixture with the custard mixture. Bake the apple cake in a preheated 375°F oven for 40 minutes. Remove the cake from the oven and let it rest for 20–30 minutes before serving.

The process of making Extra Virgin Olive Oil in Tuscany! It begins with picking the olives, sorting the olives at the community olive press, and finally the end result: liquid gold! Extra Virgin Olive Oil!

This Is Sunday Dinner

Liquid Gold:
Extra Virgin Olive Oil

The backbone of the incredibly healthy Mediterranean diet is this liquid gold: Extra Virgin Olive Oil! If you find yourself standing in front of a sea of olive oil bottles at the supermarket, not knowing which to choose, consider these important differences before you make a selection:

Extra Virgin Olive Oil This is the purest, richest olive oil you can buy, because it is minimally processed, by cold-pressing the olives, and then filtering the oil from the cold-pressed olives. The result is a pure, clean taste, yielding premium flavor and the maximum amount of nutritional benefits. I recommend Extra Virgin Olive Oil for dipping and all other noncooked dishes, such as salad dressings or garnish on soup. But I also recommend it for cooking, when you want to make a dish extra special, with a clean, pure flavor. The only downside of Extra Virgin Olive Oil is that it burns at a lower temperature than most oils. Therefore, when you are using it for cooking, be very careful or the oil will burn, the food will burn, and the oil will take on a slightly bitter taste. I always look for Extra Virgin Olive Oil from Italy, which is made only from Italian olives, rather than olives that come from other places in Europe, some of which have a bitter, heavy taste. My favorite brands of Extra Virgin Olive Oil are Partanna, Castelvetrano, DeCecco, and Lucini.

Virgin Olive Oil This oil has the same qualities as Extra Virgin Olive Oil, except the manufacturers usually use a lower grade of olive. Therefore, you do not get the premium flavor. I recommend virgin olive oil for cooking because it is not as flavorful as Extra Virgin Olive Oil, which is best used raw for dipping, salad dressings, and garnishing dishes.

Olive Oil This oil is frequently a mixture of refined oil and virgin olive oil. In other words, it is not cold-pressed and does not have a clean, fresh, fruity taste, because it has been refined or treated. While it has some of the flavor of Extra Virgin Olive Oil, I would only recommend using olive oil when combining it with a vegetable oil for frying foods such as the homemade French Fries in my first cookbook, *Whatever Happened to Sunday Dinner*. But do not use it on any dish where the pure flavor of the olive oil is important. It is also important to note that olive oil, unlike Extra Virgin Olive Oil and virgin olive oil, is partially processed, so some of the nutrients are lost and you receive less nutritional value from it.

Menu 43

SERVES 8

Triangoli di Polenta con Peperoni e Gorgonzola Polenta Triangles with Peppers and Gorgonzola

Zuppa di Farro con Funghi Farro Mushroom Soup

Frittata ai Zucchini e Scamorza Frittata with Zucchini and Scamorza

Finocchio Croccanti al Forno Crunchy Fennel Bake

Soufflé alla Nutella Nutella Soufflés

This was one of my favorite Tuscan menus to make on an autumn Sunday when my children were small. It is hearty, rustic, and satisfying.

Polenta, a dish primarily composed of cornmeal, makes for warm, rich, and satisfying meals. I especially love to serve it as an appetizer, because when you fry or broil polenta, it becomes crunchy and golden on the outside, yet remains creamy inside. With the sautéed peppers and tangy, sweet Italian Gorgonzola, your family and guests will gobble this up.

Farro is very popular in Tuscany and the best farro beans are from Garfagnana. You can find these in most specialty stores here in the United States, but I have also seen them in some major grocery store chains. Farro is basically a combination of three wheats—some people call it a first cousin to barley! Garfagnana is an area of Tuscany in the province of Lucca, about 40 minutes from Florence. The Farro Mushroom Soup in this menu, which includes porcini mushrooms, has a rich, earthy flavor.

There's a frittata in every section of this regional cookbook because we eat them all over Italy! Frittatas are healthy, easy to make, and

delicious. Scamorza cheese is very similar to mozzarella, but it is more tangy and a little saltier, too. Many pizzerias in Italy use scamorza instead of mozzarella on their pizza, and it is delicious.

As I said in my first cookbook *Whatever Happened to Sunday Dinner?*, fennel is a vegetable that is not used much here in the United States, but it is so delicious and versatile! My children love Crunchy Fennel Bake because the fennel is soft and creamy, while the cheese and breadcrumbs on top add a fun crunch.

And who doesn't love Nutella? The hazelnut is used in everything in central and northern Italy, much as the pine nut and pistachio are used in southern Italy. This delicious hazelnut-chocolate spread makes the soufflés heavenly! So curl up by the fire on a brisk Sunday in the fall and enjoy every bite of this comforting menu!

Buon appetito!

Triangoli di Polenta con Peperoni e Gorgonzola
Polenta Triangles with Peppers and Gorgonzola

- 1 (14-ounce) box instant polenta, imported from Italy
- 4 tablespoons extra virgin olive oil, plus more for greasing the casserole dish and baking sheet
- 2 red bell peppers, cored, seeded, and cut into strips
- 1 yellow bell pepper, cored, seeded, and cut into strips
- 1 teaspoon Sicilian sea salt, fine
- 1 teaspoon sugar
- 1 teaspoon freshly ground black pepper
- 8 ounces Gorgonzola cheese, imported from Italy

1. Prepare the polenta according to the instructions on the package. Pour the polenta into a lightly oiled 13 × 9-inch casserole. Cover the casserole with plastic wrap and refrigerate it for at least 1 hour.

2. Place the olive oil in a large frying pan, and add the bell peppers and salt. Cook the peppers over medium heat until they are tender and soft, approximately 15 minutes.

3. While the peppers are cooking, add the sugar to the pan, and stir the mixture to ensure that it dissolves. Remove the polenta from the refrigerator, and, with a paring knife, cut the polenta into triangles, approximately 2 to 3 inches long.

4. Lightly oil a baking sheet with olive oil. Lay the polenta triangles on the baking sheet, sprinkle them with the black pepper, and place the baking sheet under the broiler. Toast the polenta triangles for 4 minutes on each side, and then transfer them to a platter. With a butter knife, spread some of the Gorgonzola on top of each polenta triangle, and then place a teaspoon of the sautéed pepper mixture on top of the cheese.

Zuppa di Farro con Funghi
Farro Mushroom Soup

- 2 cups farro, preferably imported from Tuscany
- ½ cup dried porcini mushrooms
- 6 cups vegetable broth (may be store-bought, if excellent quality, or made from vegetable bouillon cubes)
- 1 stick unsalted butter
- 2 large onions, chopped
- 6 cloves garlic, chopped
- 1 pound button mushrooms, sliced
- 1 pound Cremini mushrooms, sliced
- 1 teaspoon Sicilian sea salt, coarse, plus more to taste
- ½ teaspoon freshly ground black pepper, plus more to taste
- ½ cup sherry

1. Soak the farro overnight in a pot of water, to cover, and then drain it. Place the porcini mushrooms in a small bowl and cover them with 4 cups of boiling water. Let the mushrooms rest for 15 minutes. Drain the mushrooms and reserve the liquid in which they were reconstituted. Chop the porcini mushrooms.

2. To make the farro soup, combine the farro, vegetable broth, and reserved porcini liquid in a large saucepan. Bring the mixture to a boil, and then reduce the heat to a simmer. Cover the saucepan and cook the soup until the farro is tender, about 40 minutes.

3. In another large frying pan, melt the butter. Add the onions, garlic, and porcini mushrooms, and sauté for 5 minutes. Add the button mushrooms and the cremini mushrooms, and cook the mixture over low heat for another 5 minutes. Season the mushroom mixture with the salt and pepper and stir in the sherry. Cook for 3 more minutes. Pour the mushroom mixture into the farro soup and cook another 20 minutes. Season with salt and pepper to taste.

Frittata ai Zucchini e Scamorza
Frittata with Zucchini and Scamorza

- 6 tablespoons extra virgin olive oil
- 3 tablespoons unsalted butter
- 2 small zucchini, sliced into 1/4-inch rounds
- 8 large eggs
- 2 tablespoons Italian flat leaf parsley, chopped
- 1 cup Parmigiano Reggiano cheese, grated
- 12 ounces scamorza cheese, cut in ½-inch cubes

1. Place the olive oil and the butter in a large frying pan over low heat until the butter melts. Sauté the sliced zucchini until it is golden on both sides, approximately 10 minutes.

2. Meanwhile, beat the eggs. Add the parsley, grated Parmigiano, and the scamorza cubes to the egg mixture. When the zucchini are fully cooked, pour the egg mixture over the zucchini in the frying pan. Cook the frittata for 4 minutes, and then gently lift an edge of the frittata with a spatula to check and make sure the bottom is completely cooked.

3. Place a dinner plate upside down over the frying pan. Flip the frittata onto the plate and slide the uncooked side back into the frying pan. Cook it for an additional 4 minutes, and then slice and serve the frittata.

Finocchio Croccanti al Forno
Crunchy Fennel Bake

- 6 large fennel bulbs
- 1 cup extra virgin olive oil, plus more for greasing the casserole dish
- 1 teaspoon Sicilian sea salt, fine
- ½ teaspoon freshly ground black pepper
- 3 cups breadcrumbs, made from day-old bread, or use excellent-quality store-bought breadcrumbs
- 6 cloves garlic, chopped
- 2 cups Pecorino Romano cheese, grated
- 1 cup Italian flat leaf parsley, chopped

1. Preheat the oven to 350°F.

2. Slice the fennel bulbs lengthwise and discard the stems. Place the olive oil in a large frying pan and sauté the fennel until it has softened slightly. Add the salt and pepper, and cook the fennel over medium heat for 10 minutes.

3. Oil the bottom of a 13 × 9-inch casserole or other ovenproof dish. Sprinkle 3 tablespoons of the breadcrumbs on the bottom of the dish. Mix the remaining breadcrumbs with the garlic, Pecorino Romano, and parsley. Place a layer of the fennel in the baking dish and top it with some of the breadcrumb mixture. Repeat this process until you have used up all the ingredients. Bake the fennel in the preheated oven for 45 minutes

Soufflé alla Nutella
Nutella Souffles

- 1 cup Nutella
- 8 eggs
- 1 cup granulated sugar
- 2 teaspoons pure vanilla extract
- ¼ cup cornstarch
- 3 tablespoons butter for greasing the ramekins or soufflé dishes
- Confectioners' sugar, for garnish

1. Melt the Nutella in a double boiler or in a heat-proof glass bowl, set over a pan of gently boiling water. Crack the eggs and separate the yolks from the whites. Add the egg yolks to the melted Nutella, mixing them in with a wire whisk, and then add ½ cup of the sugar, the vanilla extract, and cornstarch.

2. Preheat the oven to 400°F. In a large bowl, beat the egg whites with a handheld mixer until they form stiff peaks, and then fold the remaining ½ cup of sugar into the egg whites. Remove the Nutella mixture from the stove and gently fold the beaten egg whites into the mixture. Do not overmix the egg whites into the Nutella mixture. Butter 8 individual ceramic ramekins or small soufflé dishes. Pour the mixture into the dishes and bake the soufflés for 30 minutes in the preheated 400°F oven. Remove the soufflés from the oven, sprinkle them with confectioners' sugar, and serve.

Menu 44

SERVES 8

Formaggio di Capra Marinato Marinated Goat Cheese
Pappa al Pomodoro Tuscan Tomato Soup
Pollo Arrosto con Funghi Pan-Roasted Chicken with Mushrooms
Torta di Patate al Formaggio Cheesy Potato Torte
Biscotti per il Matrimonio Italiano Italian Wedding Cookies

Pappa al Pomodoro is a classic example of the *cucina povera* for which Tuscany is famous—it utilizes everything and makes delicious dishes! Traditionally, it is made with day-old bread, but if you have only fresh Italian bread, pop it in the oven for 15 minutes or so, cut it into cubes, and let it stand for about 30 minutes. There is a very old, traditional children's song in Tuscany about this famous soup, "*Viva la Pappa al Pomodoro.*" It was also the theme song of the classic children's series *Il Giornalino di Gian Burrasca.* I still remember that it was one of the first children's songs my daughter Felicia learned, at the age of six, when we moved to Florence, so, of course, this soup has a special place in our home!

A great number of dishes from Tuscany—known for its rustic cuisine—are cooked on the stovetop, not in the oven, because in the countryside cooking was always done outdoors over an open fire. The pan-roasted chicken in this menu calls to mind this historic cuisine, and the flavors from the slow roasting over a flame are amazing.

Italian Wedding Cookies go way back to my childhood—and probably the childhood of every Italian-American! They melt in your mouth and are perfect with after-dinner espresso. Make a double or triple batch with your children as these freeze beautifully!

Formaggio di Capra Marinato
Marinated Goat Cheese

- 1 (8-ounce) log of goat cheese
- 4 tablespoons Italian flat leaf parsley, chopped
- 2 garlic cloves, chopped
- ½ teaspoon crushed red pepper flakes
- 4 tablespoons extra virgin olive oil
- 2 tablespoons grappa or vodka
- 1 thin loaf Italian bread, such as a baguette (which we call *filone* in Italian), cut into ¼-inch slices and toasted

Slice the goat cheese log into 8 pieces and place them in a deep glass or ceramic casserole dish. Cover the cheese with the parsley, garlic, red pepper flakes, olive oil, and grappa (or vodka) and refrigerate the dish for a minimum of 2–4 hours. Remove the dish from the refrigerator at least 1 hour before serving. Place each round of goat cheese on a small plate and serve with the toasted Italian bread.

Pappa al Pomodoro
Tuscan Tomato Soup

    1 large leek, chopped

    1 hot pepper (preferably a hot cherry
      pepper), seeds removed and
      chopped

    1 cup extra virgin olive oil

    2 (26-ounce) cans crushed, imported
      San Marzano tomatoes

    2 cups vegetable broth

   10 slices good Italian bread (such as
      Lisa's Country Rustic Bread, page
      186) or excellent-quality store-
      bought)

    4 tablespoons fresh basil leaves,
      chopped

1. In a Dutch oven or a 6-quart pasta pot, cook the leek and the hot pepper in half the olive oil for about 7 minutes until the leek has softened. Add the tomatoes and the vegetable broth. Bring the mixture to a boil and then lower the heat to a simmer for 30 minutes.

2. Tear the slices of bread into pieces and stir them into the soup. Add the basil and stir it in. Remove the soup from the stove. Cover the pot with a lid and let it rest for 10 minutes. Stir the soup with a large whisk until all the ingredients are well combined. The soup will be very thick.

3. Divide the soup among 8 bowls and drizzle a little olive oil on each of them.

Pollo Arrosto con Funghi
Pan-Roasted Chicken with Mushrooms

8– 10 pieces of chicken of your choice (if you like all white meat, you can have 4 breasts and 4 wings; otherwise you can mix with thighs and legs)

2 cups white wine vinegar

1 cup extra virgin olive oil

4 carrots, peeled and chopped

4 celery stalks, chopped

2 onions, chopped

2 tablespoons fresh sage leaves, chopped

2 cups dry white wine

2 pounds cremini mushrooms, sliced

1 teaspoon Sicilian sea salt, fine

½ teaspoon freshly ground black pepper

1. Place the chicken pieces in a large bowl and cover them with the vinegar. Allow the chicken to rest for 10 minutes. Pour the olive oil into a large frying pan over medium-high heat, and place the chicken, skin side down, in the hot oil to brown for 4 minutes. Turn the chicken pieces over and brown them on the other side for 4 more minutes. Remove the chicken pieces from the pan and place them on a platter. Leave the oil in the pan. Add the carrots, celery, onion, and sage to the pan, and sauté them for 5 minutes, stirring frequently.

2. Place the chicken back in the pan with the vegetables. Pour in the wine. Add the mushrooms, salt, and pepper. Cook the mixture over medium to high heat for 40 minutes, until all the vegetables are very soft and the chicken is cooked through. Transfer the chicken and vegetables to a platter and serve.

Torta di Patate al Formaggio
Cheesy Potato Torte

4 pounds Yukon gold potatoes

4 eggs

1 teaspoon Sicilian sea salt, fine

½ teaspoon freshly ground black pepper

12 tablespoons unsalted butter

1 cup Parmigiano Reggiano

6 ounces Mozzarella

6 ounces smoked Provolone

1½ cups breadcrumbs

1. Peel the potatoes, cut them into cubes, and boil them for approximately 20 minutes until they're soft. Drain the potatoes and mash them in a large bowl with a potato masher. Add the eggs, salt, pepper, half the butter, and all the Parmigiano Reggiano to the potatoes in the bowl. Stir the mixture until all the ingredients are well blended.

2. Slice the mozzarella and the smoked provolone and set it aside.

3. Butter a 13 × 9-inch casserole dish and sprinkle the bottom with the breadcrumbs. Add half the potato mixture to the dish and flatten it with the back of a spatula. Arrange the slices of mozzarella and provolone on top of the potato mixture. Add the remaining potatoes and flatten them with the spatula. Top the potatoes with the rest of the breadcrumbs and a few pads of the remaining butter. Bake the torte in a preheated 400°F oven for 10–15 minutes, or until it is golden on top.

Biscotti per il Matrimonio Italiano
Italian Wedding Cookies

For the Cookie Batter

6 eggs

1 cup granulated sugar

2 teaspoons pure vanilla extract

1 cup butter, unsalted and melted

4 cups all-purpose flour, unbleached

4 teaspoons baking powder

½ teaspoon Sicilian sea salt, fine

For the Frosting

½ tablespoon unsalted butter, softened

2 cups confectioners' sugar

2 teaspoons pure vanilla extract

1 cup whole milk

1 jar (about 1 ounce) rainbow nonpareils/
sprinkles for decoration (optional)

1. *To make the cookies:* Beat the eggs, sugar, vanilla, and butter in the bowl of an electric mixer until all the ingredients are well combined. Add the flour, baking powder, and salt to the egg mixture and blend well.

2. Preheat the oven to 375°F.

3. Drop the dough, ½ tablespoon at a time, onto an ungreased baking sheet. Bake the cookies for 10 minutes, and then transfer them to a cooling rack.

4. *To make the frosting:* Mix the butter, confectioners' sugar, and vanilla in a medium-size bowl, and add just enough of the milk to make a soft, creamy frosting. Spread the cookies with the frosting and sprinkle the nonpareils on top, if you like.

My children on our balcony in Florence, overlooking the Ponte Vecchio, when they were young.

Funghi Ripieni con Spinaci Spinach-Stuffed Mushrooms

Ribollita Tuscan Bread and Bean Soup

Involtino di Manzo con Ricotta e Spinaci
Pork Rolls Stuffed with Ricotta and Spinach

Rucola con Pecorino Arugula with Pecorino

Torta di Pera e Cioccolato Chocolate and Pear Tart

I had the very good fortune of making some wonderful friendships when I lived in Tuscany. The most enduring friendships were with the mothers of my children's friends, one of whom was raised on a beautiful farm just outside of Florence. Her daughter and my son Guido are the same age, and have been friends since they were born. One evening, she made the best *ribollita* I had ever had, and told me it was her mother's recipe. I have treasured the recipe ever since, and not a fall goes by that I don't make it!

The two most famous Tuscan soups are *Pappa al Pomodoro* (page 268) and *Ribollita*, both of which are delicious and healthy. The black Swiss chard, which is called for in the ribollita, grows in Tuscany, but it really doesn't exist in the United States. I have searched all the farmers' markets in my area of the Midwest, but to no avail. The closest thing I've found, in texture and taste, is Tuscan kale. This soup is excellent the next day or two days after you first serve it, so make a double batch and have it on Tuesday!

Mangia bene, ridi spesso, ama molto! (Eat well, laugh often, and love much!)

Funghi Ripieni con Spinaci
Spinach-Stuffed Mushrooms

16 ounces fresh spinach or 12 ounces frozen spinach, thawed

4 tablespoons unsalted butter, plus more for greasing the baking dish

2 tablespoons onion, chopped

¼ cup prosciutto, chopped

⅓ cup heavy cream

½ cup Parmigiano Reggiano, grated

⅛ teaspoon ground nutmeg

1 teaspoon Sicilian sea salt, fine

½ teaspoon freshly ground black pepper

14–16 large white button mushrooms, stems removed

1. Preheat the oven to 400°F. Butter a 13 × 9-inch baking dish.

2. Place the spinach in a large frying pan and cook it for about 3 minutes over medium heat until the spinach has wilted. When the spinach is done, place it in a colander to drain off any liquid from the spinach, and let it cool at room temperature. Wrap the spinach in paper towels and squeeze them over the kitchen sink to extract all the liquid from the spinach. Finely chop the spinach.

3. Heat 2 tablespoons of the butter in a large skillet and cook the onion for 5 minutes over medium heat. Stir in the spinach and the prosciutto. Add the cream and bring the mixture to a low boil. Turn off the heat under the pan, stir in the cheese, nutmeg, salt, and pepper. Arrange the mushroom caps in the casserole dish and spoon the spinach mixture into the mushroom caps. Melt the remaining 2 tablespoons of butter and brush it over the mushrooms. Bake the mushrooms in the oven for 30 minutes.

Ribollita
Tuscan Bread and Bean Soup

1 pound (5–6 cups) country-style Italian rustic bread (either purchased or make Lisa's Country Rustic Bread, page 186), torn into 1-inch pieces

1 cup extra virgin olive oil

2 onions, chopped

10 garlic cloves, chopped

4 parsnips (about 2 cups), peeled and cut into ½-inch cubes

2 carrots, peeled and chopped

2 celery stalks, chopped

1 teaspoon crushed red pepper

2 (28-ounce) cans crushed San Marzano tomatoes

1 sprig rosemary

1 sprig sage

6 sprigs thyme

1 large piece (about 4 inches long and 2 inches high) Parmigiano Reggiano cheese rind (see Tip)

½ cup Italian flat leaf parsley, chopped

2 pounds Tuscan kale (or green kale)

2 (15-ounce) cans large cannellini beans, preferably imported, rinsed and drained

2 teaspoons Sicilian sea salt, fine

1 teaspoon freshly ground black pepper

1 cup Parmigiano Reggiano cheese, grated

1. Place the torn bread on a jelly-roll pan and bake it at 300°F for about an hour, or until it is crisp, but not brown.

2. Add the olive oil to a large (8- to 10-quart) stockpot. Add the onions and cook them over medium heat for 8–10 minutes, or until they are translucent. Add the garlic and cook the mixture for 3 more minutes. Stir in the parsnips, carrots, and celery. Sauté the mixture for 5 more minutes, and then add the crushed red pepper and the tomatoes.

3. Tie the rosemary, sage, and thyme into a bunch with some kitchen twine. Add the herbs to the pot, along with the rind of the Parmigiano, and add the chopped parsley. Add enough water to cover all the vegetables (approximately 10 cups), and bring the mixture to a simmer over medium to high heat. Cover the pot, reduce the heat to low, and simmer the mixture for 1 hour. Discard the herb bundle and the rind of Parmigiano Reggiano. Stir in the chopped kale or Swiss chard and the beans. Cook the soup for 20 more minutes. Stir in the toasted bread until it is soaked, and add the salt and pepper. Ladle the soup into bowls and serve.

Soups in Italy are delicious! They seem to have an extra layer of flavor. Here's one of the secrets to that extra flavor: After you have grated your Parmigiano cheese down to approximately ¼ inch from the rind, set the rind aside and save it for making homemade soup. If you won't be making soup for a while, freeze the rind. When you are making soup such as Ribollita, and you allow the Parmigiano Reggiano rind to simmer in the soup as it cooks, the cheese melts off the rind into the soup, giving it an extra dimension of flavor, and the rind itself melts and becomes stringy, almost like mozzarella cheese. The rind is completely edible, as it is simply the outside layer of the cheese that forms during the aging process.

In typical Tuscan tradition, Ribollita is served to the olive grove workers, after a long day of harvesting the olives.

Involtino di Manzo con Ricotta e Spinaci
Pork Rolls Stuffed with Ricotta and Spinach

1 cup whole milk ricotta cheese

16 ounces spinach, chopped

1 teaspoon Sicilian sea salt, fine

½ teaspoon freshly ground black pepper

1 teaspoon ground nutmeg

2 pounds boneless pork loin, sliced into 16 pieces

16 slices pancetta (Italian bacon) or use good-quality American bacon if you can't find pancetta

1 cup extra virgin olive oil

2 cups white wine

1. In a medium-sized bowl, mix the ricotta, spinach, salt, pepper, and nutmeg. Mix well.

2. Place a slice of pork between 2 pieces of parchment paper and pound it with a rolling pin until it is about ¼ inch thick. Repeat with all the pork slices. Place a layer of the spinach mixture on each slice of pork, and roll it up. Wrap the rolled pork with a slice of pancetta and secure the roll with a toothpick. Repeat with the rest of the pork slices.

3. Place the olive oil in a large frying pan over medium heat and sear the pork rolls for approximately 2 minutes on each side. Add the wine, stir, and use a wooden spoon to scrape up the brown bits from the bottom of the pan. Turn the rolls over a few times in the pan to ensure that they cook evenly, over medium heat, for about 10 minutes.

Rucola di Pecorino
Arugula with Pecorino

For the Dressing

1 teaspoon Sicilian sea salt, fine

3 tablespoons red wine vinegar

½ cup extra virgin olive oil

½ teaspoon freshly ground black pepper

For the Salad

8 cups arugula

2 ripe, but firm pears (Bosc or d'Anjou), cored and thinly sliced

1½ cups Pecorino Romano cheese, finely shaved or grated

1. To make the dressing: Place the salt in a small bowl. Pour the vinegar over the salt and whisk until the salt has dissolved into the vinegar. Add the olive oil slowly into the vinegar, whisking constantly until the mixture thickens. Stir in the black pepper.

2. *To assemble the salad*: Combine the arugula and pears in a large bowl and toss them with the dressing. Top the salad with the shaved Pecorino Romano and serve.

This Is Sunday Dinner

Torta di Pera e Cioccolato
Chocolate and Pear Tart

For the Pastry

1¼ cups flour

¼ teaspoon baking powder

Pinch of salt

⅓ cup sugar

1 stick, plus 1 tablespoon butter, cold, sliced

1 egg yolk

For the Filling

4 ripe pears

4 tablespoons sugar

6 tablespoons Grand Marnier (or another orange liqueur of excellent quality)

6 ounces semisweet chocolate

6 tablespoons unsalted butter

½ cup heavy cream

½ cup almonds, chopped

1. *To make the pastry:* Combine the flour, baking powder, salt, and sugar. Make a well in the center of the flour mixture and add the butter and egg yolk. Knead the mixture into a soft dough, adding a few drops of ice water, if the dough becomes too stiff. Work the ingredients together by hand or with a pastry blender. (This can be done in a stand mixer by simply placing all the ingredients in a mixing bowl, with the paddle on medium speed.)

2. Roll out the dough to about ⅛-inch thickness. Line a 9- or 9½-inch fluted, loose-bottomed tart or quiche mold with the dough and prick it with a fork. Cover the pastry and chill it in the fridge for 30 minutes.

3. Preheat the oven to 325°F.

4. *To make the tart:* Preheat the oven to 325°F. Sprinkle 2 tablespoons of the sugar over the crust. Peel, core, and slice the pears. Place the pears on the crust and sprinkle them with the Grand Marnier and the remaining sugar. Bake the tart for 15 minutes.

5. Melt the chocolate and butter in a small saucepan over very low heat for approximately 5 minutes. Remove the pan from the heat and let it cool. Remove the pears from the oven. Place the pears in the pie pan, directly on the crust.

6. Using a whisk or a handheld mixer, whip the heavy cream until it forms stiff peaks, and gently fold it into the chocolate mixture. Spread the chocolate mixture over the pears, sprinkle the almonds on top, and serve.

Menu 46

SERVES 8

Involtini di Prosciutto Prosciutto Roll-ups

Rotelle con Ragù alle Salsiccie Rotelle with Sausage Ragù

Arista con Fichi e Salsa di Chianti di Lisa
Lisa's Pork Loin with Fig and Chianti Sauce

Piselli Fiorentini Peas, Florentine Style

Mousse al Cioccolato e Grand Marnier di Guido
Guido's Grand Marnier Chocolate Mousse

As I've mentioned, my daughter Felicia's Sicilian Tomato Sauce (page 229) makes me so proud, and in this menu, my son Guido, who is an outstanding cook, shares his decadent, melt in your mouth, chocolate mousse recipe. He makes this every Christmas Day for our family and everyone looks forward to it!

Cooking with your children is a gift you give to them and to yourself: It creates memories for you both and (if you're lucky!) your children become wonderful cooks, and continue to cook with you, even when they are grown!

The *pork dish* in this menu has become one of my signature dishes. I learned how to make and use a wonderful Chianti reduction when I lived in Tuscany and, since I love fig with pork, I decided to combine the two—now I am known for my fig and Chianti sauce. The bold taste of the wine reduces to a velvety consistency and the sweetness of the fig lends just the right contrast. This dish will quickly become a "regular" on your Sunday dinner table.

Che bontá! (Such goodness!)

Involtini di Prosciutto
Prosciutto Roll-ups

- 6 ounces (½ cup) ricotta cheese
- 6 ounces (½ cup) Gorgonzola cheese, crumbled
- 2 tablespoons heavy cream
- 18 slices prosciutto, sliced very thin
- 2 pears, cored, peeled, and cut lengthwise into ⅛-inch-thin slices

In a small bowl, blend the ricotta, the gorgonzola, and the heavy cream. With a butter knife, spread the cheese mixture evenly over each slice of the prosciutto and place 1 slice of pear on top. Roll up the prosciutto and serve.

Rotelle con Ragù alle Salsiccie
Rotelle with Sausage Ragù

For the Ragù

- ¾ cup extra virgin olive oil
- 1 carrot, peeled and minced
- 1 celery stalk, minced
- 1 onion, minced
- 4 cloves garlic, minced
- ½ cup Italian flat leaf parsley, minced
- 4 Italian sausages, casings removed (may be sweet, hot, or mixed)
- 1 teaspoon Sicilian sea salt, fine
- ⅛ teaspoon crushed red pepper
- ½ teaspoon freshly ground black pepper
- 1½ cups red wine
- 2 tablespoons tomato paste (preferably imported Italian *concentrato di pomodoro*)
- 2 cups crushed San Marzano tomatoes

For the Pasta

- 2 pounds rotelle or pasta wheels

1. *To make the ragù:* Pour the olive oil into a 4- to 6-quart soup pot and sauté the carrot, celery, onion, garlic, and parsley. Add the sausage, salt, crushed red pepper, and black pepper. Sauté the mixture until the sausage is brown, stirring often. Add the red wine and cook over medium-low until approximately half the wine evaporates. Add the tomato paste and stir it into the wine and sausage mixture. Add the San Marzano tomatoes. Simmer the ragù over low heat for approximately 40 minutes.

2. *To make the pasta:* About 10–15 minutes before the sausage ragù is done, cook the pasta according to the directions on the package. When it is *al dente*, drain the pasta and toss it with the ragù.

Arista con Fichi e Salsa di Chianti di Lisa

Lisa's Pork Loin with Fig and Chianti Sauce

For the Fig and Chianti Sauce

3 cups Chianti

2 cups vegetable broth

16–18 black figs, dried, chopped

4 sprigs fresh rosemary

6 tablespoons unsalted butter

1 teaspoon Sicilian sea salt, fine

½ teaspoon freshly ground black pepper

1 (12-ounce) jar imported Italian fig jam, such as Casa Giulia

For the Pork

1 (5-pound) boneless pork loin

4 tablespoons extra virgin olive oil

2 teaspoons freshly ground black pepper

2 teaspoons Sicilian sea salt, fine

1. *To make the Fig and Chianti sauce:* In a medium-size saucepan combine the Chianti, vegetable broth, figs, and rosemary. Simmer the mixture over medium to high heat until it has reduced by half. Remove the rosemary (reserve it to use on the pork) and puree the mixture in a blender until it is smooth. Return the mixture to the saucepan and blend in the butter until it has melted. Add the salt and pepper to the sauce. Add 4 large tablespoons of the fig jam to the saucepan. Heat the sauce over low heat until the jam dissolves.

2. Preheat the oven to 400°F.

3. Cover the pork loin with the extra virgin olive oil, rosemary, salt, and pepper. Place the pork on a rack in a large 16 × 12 roasting pan and roast it for 1 hour. Slice the pork on a platter and pour the Fig and Chianti sauce over the top.

Piselli Fiorentini

Peas, Florentine Style

2 pounds fresh peas

½ cup extra virgin olive oil

3 garlic cloves, chopped

½ pound pancetta

¼ cup Italian flat leaf parsley, chopped

1 teaspoon sugar

1 teaspoon Sicilian sea salt, fine

1. Cook the peas in a medium-size saucepan with enough water to cover the peas. Simmer on low for 30 minutes. Drain the peas and set them aside.

2. Place the oil in a medium-size frying pan and sauté the garlic, pancetta, parsley, sugar, and salt. Pour the peas into the frying pan and sauté them for 2–3 minutes in the garlic and pancetta sauce.

Mousse al Cioccolato e Grand Marnier di Guido

Guido's Grand Marnier
Chocolate Mousse

8 ounces semisweet chocolate, chopped

4 ounces bittersweet chocolate, chopped

½ cup Grand Marnier liqueur

¼ cup water

1 teaspoon pure vanilla extract

1 teaspoon grated orange zest

2 sticks unsalted butter, softened at room temperature, but not melted

10 extra-large eggs, separated

¾ cup sugar

¾ cup heavy cream

1. Combine the semisweet and bittersweet chocolate, Grand Marnier, water, and vanilla in a heat-proof bowl. Place the bowl over a simmering pan of water until the chocolate melts. Let the mixture cool, and then whisk in the orange zest and butter until well mixed.

2. Beat the egg yolks and half the sugar in an electric mixer on high, until the mixture is very thick. With the mixer speed on low, add the chocolate mixture. Transfer the egg yolk and chocolate mixture to a large bowl.

3. In a separate bowl, whip the heavy cream until soft peaks form, adding the remaining sugar to the cream.

4. Place the egg whites in the bowl of an electric mixer and whisk or beat them on high, until firm peaks form. Very gently fold the beaten egg whites (meringue) and the whipped cream into the egg yolk–and–chocolate mixture. Pour the mousse into individual dishes or a large bowl and chill for approximately 30 minutes before serving.

Menu 47

Bruschetta di Formaggio e Pomodori Secchi
Cheese and Sun-Dried Tomato Toasts

Pasta al Forno Baked Pasta

Cotoletti di Vitello Cotte Due Volte Twice-Cooked Veal Cutlets

Cipolline con Pomodori Arrostiti Roasted Tomatoes with Cipolline

Ciambellone con Mascarpone Ciambellone with Mascarpone

From north to south, east to west, if there is one dish that unites all of Italy it is *Pasta al Forno*! Each region makes it slightly differently, but I love the Tuscan version: the *besciamella*, plus my three-meat *ragù*, makes this *Pasta al Forno* absolutely perfect! It has been my go-to dish with my children ever since they were small—it has everything everyone loves: creamy *besciamella*, hearty meat sauce, and lots of cheese! And everyone can contribute to making this dish—one person can make the pasta, another can make the ragù, and a third can grate the cheese. It is definitely a family dish!

The signature dessert of Tuscany is *ciambellone*. This is not a dessert that you eat in the city of Florence, but rather in the outlying areas of Tuscany. Since my children and I love to go to *sagre* (food festivals) in the countryside, we always end with a slice of *ciambellone*. The word literally means a large doughnut, as it is shaped just like a large doughnut. The consistency is similar to pound cake and I love to serve it with a dollop of mascarpone, for a little elegance. In the countryside, *ciambellone* is frequently served with chocolate sauce, which is also delicious!

Bruschetta di Formaggio e Pomodori Secchi

Cheese and Sun-Dried Tomato Toasts

- 1 filone (long, thin Italian bread, resembling a baguette)
- ¼ cup extra virgin olive oil
- 1 cup sun-dried tomato paste
- 1 pound fresh mozzarella, drained and diced into cubes
- 2 teaspoons dried oregano
- ¼ teaspoon freshly ground black pepper

1. Preheat the oven to 400°F.

2. Slice the bread on a diagonal, about ½ inch thick. Brush the oil on one side of each of the slices, using a pastry brush, and then toast them under the broiler until they turn golden brown.

3. Spread the sun-dried tomato paste on the toast and top with a few cubes of the fresh mozzarella. Sprinkle with oregano and ground black pepper. Place the toasts back on the large baking sheet, drizzle with olive oil and bake in the preheated oven for 5 minutes until the cheese has melted. Serve.

Pasta al Forno

Baked Pasta

For Lisa's Besciamella Sauce

- ¼ cup butter
- 1 cup all-purpose flour
- 2 cups whole milk

For Lisa's Ragù

- 1 cup extra virgin olive oil
- 1 cup white onion, chopped
- 1 green bell pepper, chopped
- 1 pound ground veal
- 1 pound ground Italian sausage
- 1 pound ground sirloin
- 6 ounces tomato paste (*concentrato di pomodoro*, preferably imported from Italy in the tube)
- 1 (26-ounce) can imported San Marzano tomatoes, chopped
- 1 (26-ounce) can crushed imported San Marzano tomatoes
- 1 teaspoon chopped fresh basil
- 1 teaspoon oregano
- 1 teaspoon Sicilian sea salt, fine
- ½ teaspoon freshly ground black pepper
- 2 tablespoons sugar
- 2 garlic cloves, chopped
- 1 cup Parmigiano Reggiano, grated
- 1 cup Pecorino Romano, grated

For the Pasta

- 2 pounds rigatoni

1. To make the besciamella: Melt the butter in a large frying pan. With a wooden spoon, stir the flour into the butter until it is well combined. Slowly pour in the milk, stirring constantly with a wooden spoon, until you have a thick, velvety sauce that coats the back of the spoon.

2. *To make the ragù:* Place the olive oil in a large frying pan and sauté the onion and green pepper until the onion is transparent. Place the onion and the green pepper into a large 6-quart pasta pot.

3. In the same frying pan in which you sautéed the onion and green pepper, brown the veal, Italian sausage, and ground sirloin. Add the meat to the pasta pot. Add the tomato paste, chopped tomatoes, crushed tomatoes, basil, oregano, salt, pepper, sugar, and garlic, and cook the mixture over low heat for at least 1 hour.

4. *To make the pasta and assemble the dish:* Cook the rigatoni for 4 minutes less than the directions on the package. Drain the pasta and toss it with the ragù and 1½ cups of the Parmigiano and Pecorino.

5. Preheat the oven to 350°F.

6. Lightly oil a 13 × 9-inch baking dish, at least 3- to 4-inches deep. Spread half the besciamella on the bottom of the baking dish. Pour the tossed pasta on top of the besciamella. Cover the top of the pasta with the remaining besciamella. Smooth the top and sprinkle it with ½ cup of Parmigiano Reggiano. Bake the pasta for 30 minutes, until it is lightly browned on top, and serve.

Cotoletti di Vitello Cotte Due Volte
Twice-Cooked Veal Cutlets

For the Sauce

1 cup extra virgin olive oil

4 cloves garlic, chopped

½ cup Italian flat leaf parsley, chopped

8 basil leaves, chopped

2 pounds fresh tomatoes, chopped

1 teaspoon Sicilian sea salt, fine

½ teaspoon freshly ground black pepper

¼ teaspoon crushed red pepper

½ teaspoon dried rosemary

½ teaspoon dried sage

For the Veal

2 cups extra virgin olive oil

2 cups breadcrumbs

3 large eggs, beaten

8 veal cutlets, lightly pounded, ¼-inch thick

1 teaspoon Sicilian sea salt, fine

1. *To make the sauce:* Pour the olive oil into a large frying pan. Add the garlic, parsley, and basil to the pan, and sauté over low heat for 4 minutes. Add the tomatoes to the pan, and let the mixture simmer for 20 minutes. Add the salt, black pepper, and crushed red pepper. Set the sauce aside.

2. *To prepare the veal and assemble the dish:* Heat the oil over medium heat in a large, deep, frying pan. Place the breadcrumbs in a shallow bowl and the eggs in another shallow bowl. Dip the veal cutlets, on both sides, into the egg and then into the breadcrumbs. Place the cutlets into the hot oil in the frying pan and cook them for about 3 minutes on each side, until both sides are a light-golden brown. Transfer the cutlets to a platter covered with paper towels, and let them drain. Arrange the cutlets on an ovenproof platter or casserole dish, pour the sauce on top, place the cutlets in a 350°F oven for 10 minutes, and serve.

Cipolline con Pomodori Arrostiti
Roasted Tomatoes with Cipolline

2 pounds Yukon gold potatoes, peeled and cut into ½-inch cubes

2 pounds cipolline onions* (see description below)

1 fennel bulb, cored and cut in slices

1 cup extra virgin olive oil

1 teaspoon Sicilian sea salt, fine

½ teaspoon freshly ground black pepper

2 cups cherry tomatoes, halved

2 cups cooked cannellini beans, preferably imported

1 teaspoon thyme

1. Preheat the oven to 400°F.

2. Place the potatoes, onions, and fennel in a roasting pan. Add the olive oil to the vegetables and coat them well. Season the mixture with the salt and pepper.

3. Roast for 30 minutes. Remove the pan from the oven, add the tomatoes, and roast the mixture for another 10 minutes. Remove the pan from oven, add the cannellini beans and thyme, and roast the mixture for another 5 minutes. Serve.

This Is Sunday Dinner

★ Cipolline onions are small, flat round onions with
a delicate, sweet taste. They are very popular in
Tuscany and, fortunately, are now readily available
at Farmer's Markets here in the US.

Ciambellone con Mascarpone
Ciambellone with Mascarpone

For the Ciambellone Cake

Butter, for greasing the pan

5 cups unbleached all-purpose flour,
plus more for dusting the pan

5 large eggs

2½ cups sugar

1 cup whole milk

1 cup extra virgin olive oil

1 tablespoon lemon zest

2 tablespoons fresh lemon juice

1½ teaspoons baking powder

½ teaspoon Sicilian sea salt, fine

8 ounces mascarpone cheese,
preferably imported from Italy

For the Topping and Garnish

½ cup heavy cream

3 tablespoons sugar

6 ounces fresh blackberries

6 ounces fresh raspberries

1. *To make the cake:* Preheat the oven to
400°F.

2. Lightly butter and flour a 12-inch tube pan
(or a Bundt pan, if you don't have a tube pan).
Whisk the eggs in the bowl of a stand mixer or
in a large mixing bowl with a handheld mixer,
and add the sugar. Stir in the milk, olive oil,
lemon zest, and lemon juice. Slowly mix in the
flour, baking powder, and salt.

3. Pour the batter into the prepared pan and
bake the cake for 45 minutes, or until the top
is golden. Remove the cake from the oven and
let it cool completely. Invert the cake onto a
platter.

4. *To prepare the topping and garnish:* Place the
heavy cream in a mixing bowl and beat until
soft peaks begin to form. Add the sugar. To
serve, place a dollop of the mascarpone cheese
on each slice of the cake, and then a dollop of
cream on top of the mascarpone. Sprinkle the
berries over the top.

I had a wonderfully kind, generous, and sweet uncle Mark, from Sicily. Of course, as is typical in Italian families, he really wasn't my uncle. He was married to my Sicilian grandmother's cousin, but out of respect we called him "Uncle Mark". He had a very heavy Italian accent, and also had an absolutely magnificent vegetable garden in his backyard, on the famous hill (the Italian neighborhood) of Saint Louis.

My father adored Uncle Mark. Each time we arrived at Uncle Mark's house, he would insist that my father come out to the garden so he could show him his beautiful vegetables. He would pick a huge tomato, hold it up in the air, and say to my father, "Roberto, this is a som-a-na-gun tomato!" My father would laugh every time he did this, and whenever we would see a large vegetable, we would all imitate Uncle Mark and call it a som-a-na-gun. So when I started making my meatballs, which are a little on the large side, my father would say, "Lisa! That's a som-a-na-gun meat-a-ball!," as Uncle Mark would say. Both my father and Uncle Mark are gone now, but every time I make meatballs or see a very large tomato, I can't help but smile and think of the two of them.

Antipasto ai Fagioli, Patate e Cipolle Rosse
Green Bean, Potato, and Red Onion Antipasto

- 1 tablespoon Sicilian sea salt, coarsely ground
- 2 pounds green beans, trimmed and cut into 1-inch pieces
- 6 large Yukon gold potatoes, cut into 1-inch cubes
- 1 cup extra virgin olive oil
- ¼ cup red wine vinegar, preferably imported
- 1 teaspoon Sicilian sea salt, fine
- ½ teaspoon freshly ground black pepper
- 1 red onion, thinly sliced
- 2 tablespoons Italian flat leaf parsley, chopped

1. Place the salt in a large pot of boiling water and cook the green beans for approximately 6 minutes, and then drain them. Fill another large pot with water and boil the potatoes for 20 minutes, or until they are tender.

2. In a measuring cup, mix the oil, vinegar, salt, and pepper. Place the green beans, potatoes, and onion in a large bowl and gently toss them together with the oil and vinegar in the bowl. Garnish with the fresh parsley and serve.

Pappardelle con Agnello e Ragù di Chianti
Pappardelle with Lamb and Chianti Ragù

For the Chianti Ragù
- ½ cup extra virgin olive oil
- 3 pounds ground lamb
- ½ cup carrots, chopped
- ½ cup onions, chopped
- ½ cup celery, chopped
- 3 tablespoons tomato paste, *concentrato di pomodoro*, preferably imported
- 2 cups Chianti
- 3 cups (24 ounces) imported, crushed San Marzano tomatoes
- 2 cups vegetable broth
- 2 sprigs fresh thyme
- 2 sprigs fresh rosemary
- 4 garlic cloves, chopped
- 1 teaspoon ground fennel seeds
- ½ teaspoon crushed red pepper flakes

For the Pasta
- 2 pounds pappardelle pasta
- 1 cup Pecorino Romano, grated
- 2 tablespoons unsalted butter
- 1 teaspoon Sicilian sea salt, fine
- ½ cup fresh mint, chopped

1. In a large 8- to 10-quart pot, heat the olive oil over medium to high heat. Brown the lamb in the oil, breaking it up into small pieces with the back of a wooden spoon while it cooks. Thoroughly cook the lamb until it turns brown. Place the lamb in a colander to drain off the fat.

2. Place the lamb back into the pot. Add the carrots, onions, and celery, and cook the vegetables on high until they're soft, approximately 3 minutes. Add the tomato paste and the Chianti, mixing them together thoroughly, until the wine reduces to about half. The heat should still be on high. Use a wooden spoon to continuously scrape brown bits of meat from the sides and off the bottom of the pan, into the mixture. Add the tomatoes, vegetable broth, thyme, rosemary, cloves, fennel, crushed red pepper flakes, butter, salt, and mint. Simmer the ragù for 2 hours over low to medium heat.

3. Fill a large pasta pot with water and bring it to a rolling boil. Add a handful of coarse Sicilian sea salt. Cook the pappardelle for 2 minutes. Drain the pasta and toss it with the lamb and Chianti ragù. Generously top with Pecorino Romano and serve.

LISA'S TIP

Pappardelle is fresh pasta. I would suggest you purchase it in the deli section of your supermarket or specialty store, and only purchase fresh pasta from Italy, such as Rana or Buitoni. If I can find pappardelle in Indiana, I'm sure you can find it anywhere! Using fresh pasta from Italy with this recipe makes all the difference in the world, and that is why it is only cooked for 2 minutes—because it is fresh, not dry.

Polpettone
Lisa's Som-a-na-gun Meat-a-balls

- 3 pounds ground sirloin (85% lean)
- 2 pounds ground veal
- 2 pounds ground pork
- 2 cups breadcrumbs with Italian seasonings, plus more for rolling the meatballs
- 10 eggs
- 1 cup whole milk
- 1 cup Parmigiano Reggiano, grated
- 4 garlic cloves, chopped
- 2 teaspoons Sicilian sea salt, fine
- 1 teaspoon freshly grated black pepper
- ¼ cup Italian flat leaf parsley, chopped
- 2 cups extra virgin olive oil

1. In a large bowl, combine the ground sirloin, veal, and pork with the 2 cups of breadcrumbs, the eggs, milk, Parmigiano Reggiano, garlic, salt, pepper, and parsley. Shape the mixture into meatballs, each one a little larger than a golf ball.

2. Place the extra breadcrumbs in a large shallow bowl. Roll each meatball in the breadcrumbs.

3. Pour the oil into a large, deep frying pan over medium high, and fry each meatball, turning it to ensure that it is golden brown on all sides. Transfer the meatballs to 13 × 9-inch heat-proof glass casserole and bake them in a preheated 350°F oven for 20 minutes.

This Is Sunday Dinner

Sformato di Carciofi
Artichoke Tort

- ½ cup extra virgin olive oil
- 2 pounds frozen artichoke hearts
- 2 cloves garlic, chopped
- 1 tablespoon Italian flat leaf parsley, chopped
- 1 teaspoon Sicilian sea salt, fine
- ½ teaspoon freshly ground black pepper
- 1 cup white wine
- ½ teaspoon dried marjoram
- 1 pound whole milk ricotta
- 3 eggs
- 1 cup Parmigiano Reggiano, grated
- 4 tablespoons unsalted butter, plus more for greasing the baking dish
- 1 cup breadcrumbs

1. Place the olive oil in a large frying pan and fry the artichoke hearts with the garlic and parsley. Add the salt and pepper, the white wine, and the marjoram. Cook the mixture over medium heat for about 10 minutes until the wine reduces by half. Spoon the artichoke mixture into a large bowl and let it cool for 10 minutes.

2. Add the ricotta, eggs, and grated cheese to the artichoke mixture in the bowl and mix it well. Pour the mixture into a buttered 13 × 9-inch baking dish and sprinkle the breadcrumbs on top. Cut the 4 tablespoons of butter into small pieces and place them on top of the breadcrumbs. Bake the mixture at 300°F for 30 minutes.

Biscotti Intrecciati al Limone
Lemon-Knot Cookies

For the Cookie Dough

- 1 cup unsalted butter
- 1 cup granulated sugar
- 4 teaspoons grated lemon zest
- 4 large eggs
- ½ cup whole milk
- 2 tablespoons fresh lemon juice
- 4 cups all-purpose flour
- 1 teaspoon Sicilian sea salt, fine
- 3 teaspoons baking powder

For the Glaze

- 2 cups confectioners' sugar
- 2 tablespoons fresh lemon juice
- 2 teaspoons grated lemon zest

Decoration (Optional)

- 1 one-ounce package colored nonpareils

1. *To make the cookies:* Preheat the oven to 350°F.

2. In a stand mixer or with a handheld mixer, beat together butter and sugar until the mixture is light and fluffy. Add the lemon zest and the eggs, one at a time, until the mixture is well blended. Add the milk and the lemon juice and then add the flour, salt, and baking powder. Chill the cookie dough for at least 3 hours.

3. Line a baking sheet with parchment paper. Divide the dough into 3 balls. Cut each ball into 12 pieces. With your hands, roll each piece into a 6-inch snake or rope and tie it into a loose knot. Place the knots on the baking sheet, about 1 inch apart. Bake the cookies for 10–12 minutes and then let them cool for 5 minutes.

4. *To make the glaze and decorate the cookies:* Combine the confectioners' sugar, lemon juice, and lemon zest. The glaze will be thick. After the cookies have cooled, either brush the glaze on the cookies with a pastry brush or dip them upside down into the glaze. Add colorful nonpareils, if you like.

Menu 49

SERVES 8

Tortini di Funghi e Pecorino Mushroom and Pecorino Tarts
Zuppa Frantoiana Olive Harvest Soup
Pollo Arrostito con Vin Santo Roasted Chicken with Vin Santo
Timbalo di Verdure Verdi Green Vegetable Timbalo
Torta Capovolta di Prugne Upside-Down Plum Cake

Roasted chicken with Vin Santo! This is one of the most heavenly sauces you will ever make. Those of you who are familiar with Tuscan wines may know that Vin Santo is a dessert wine. The Tuscans use white grapes, such as the Trebbiano, and dry the grapes to make this sweet wine. The name Vin Santo literally means "holy wine," because it is believed that this wine was used for Mass in Renaissance Florence. One of my favorite desserts involves a very simple "ritual" we have in Tuscany—after dinner we have a glass of Vin Santo and dip our crunchy biscotti into the wine. This is one of the simplest, yet most delicious, desserts you will ever have. In this menu, I also make a delectable, golden reduction for roasted chicken with Vin Santo.

Zuppa Frantoiana means "Olive-Pressers' Soup," and it comes by its name because it is made during the harvest season, while everyone is pressing the olives for a new batch of olive oil! It's a fabulous soup because it is hearty and delicious but, best of all, you can put everything in the pot at once, and let it cook!

Alla vostra! (To you!)

Tortini di Funghi e Pecorino
Mushroom and Pecorino Tarts

1 package puff pastry (2 sheets)

6 tablespoons extra virgin olive oil

8 ounces cremini mushrooms

8 ounces white button mushrooms

4 tablespoons pine nuts

1 tablespoon oregano

1 teaspoon Sicilian sea salt, fine

½ teaspoon freshly ground black pepper

1 cup Pecorino Romano, grated

1. Roll out the puff pastry. Cut each sheet into 8 squares.

2. Preheat the oven to 400°F.

3. Heat the olive oil in a large frying pan. Add the cremini and white button mushrooms and cook them over low heat until they are soft. Drain the mushrooms in a colander to dispose of all the liquid. Let the mushrooms cool. Transfer the mushrooms to a medium-size bowl. Mix in the pine nuts, oregano, and salt and pepper.

4. Line 2 baking sheets or jelly-roll pans with parchment paper or a silpat. Place the puff pastry squares on the baking sheets or jelly-roll pans and prick the pastry with a fork 2 or 3 times. Place 1–1½ teaspoons of the mushroom mixture on each of the squares, leaving a ½-inch border of the pastry uncovered. Place the grated cheese on top of the mushroom mixture. Bake the tarts in the oven for 10 minutes until the pastry is golden.

Zuppa Frantoiana
Olive Harvest Soup

2 cups extra virgin olive oil, plus more for brushing on the bread

2 onions, chopped

3 carrots, peeled and chopped

4 celery sticks, chopped

6 slices pancetta (or bacon)

4 garlic cloves, chopped

12 large individual leaves Swiss chard

2 cups butternut squash, peeled, seeded, and cubed

4 potatoes, cut into ½-inch cubes

2 (12-ounce) cans Italian borlotti beans

2 teaspoons fennel seeds

2 teaspoons Sicilian sea salt, fine

1 teaspoon freshly ground black pepper

Rustic Italian bread (either purchased or make Lisa's Country Rustic Bread, page 186), cut into 12 (½-inch-thick) slices

1. Pour the olive oil into an 8-quart pot. Place the onions, carrots, celery, pancetta or bacon, and the garlic in the olive oil, and cook over medium heat for 8 minutes. Add the Swiss chard, butternut squash, and the potatoes and cook for 20 more minutes, or until the vegetables are wilted and soft. Add the borlotti beans, the fennel seeds, and the salt and pepper. Cook the soup for 30 minutes over medium heat.

2. Meanwhile, brush the bread with olive oil and sprinkle a little salt and pepper on top. Toast the bread in the oven for 5 minutes. To serve, place 1 slice of the bread in a deep soup bowl and ladle the soup over the bread.

Pollo Arrostito con Vin Santo
Roasted Chicken with Vin Santo

½ cup extra virgin olive oil, plus more
for greasing the pan or casserole
dishes

2 garlic cloves, chopped

3 tablespoons Italian seasoning (see
Note)

5 pounds chicken, cut in pieces

2 teaspoons Sicilian sea salt, fine

1 teaspoon freshly ground black
pepper

3 cups Vin Santo

★ *Note:* Italian seasoning is a blend that you can buy in
the spice aisle of your supermarket. It is a mixture of
dried herbs that includes basil, oregano, rosemary,
marjoram, sage, and thyme.

1. Preheat the oven to 400°F.

2. Oil 1 large roasting pan or 2 medium-size
casserole dishes.

3. In a medium-size bowl, combine the garlic
and Italian seasonings. Loosen the skin from
each piece of chicken and place the herb
mixture and garlic between the meat of the
chicken and the skin. Rub the chicken very
well with the olive oil and season it generously
with salt and pepper. Place the chicken, skin
side down, on the roasting pan or casserole
dishes and roast it for 15 minutes. Turn the
pieces over and roast them for 15 minutes
more. Turn the chicken again, skin side down,
and roast it for 30 minutes more.

4. Transfer the chicken pieces to a serving
platter and cover them with aluminum

foil. Leave the juice from the chicken in the
roasting pan (or the casserole dishes, if you
used them) and add the wine simmering over
medium to high heat. Scrape up the brown
bits from the bottom of the pan. Increase the
flame to high and cook the liquid until it is
reduced by half. The Vin Santo will make the
liquid thick and golden. Drizzle the Vin Santo
sauce over the roasted chicken and serve.

Timbalo di Verdure Verdi
Green Vegetable Timbalo

2 pounds white or yellow potatoes

2 pounds fresh spinach

4 tablespoons extra virgin olive oil

2 medium onions, chopped

4 cloves garlic, chopped

4 tablespoons unsalted butter, cut into ½-inch cubes, plus more for greasing the pan

3 tablespoons Italian flat leaf parsley, chopped

1 teaspoon Sicilian sea salt, fine

½ teaspoon freshly ground black pepper

½ teaspoon freshly grated nutmeg

4 eggs

½ cup heavy cream

1 cup Parmigiano Reggiano, grated

1. Wash the potatoes very well and cut them into 1-inch cubes. Place the potatoes in a large pot of boiling water and cook them for 20 minutes, or until they are very soft. Wash the spinach thoroughly and dry it off with paper towels. Chop the spinach and set it aside.

2. Place the oil in a large frying pan, and sauté the spinach with the onions and garlic over medium heat, being careful not to burn the garlic. Drain the liquid out of the pan from the spinach.

3. Preheat the oven to 350°F. Grease a round, 8-inch heat-proof glass or ceramic baking dish. Place the spinach and the parsley in a blender and puree it. Transfer the mixture to a bowl and season it with the salt, pepper, and nutmeg.

4. In a large bowl, use a handheld whisk to combine the eggs and cream. Add the potatoes, the spinach puree, and half the grated Parmigiano to the bowl. Fill the baking dish with the potato-spinach mixture and sprinkle the remaining Parmigiano over the top. Dot the top of the timbalo with the butter and bake it in the oven for 20 minutes.

Torta Capovolta di Prugne
Upside-Down Plum Cake

For the Cake

- 1 cup sugar
- 1 cup water
- 2 sticks unsalted butter, softened
- 8 medium-size plums, pitted and cut into wedges
- ½ cup mascarpone
- 4 tablespoons whole milk
- 2 teaspoons pure vanilla extract
- 2 cups unbleached all-purpose flour
- 1 cup sugar
- 1 teaspoon baking powder
- ½ teaspoon baking soda
- ½ teaspoon Sicilian sea salt, fine
- 2 large eggs

1. Combine the sugar and water in a small saucepan and bring it to a boil. Turn off the heat and whisk in 1 stick of the butter. Pour the mixture into a deep 9-inch round metal or heat-proof glass cake pan. Arrange the plum wedges in the sugar and butter mixture in a circular design.

2. Preheat the oven to 350°F.

3. Combine the mascarpone with the milk and vanilla in large bowl, using a handheld or stand mixer. Mix in the flour and sugar, baking powder, baking soda, and salt. Add the remaining stick of butter until the mixture is very crumbly. Then beat in the eggs until they're well incorporated. Beat the batter for another 2 minutes until it is light and fluffy.

4. Pour the batter over the plums and bake the cake for 45 minutes or until a toothpick comes out clean from the center of the cake. To serve, place a slice of the cake upside down on a plate, so that the plums are visible.

Menu 50

SERVES 8

Crostini con Salsiccie Sausage Crostini

Zuppa di Pomodoro con Pecorino Romano
Tuscan Tomato Soup with Pecorino Romano

Filetto di Manzo con Porcini e Salsa di Scalogni
Beef Tenderloin with Porcini and Shallot Sauce

Zucchini Ripieni con Salsa di Pecorino
Stuffed Zucchini with Pecorino Sauce

Involtino di Mandorle Almond Roll with Strawberry Sauce

Pecorino Romano is one of my favorite cheeses because of its tangy bite. It is a wonderful complement to the flavors of the zucchini and tomatoes in this menu. Stuffed Zucchini with Pecorino Sauce is another example of creative Tuscan cooking that includes a decadent, creamy pecorino sauce to spice up an otherwise bland zucchini dish. The key to this sauce—a trick I learned while living in Tuscany—is to add hard-boiled egg yolks to the sauce, which gives it a delicious thickness and richness. With the addition of eggs, there is no reason to add cream, which would make the sauce heavy.

Tuscany is home to the porcino mushroom, and there is no flavor or texture on earth quite like it. During the fall months, the hills surrounding Tuscany come alive with gentlemen in quilted coats or tweed jackets, carrying walking sticks and accompanied by their dogs, as they forage the woods for the porcini. I have accompanied some of my Tuscan friends on these outings with my children, when they were young, and there is truly an art to hunting the porcini! The aroma of

porcini mushroom soup, pasta with porcini, crostini with porcini (you name it!) coming out of the kitchens of homes and trattorie is amazing!

The Beef Tenderloin with Porcini and Shallot Sauce in this menu will become one of your favorite, go-to, easy yet elegant, Tuscan entrées.

End the meal with a scrumptious and typically Tuscan dessert. Almond Roll is not too sweet, thanks to the nuts, which are so prevalent in Tuscany, and the Strawberry Sauce is perfect!

Buon appetito!

Crostini con Salsiccie
Sausage Crostini

   4 Italian sausages, casings removed

   8 ounces stracchino cheese, chopped
      (if you can't find stracchino, you can
      use mozzarella)

   2 tablespoons fennel seeds

   2 teaspoons Sicilian sea salt, fine

   8–10 slices rustic Italian bread

1. Preheat the oven to 350°F.

2. Crumble the sausage meat into a bowl. Add the cheese and fennel seeds and mix them in with the meat. Season the mixture with the salt and stir well.

3. Spread the sausage mixture on the slices of bread and place them on a baking sheet. Bake the bread for 15 minutes, or until it is crisp and golden.

4. Arrange the crostini on a platter and serve.

Zuppa di Pomodoro con Pecorino Romano
Tuscan Tomato Soup with Pecorino Romano

   4 tablespoons extra virgin olive oil

   4 pounds fresh tomatoes, chopped

   2 onions, chopped

   2 stalks celery, chopped

   6 cups vegetable broth

   2 tablespoons fresh lemon juice

   3 teaspoons Sicilian sea salt, fine

   2 cups Pecorino Romano, grated

   1 batch Lisa's Famous Homemade
      Croutons (recipe below)

   Salt and pepper, to taste

1. Place the olive oil in a large 6- to 8-quart pot and add the tomatoes, onions, celery, and broth. Bring the mixture to a boil, reduce the heat, and let it simmer for 20 minutes. Add the lemon juice and salt and simmer the mixture for another 15 minutes. Add salt and pepper to taste. Allow the vegetable mixture to cool.

2. Puree the mixture in a blender. Return it to the pot and warm it up over low heat.

3. In the meantime, make a batch of homemade croutons (see below).

4. Ladle the soup into individual soup bowls and top them with the grated pecorino and croutons.

Lisa's Famous Homemade Croutons (From *Whatever Happened to Sunday Dinner*)

   1 loaf Italian bread, cubed

   ½ cup extra virgin olive oil

   ¼ cup garlic, chopped very finely

   1 teaspoon Sicilian sea salt, fine

Place the bread, oil, garlic, and salt in a large bowl and mix them together. Bake the croutons in the oven at 350°F for about 10 minutes, or until they are golden and crunchy.

Filetto di Manzo con Porcini e Salsa di Scalogni

Beef Tenderloin with Porcini and Shallot Sauce

2 ounces dried porcini mushrooms

½ cup extra virgin olive oil

6 shallots, peeled and chopped

4 cloves garlic, chopped

½ cup balsamic vinegar, excellent quality, imported from Italy

2 sprigs fresh rosemary

2 cups beef broth

2 beef tenderloins, approximately 3 lbs each

4 tablespoons unsalted butter

1. Place the dried porcini mushrooms in 2 cups of boiling-hot water and allow them to reconstitute for 30 minutes.

2. Place ¼ cup of the olive oil in a large frying pan and sauté the shallots, garlic, vinegar, and rosemary until the liquid is syrupy and the shallots and garlic are very soft and beginning to brown, approximately 20 minutes. Discard the rosemary. Puree the shallot and garlic liquid in a blender until the mixture is smooth.

3. Pour the beef broth into a large saucepan and bring it to a boil. Add the shallot and garlic puree. Drain and chop the porcini mushrooms, and add them to the beef broth and shallot puree. Lower the heat to a simmer and cook the sauce for another 20 minutes—it should reduce to approximately 2 cups of sauce.

4. Preheat the oven to 300°F. In a large frying pan, sear the beef tenderloins on all sides for 5 minutes. Place the beef tenderloins in a roasting pan and roast the meat for 35–40 minutes. Remove the pan from the oven and transfer the meat to a cutting board. Cut the meat into ¾-inch slices. To serve, place the meat on a platter and generously top it with the porcini and shallot sauce.

Zucchini Ripieni con Salsa di Pecorino
Stuffed Zucchini with Pecorino Sauce

For the Zucchini

12 firm zucchini, approximately
    1½ inches in diameter

4 tablespoons unsalted butter

4 tablespoons extra virgin olive oil

2 large shallots, chopped

1 tablespoon Italian flat leaf parsley

1 tablespoon dried thyme

½ cup Parmigiano Reggiano, grated

1 teaspoon Sicilian sea salt, fine

½ teaspoon freshly ground black
    pepper

2 eggs, lightly beaten

For the Pecorino Sauce

2 large, hard-boiled egg yolks

½ cup extra virgin olive oil

3 cups Pecorino Romano, grated

Salt and pepper, to taste

1. *To make the zucchini:* Wash the zucchini well. Cut off both ends of the zucchini and discard them. Cut each zucchini into 1½-inch-thick slices. With a melon baller, scoop out the center area of the zucchini, where the seeds are (see Note). Place the scooped-out part of the zucchini in a bowl and do not discard.

2. Place the hollowed-out zucchini slices in a 13 × 9-inch heat-proof casserole dish, hollowed-out side facing up.

3. Melt the butter and oil in a large frying pan. Add the shallots and cook them over medium heat for 3 minutes. Add the zucchini meat, which you scooped out of the center of each zucchini slice, to the pan, and cook until it is tender and brown, approximately 15–20 minutes. Stir in the parsley and thyme. Transfer the zucchini filling to a medium-size bowl, stir in the Parmigiano Reggiano, and season with salt and pepper. Let the filling cool, and then stir in the two eggs.

4. Preheat the oven to 350°F. Grease a large 13 × 9-inch heat-proof baking dish and place the hollowed-out zucchini cups in the dish, hollow side up. Spoon the filling into the cups and bake the stuffed zucchini for 1 hour, or until it is tender and light brown.

5. To make the Pecorino sauce: In a food processor or a blender, pulse the hard-boiled egg yolks with the olive oil until a smooth paste forms. Add the Pecorino and ⅓ cup of water. The sauce should have the consistency of heavy cream. If it is too thick, add a little more water. Season the sauce with salt and pepper, to taste.

6. To serve, arrange 2 or 3 zucchini cups on each plate and top the cups with a tablespoon or two of the Pecorino sauce.

To scoop out the center of the zucchini properly, place the melon baller in the middle of each zucchini slice and apply pressure straight down, until the melon baller is halfway submerged into the flesh of the zucchini. Then begin to twist the melon baller. In this way, you make a perfect hole in each zucchini slice while removing the meat of the zucchini. Remember: Do not go all the way through to the bottom of the zucchini—you want to leave approximately ⅛ to ¼ inch on the bottom of the zucchini slice so the breadcrumb filling does not fall out the other side.

Involtino di Mandorle
Almond Roll with Strawberry Sauce

For the Cake

Butter, for greasing the pan

4 eggs, separated

1 cup sugar

1 teaspoon pure vanilla extract

½ teaspoon almond extract

⅔ cup unbleached flour

½ teaspoon baking powder

1 cup sliced toasted almonds

For the Filling

2 cups heavy cream

4 tablespoons sugar

1 teaspoon pure vanilla extract

For the Strawberry Sauce

2 pints fresh strawberries, rinsed and chopped

8 tablespoons sugar

1 tablespoon fresh lemon juice

1. *To make the cake:* Preheat the oven to 375°F.

2. Butter a 13 × 9-inch baking or casserole dish. In a stand mixer or with a handheld mixer, beat the egg yolks until they are light. Gradually beat in ¾ cup sugar, vanilla, and almond extract. Add the flour and baking powder.

3. In a bowl, beat the egg whites until they're foamy. Add the remaining ¼ cup of sugar to the egg whites and beat them until soft peaks form. Gently fold the egg white mixture into the egg yolk mixture. Add the sliced toasted almonds. Spread the batter in the prepared pan. Bake the cake for 20 minutes, or until it is light brown on top and the cake springs back when you touch the center.

4. *To make the filling:* In a bowl, whip the heavy cream, sugar, and vanilla extract until the cream forms soft peaks.

5. *To make the strawberry sauce:* Place the strawberries, sugar, and lemon extract in a food processor and blend to combine all the ingredients until the mixture is smooth.

6. *To serve:* To serve, cut the Almond Torte into squares. Top each piece of cake with the cream and pour a tablespoon of Strawberry Sauce over the cream filling.

Menu 51

SERVES 8

Torta di Carote Carrot Torte

Rigatoni al Rosé di Bobby Bobby's Rigatoni al Rosé

Salsiccia di Campagna con Lenticchie e Finocchi
Country Sausage with Lentils and Fennel

Cavolini di Bruxelles Cremosi al Parmigiano
Creamy Brussels Sprouts with Parmigiano

Bavarese Italian Bavarian Cake

This is a very special menu for me because it features my son Bobby's favorite pasta: Rigatoni al Rosé. I learned to make this dish in Tuscany, where it is very popular to combine a red sauce with a cream sauce, hence the rosé name and color. The sauce is very delicate, very versatile, and it is delicious, not just on pasta, but on chicken or vegetables as well.

In Italy, we serve lentils as a garnish—for example, under a piece of fish or meat—not only in lentil soup. On our weekend explorations of Tuscany, when my children were small, lentil soup was a typical dish that we would find at *sagre* (outdoor food festivals).

The sausage and fennel were prepared outside on a massive grill, while the lentils were served from a giant pot. At a typical *sagra*, you would have five or six fun-loving, boisterous Tuscan men running the grill, shouting and singing. The women would stand behind huge pots that were full of lentils, vegetables, or soup.

One of my favorite aspects of fall in Tuscany are all the *sagre*, one for the porcini mushrooms, where a variety of dishes with porcini,

such as Tagliatelle con Porcini and Porcini Trifolati (sautéed Porcini) are served; one for roasted pork; and one for sausage, which features a dish like the one in this menu. My children loved the *sagra* of ravioli! In short, in Italy they have *sagre* for every food imaginable that is native to that region, at that particular time of year. A *sagra* is not only a fun, rustic, native custom in which to partake, it is also a wonderful way to eat the regional foods of an area in Italy at the peak of the season.

    Cent'anni! (May you live to one hundred years!)

Torta di Carote
Carrot Torte

For Lisa's Pasta Salata

1 cup flour

½ cup butter

Pinch Sicilian sea salt, fine

3 tablespoons milk

For the Filling

1 pound carrots, peeled and sliced

2 tablespoons unsalted butter

1 teaspoon sugar

1 teaspoon Sicilian sea salt, fine

1 cup Parmigiano Reggiano, grated

3 ounces Fontina cheese, grated

3 large egg yolks

2 large eggs

1 teaspoon marjoram

1 teaspoon Sicilian sea salt, fine

½ teaspoon freshly ground black pepper

1. *To make the pasta salata:* Mix together the flour, butter, salt, and milk in a bowl until the dough comes together and refrigerate the dough for 1 hour.

2. Preheat the oven to 350°F. Break the ball of dough into 2 pieces: 1 large and 1 small. Roll out the large ball of dough to about ¼-inch thick and place it in a 10½-inch pie plate, approximately 1½ inches deep. (Refrigerate the small ball for later use.) Bake the pastry in the preheated oven for approximately 15 minutes. Remove the crust and allow it to cool.

3. *To make the filling:* Place the carrots, butter, sugar, salt, and ½ cup water in a large frying pan. Cook the carrots for about 15 minutes. Transfer the mixture to a food processor or a blender and puree it. Add the cheeses, egg yolks, 1 of the 2 whole eggs, and the marjoram. Puree the mixture until it is smooth. Add the salt and pepper.

4. *To assemble the torte:* Pour the filling into the pie crust. Reduce the oven temperature to 325°F. Roll out the remaining small piece of dough into a rectangle and cut it into ¼-inch strips. Make a lattice across the top of the carrot mixture with the strips. Place the pie pan on a baking sheet, and bake the torte for 20 minutes.

Rigatoni al Rosé di Bobby
Bobby's Rigatoni al Rosé

For the Rosé Sauce

½ cup extra virgin olive oil

4 tablespoons unsalted butter

2 garlic cloves, chopped

2 (26-ounce) cans crushed imported San Marzano tomatoes

6 basil leaves, chopped

2 tablespoons Italian flat leaf parsley, chopped

1 teaspoon Sicilian sea salt, fine

½ teaspoon freshly ground black pepper

1 cup Parmigiano Reggiano, grated

1 cup heavy cream

1 tablespoon sugar

For the Pasta

Handful Sicilian sea salt, coarse

2 pounds rigatoni

1 teaspoon freshly ground black pepper

2 tablespoons red wine vinegar

1. *To make the rosé sauce:* Place the olive oil and the butter in a large saucepan. Melt the butter over low heat. Add the garlic and cook it until it is soft, but not brown. Add the tomatoes, basil, parsley, salt, and pepper. Cook the mixture for 10 minutes over low heat. Slowly stir the Parmigiano and the cream into the tomato mixture. Blend it well. Add the sugar. Reduce the heat, never allowing the sauce to boil, once you have added the cream.

2. *To make the pasta:* Fill a large pasta pot with water and bring it to a boil. Add a generous handful of coarse Sicilian sea salt. Cook the rigatoni according to the directions on the package and toss with the sauce.

Salsiccia di Campagna con Lenticchie e Finocchi
Country Sausage with Lentils and Fennel

2 cups (12–14 ounces) dried lentils

3 teaspoons Sicilian sea salt, fine

2 fennel bulbs

8 tablespoons extra virgin olive oil, plus more for drizzling (optional)

2 onions, chopped

2 carrots, chopped

2 teaspoons fennel seeds

3–4 pounds sweet Italian sausages

4 tablespoons Italian flat leaf parsley, chopped

1. Bring the lentils, 8 cups of cold water, and 1 teaspoon of the salt to a boil in a heavy, 2- to 4-quart saucepan. Reduce the heat to a simmer and cook the lentils until they are tender, approximately 30 minutes.

2. While the lentils are simmering, cut the fennel bulbs into ¼-inch chunks. Place 4–5 tablespoons of the olive oil in a large frying pan over medium heat and stir in the onions, carrots, fennel, fennel seeds, and another teaspoon of the salt. Cook the vegetables until they're tender, approximately 10–12 minutes. Set them aside.

3. Place ¼-inch of water in a large, 10-inch frying pan and cook the sausages, turning them occasionally, for 15 minutes, or until they become brown and crisp on the outside. Transfer the sausages to a cutting board and cut them into 1- to 2-inch pieces.

4. Drain the cooked lentils in a colander. Stir the vegetables into the lentils. Stir in the parsley, pepper, vinegar, and the remaining teaspoon of salt. Mix the sausage with the lentil mixture and serve. Drizzle with a little extra olive oil, if desired.

Cavolini di Bruxelles Cremosi al Parmigiano

Creamy Brussels Sprouts with Parmigiano

6 slices bacon

2 pounds Brussels sprouts, stems removed and cut in half

1 cup vegetable broth

1 teaspoon Sicilian sea salt, fine

½ teaspoon freshly ground black pepper

¾ cup heavy whipping cream

¾ cup Parmigiano Reggiano, grated

Cracked black pepper, to taste

1. Cut the bacon strips into ½-inch pieces with a pair of kitchen shears. Cook the bacon in a large frying pan, until it is brown and crisp. Drain the bacon on paper towels. Set it aside. Reserve 2 tablespoons of the bacon drippings in the frying pan.

2. Add the Brussels sprouts to the pan with the bacon drippings and cook them over medium heat. Add the vegetable broth and the salt and pepper. Raise the heat under the pan until the mixture starts to boil and then reduce the heat and let the mixture simmer for 5–6 minutes. The liquid should be nearly evaporated.

3. Add the cream and the Parmigiano Reggiano and cook the mixture for 5 more minutes until it has thickened. To serve, transfer the Brussels sprouts to a platter and sprinkle them with the bacon and cracked black pepper.

Bavarese

Italian Bavarian Cake

- 12 vanilla wafers, ground into fine crumbs in a blender or food processor
- 1 stick unsalted butter, melted
- 6 egg yolks
- 1 cup sugar
- 1 (15-ounce) container whole milk ricotta
- 1 cup chopped almonds, toasted
- 3 tablespoons Grand Marnier
- ½ cup heavy cream, not whipped
- 2½ packets (¼ ounce) unflavored gelatin
- 1 cup heavy cream, whipped to soft peaks
- 3 egg whites, whipped

1. Combine the ground vanilla wafers and melted butter in a mixing bowl and mix thoroughly. Press the crust mixture evenly into the bottom of a 10-inch springform pan or a 10-inch pie plate.

2. Using a handheld mixer on medium speed, beat the egg yolks until they become thick. While beating the eggs with the mixer, add the sugar. Beat in the ricotta, almonds, and Grand Marnier.

> ### LISA'S TIP
> Remember when you are beating cream to add the sugar when the cream is almost completely whipped. Otherwise, the weight of the sugar prohibits the complete whipping of the cream.

3. Meanwhile, pour the unwhipped heavy cream into a small saucepan. Sprinkle in the gelatin. Place the saucepan over medium heat and stir the mixture until it is smooth, thick, and lump-free. Beat the gelatin mixture into the ricotta mixture. With a spatula, carefully fold the whipped cream, and then the whipped egg whites, into the ricotta mixture. Pour the mixture into the prepared pan and refrigerate it for at least 4 hours. Remove the Bavarese from the refrigerator 15 minutes before slicing and serving.

Menu 52

Torta di Cipolla Onion Pie

Penne con Noci e Ricotta Penne with Walnuts and Ricotta

Cosciotto di Agnello alla Toscana Leg of Lamb, Tuscan Style

Zucca con Glassa al Balsamico e Pinoli Tostati
Acorn Squash with Balsamic Glaze and Toasted Pine Nuts

Torta di Baci Baci Torta

The warmth and heartiness of Tuscan autumn fare definitely comes through in this menu. Penne with smooth, whole milk ricotta is satisfying and comforting, with crunchy walnuts and arugula thrown in for just the right kick. A menu like this makes me—a southern Italian girl who would never have eaten dishes like this!—so grateful to have lived in Tuscany for so many years, and to have learned so much about the authentic, country recipes that real Tuscans eat. What I would have missed!

Nothing is more flavorful than a leg of lamb cooked on the grill. Lamb is one of my favorite meats to grill, as the sweetness of the lamb is really brought out by the flames. Here, I've provided instructions to prepare the lamb in the oven, since grilling it may not be an option for some. But if you can grill it, do so, by all means!

Dressing vegetables with balsamic glaze is another popular technique in Tuscany that really brings out the flavor of the vegetables. Although balsamic vinegar comes from the region of Emilia Romagna, specifically the area around the city of Modena, Tuscany is the region

just south of Emilia Romagna, and hence balsamic is used in many Tuscan recipes. You will fall in love with this velvety glaze. Feel free to serve it with any vegetable you like.

On the corner of the Ponte Vecchio in Florence, where we lived, there is a *giornalaio* (a man who runs a newspaper stand). When my daughter Felicia was small, he thought she was the sweetest thing he had ever seen. Every morning, while she waited for her school bus, he would give her one bacio chocolate, and he would say, "*Un bacio per la bambina piu bella del Ponte Vecchio!*" (A kiss for the prettiest little girl on the Ponte Vecchio!") Baci are the famous chocolates made by Perugina, each of which is topped with a whole hazelnut. Of course, *bacio* also means "kiss" in Italian. Massimo, the *giornalaio*, was a lovely man, and he made a lasting impression on my daughter with his kindness. So, every time my daughter and I make the Baci Torte in this menu, we toast Massimo. Wonderful memories for Sunday dinner!

Sempre famiglia! (Family forever!)

Torta di Cipolla
Onion Pie

For the Pasta Salata

1 cup flour

½ cup butter

Pinch Sicilian sea salt, fine

3 tablespoons milk

For the Filling

½ cup extra-virgin olive oil

3 pounds sweet yellow onions, chopped

1 cup green olives, sliced

½ cup anchovies, chopped

1 teaspoon freshly ground black pepper

1. *To make the pasta salata:* Mix together the flour, butter, salt, and milk in a bowl until it forms a dough and refrigerate the dough for 1 hour. Roll out the pastry and place it in a buttered 9-inch pie pan.

2. Place the olive oil in a large frying pan and sauté the onions over medium heat, until they are soft and translucent. Allow the onions to cool in the pan. Add the olives, anchovies, and pepper. Pour the onion mixture into the pie crust. Place the pie pan in a preheated 400°F oven and bake for 40 minutes until the crust is golden. Slice and serve.

Penne con Noci e Ricotta
Penne with Walnuts and Ricotta

½ cup extra virgin olive oil

1 cup onion, chopped

3 cups arugula and spinach, mixed and chopped

1 cup whole milk ricotta

1 cup grape tomatoes, cut in half

1 cup Parmigiano Reggiano, grated

1 teaspoon Sicilian sea salt, fine

½ teaspoon freshly ground black pepper

1 cup walnuts, chopped

2 pounds penne rigate

1. Heat the oil in a large frying pan. Add the onion and cook it over medium heat until it turns translucent. Add the arugula and spinach to the pan, stirring constantly, for about 4 minutes, until the greens are slightly wilted. Take the pan off the heat and stir in the ricotta, tomatoes, Parmigiano, salt, pepper, and walnuts.

2. While you are making the sauce, cook the penne rigate according to the directions on the package and fold it into the warm ricotta mixture.

Cosciotto di Agnello alla Toscana
Leg of Lamb, Tuscan Style

For the Green Peppercorn Sauce

6 tablespoons green peppercorns in brine, drained and rinsed

½ cup extra virgin olive oil

1 teaspoon Sicilian sea salt, fine

½ teaspoon freshly ground black pepper

2 garlic cloves, chopped

4 tablespoons unsalted butter, at room temperature

2 tablespoons unbleached flour

1 cup vegetable broth

2 tablespoons fresh lemon juice

2 tablespoons red wine vinegar, preferably imported, excellent quality

For the Lamb

2 (3–4 pound) legs of lamb, boneless, preferably from New Zealand

10–12 garlic cloves, whole

¼ cup olive oil

4 sprigs rosemary

1. *To make the sauce:* Finely chop the peppercorns and transfer them to a medium-size bowl. Add the olive oil, salt, and pepper, and mix well.

2. Place the chopped garlic in another bowl. Add the butter and flour, and combine them with the garlic to form a thick paste. Add the broth, lemon juice, and vinegar to the garlic mixture. Mix all the ingredients together thoroughly.

3. Place the chopped peppercorn mixture in a medium-size frying pan and sauté for 3 minutes, stirring occasionally. Add the garlic mixture to the pan and combine very well, making sure there are no lumps. Simmer the mixture over low heat for about 10 minutes.

4. *To prepare the lamb:* Make ten to twelve 1-inch-long and 1-inch-deep slices in the fat side of each leg of lamb with a paring knife. Insert a whole garlic clove into each of the slices. Rub the olive oil and rosemary all over the lamb. Place each leg on a roasting rack in a large roasting pan.

5. Roast the lamb in a preheated 450°F oven for 30 minutes. Reduce the heat to 350°F and cook the meat for 30–40 minutes for medium rare. Remove the lamb from the oven and let it rest for about 5 minutes before slicing it. Top each serving with 1 or 2 generous spoonfuls of green peppercorn sauce.

Zucca con Glassa al Balsamico e Pinoli Tostati

Acorn Squash with Balsamic Glaze and Toasted Pine Nuts

For the Glaze

    6 cloves garlic, chopped

    ½ cup balsamic vinegar

For the Acorn Squash

    ½ cup pine nuts

    4 acorn squash, each cut in half

    1 cup extra virgin olive oil

    2 tablespoons dried oregano

    2 teaspoons Sicilian sea salt, fine

    1 teaspoon freshly ground black pepper

1. *To make the balsamic glaze:* Combine the garlic and balsamic vinegar in a medium saucepan and cook the mixture over medium heat for 10 minutes, or until it becomes syrupy.

2. *To prepare the acorn squash:* Place the pine nuts in a small, dry frying pan and toast them over medium heat for 2–3 minutes, or until the pine nuts have turned golden (not brown or burned) on all sides. Using a tablespoon, scoop the seeds out of each acorn squash half and discard them. Pour ½ inch of water into a large casserole dish, and place the squash, hollowed side down, into the dish. Bake the acorn squash for 30 minutes in 350°F oven, or until a fork slides easily through the skin. Remove the squash from the oven and transfer it, hollowed side up, to a baking sheet or jelly-roll pan. Spoon 1 tablespoon of the balsamic reduction into the hollowed-out acorn squash and top it with the toasted pine nuts. Place the squash into a 300°F oven for 5 minutes to warm it up before serving.

Torta di Baci
Baci Torta

For the Torta

    2 sticks unsalted butter, cut into small pieces, plus more for greasing the pan

    8 ounces semisweet chocolate chips (or an 8-ounce chocolate bar, chopped coarsely)

    1 cup sugar

    6 large eggs, separated

    3 tablespoons rum

    2 cups toasted hazelnuts, chopped

For the Frosting

    8 ounces bittersweet chocolate (either chocolate chips, or in a chocolate bar, chopped)

    2 tablespoons unsalted butter

    2 tablespoons chopped, toasted hazelnuts

1. *To make the torta:* Preheat the oven to 350°F.

2. Butter and flour a 9-inch round × 2-inch high cake pan.

3. Place the chocolate in the top of a double boiler or in a heat-proof bowl over a pan of simmering water, and melt the chocolate over low heat. Remove the pan from the heat and let the chocolate cool.

4. Using a stand mixer, or with a handheld mixer, beat the butter and sugar until fluffy, about 2–3 minutes. Add the egg yolks and rum. Beat the mixture until it is smooth. Stir in the melted chocolate and the chopped hazelnuts.

5. In another bowl, beat the egg whites on medium speed until they're foamy, and then on high until soft peaks form. With a spatula, very gently fold the whites into the chocolate mixture. Place the batter into the prepared pan and bake it for 50 minutes.

6. *To make the frosting:* Combine the chocolate with the butter in the top of a double boiler or in a heat-proof bowl over a pan of simmering water until the chocolate has melted. Pour the icing over the cake, letting it spill down the sides, and sprinkle the hazelnuts on top. Refrigerate the cake for 1 hour before serving.

After dinner, an espresso on the Ponte Vecchio. Thank you for joining me for 52 Sunday dinners! *Arrivederci!*

ACKNOWLEDGMENTS

My thanks to:

- my agent, Tony Gardner, for, once again, guiding me through the rapids of publishing with his voice of experience, humor and friendship;
- the creative team at Sterling Publishing, especially my editor, Jennifer Williams;
- the marketing, publicity and sales teams at Sterling Publishing.

My love and deepest gratitude to:

- my Mother, who is always present in my life with encouragement, pride and love;
- my three children: Felicia, Bobby and Guido, whose constant love and support sustain me.

Lucky, lucky me to walk this path of life with you.

And last, but certainly not least, The Dream Team:

- My photographer, Kelly Rosenhagen;
- My hairdresser, Veronica Kennedy Kyle;
- My daughter, Felicia;

We took four regions of Italy by storm!!

INDEX

ABOUT THE AUTHOR

Lisa Caponigri is the author of *Whatever Happened to Sunday Dinner?* (Sterling Epicure), the only cookbook on the market that features 52 authentic rustic Italian menus. Each menu features five courses, from antipasto to dolce, in typical Italian Sunday dinner tradition. As part of her mantra, "The family that eats together, stays together," and her mission to get everyone, friends and family, back to the Sunday dinner table, Lisa appears on a variety of television programs. After developing Lisa's Italian Kitchen, a line of food items and sauces meant to make preparing Sunday dinner even easier, Lisa debuted on HSN and QVC. Lisa has also appeared on a variety of television programs, including Seattle's *New Day Northwest*, *Good Morning Toronto*, Chicago's *WGN Lunchbreak*, and *New England Cooks*, to name just a few. Lisa Caponigri lives in South Bend, Indiana and travels frequently to Italy to research the latest in *"la dolce vita."*

8/19·2

Black Bear's Backyard

by Julia Schaffer
illustrated by Amanda Harvey

Table of Contents

Chapter 1

Late Summer Days

Chandra laid out forks and napkins. Since her mother was away, she set only four places at the table—one each for Dad, Animesh, Dylan, and Chandra. The sizzle of onions and garlic in the pan made her hungry for her father's stir-fry. It was the only dish he ever made, but it was tasty.

Under the table a voice cooed, "Here kitty, kitty." Chandra's little brother, Animesh, was trying to pet the new cat, a stray their neighbor had found. Knowing that the Nandi family loved animals, she had brought it to them. "Here, kitty, kitty. Here, Quincy."

"Quincy?" Chandra stuck her head under the table. "Who is Quincy?"

"He's an NFL quarterback, right buddy?" Chandra's friend Dylan looked up, smiling. He was always smiling. "How did he do that?" she wondered.

Chandra's father turned to face them. "I don't think we should name her Quincy. I think we should name her after the Hindu goddess Parvati."

"You're so predictable, Dad. I think we should call her Susan B. Anthony," Chandra said. Her father fixed his eyes on Chandra's friend. "What do you think, Dylan?" Animesh peered out from under the table. Dylan smiled and said, "I like Susan B. Anthony. Susan B., for short."

With her mother visiting family in India, it fell to Chandra to help care for Animesh. After dinner Chandra tucked her brother into his bed. Already his eyelids were drooping, but as Chandra turned to go, Animesh asked, "Why did Quincy—I mean Susan B.—leave?"

"Leave where?" Chandra asked.

"Wherever she lived before?"

"I don't know, Animesh. Let's talk about it another time." Closing his bedroom door, she wondered. Maybe their neighbor would know where the stray had come from.

When Dylan left it was already dark out. Chandra stood in the doorway and watched his bicycle disappear. The summer was almost over. She hated to think it. If she had a hundred more days to swim and to go hiking in the woods, it wouldn't be enough. She dreaded going back to school and stepping into her old self. It would be like putting on someone else's clothes—too small, too wrinkled, and too dull.

When Chandra came downstairs the next morning, she heard shouts and shrieks from the TV. Animesh was watching cartoons. He looked like he'd been watching for hours. He looked, in fact, like an eight-year-old zombie.

Chandra had 12 days until school started, and she was determined to enjoy every one of them. "Do you want to go pick blueberries for pancakes?" she asked. Animesh looked at her and blinked. "C'mon," she said, "let's take Brett with us."

Basically Animesh was fun to be around, but when he got cranky there were only three things that would satisfy him: food, football, or their pets. At least they had plenty of pets.

Chandra checked to make sure her dad had fed Brett and the cats. She put sweatshirts, a bottle of water, a beach pail, and some snacks into a backpack. As she zipped up her bag, a voice behind her giggled, "Last one out of the house. . . ." Animesh flew out the front door. Chandra followed, smiling. "You're a rotten egg!" he screamed, and raced off into the woods with Brett barking at his heels.

For every handful of blueberries he picked, Animesh ate another handful. But even with him gobbling up the juiciest berries, they had more than enough for pancakes. Animesh chatted away, "This one isn't really a blueberry. It's more of a purpleberry—"

From behind a curtain of trees came a low growl and then a loud, angry bark. "What is it, Brett?" Chandra turned to look. Fifty feet from their dog was a black bear. He looked like a young bear, just a cub maybe.

Chandra tried to remember if you were supposed to look a bear in the eye and scream or drop down and play dead. And what were you supposed to do with your dog? "Brett!" she shouted. But he just kept barking until the bear backed off deeper into the woods. Chandra and Animesh stared after the retreating bear.

"I think he's a stray," said Animesh.

"What makes you say that?" Chandra asked.

"Why else would he come to the edge of the woods?"

"Maybe he's hungry," she said. Chandra knew you didn't call a bear a stray, but she couldn't think of what else it might be called.

Animesh ate berries the whole way home. "Watch it, Ani. I think you're dropping some."

"Okay," he said and grabbed another overflowing fistful.

Chapter 2

The Stray

"This is where it happened," Chandra said.

"Where what happened?" Dylan asked.

"So Animesh and I are picking berries, right?"

"You said I could tell him," Animesh interrupted.

"Fine."

"We heard Brett growl and then, standing right in front of us was a black bear."

"He was really about 50 feet away."

"Brett started barking like crazy and the bear— he got scared of Brett! And he went back into the woods."

"Were you scared?" Dylan asked.

Chandra and Animesh exchanged glances. "Not really," she said. "He was pretty far away."

Chandra pulled out the beach pail. The woods were full of raspberries and blackberries.

Chandra reached into the bushes tentatively. She had forgotten to wear long sleeves. Whenever she picked raspberries, the thorns scratched her arms. After picking a pail full of berries, she was ready for a break. "I'm going to go rinse my hands in the creek," she said, hoping Dylan would follow. He did.

They left Animesh picking berries and crouched down by the creek, cooling their hands in the clear water. They sat for awhile, talking about the summer and the school year coming up.

When Chandra and Dylan headed back, she didn't see Animesh where they had left him. But then Chandra spotted him low to the ground and staring at the black bear, who was just yards away.

Chandra screamed and ran toward her brother. The bear, startled, instantly bounded off into the woods. Chandra wrapped her arms around Animesh. He seemed so tiny and breakable, and she could feel his whole body trembling. He was whispering, "He's just a little bear."

She didn't know whether to laugh or to cry. But she let Animesh carry the pail and eat almost as many berries as he wanted, even though he was dropping berries every which way. There was just one thing she wanted from him.

"Ani," she started. "You didn't tell dad about the bear, right?"

"No," he said.

"Okay, let's just keep it between the three of us."

Animesh and Dylan nodded. Mr. Nandi was the only parent within ten miles who locked his front door and his car door at night. "Can we tell him about the pancakes?" Animesh asked.

"Let's surprise him on Saturday." Chandra swallowed a guilty feeling and walked fast.

That evening Chandra saw bears everywhere. Teddy bears were lined up on the couch where Animesh sat watching TV. Three cartoon bears were wrestling each other on the show he was watching. When the family sat down to dinner, her father actually said he was so hungry he could eat a bear. Chandra had to kick Animesh under the table to keep him from laughing.

As they ate, the sky darkened to a deep blue. "We have a surprise for you on Saturday, Dad." "Pancakes!" Animesh blurted out. "Well it was a surprise." Animesh blushed at his own mistake, but then continued to slurp down the rest of his dinner. "That's okay," her dad said. "I saw something in the back of the fridge. Not to mention in our driveway. You'd better pick up those berries tomorrow."

Something clattered in the yard. Chandra looked out the window at the rising moon. It was getting dark earlier every day. She saw a large shape cross in front of the window. It had a head—and ears. "It's the bear!" Animesh screamed, and raced to the window.

There in their backyard was the black bear, knocking over their trash can and rooting through the day's garbage. Chandra's father shouted and pounded on the window. She wondered if he knew that the language he was shouting wasn't English. When he got angry he slipped into his native language, Bengali. The bear ignored him. Her father grabbed two pots and ran to the backdoor banging them together. He shouted at the top of his lungs, and the bear understood at least his tone of voice.

Chandra's father came back sweating. "I'm calling the authorities," he announced.

"What authorities, Dad? You have to call the right one or they'll kill the bear," Chandra said.

"That's exactly what they should do. He's a danger and a pest."

"What? Dad, he just got lost."

"He didn't get lost. He knew right where he was going because there was a trail of blackberries leading him here," Animesh admitted. Chandra glanced at Animesh. His eyes were huge and his face was bright red. She couldn't believe it. He'd dropped those berries on purpose! She knew later she'd feel angry, even betrayed, but right now all she felt was sympathy for the panicked look on her brother's face.

Her father picked up the phone. "No, Dad. Please don't call," she pleaded. "You've said it yourself about strays. Some people think any loose animal is dangerous."

"But this is a bear, Chandra."

Chandra took a deep breath. "I know that," she said. "And there's a right way and a wrong way to handle a bear. If you'll just give me a day, I'll find the proper authorities and have the situation dealt with correctly." Chandra smiled to herself. Spoken like a grownup, she thought. Her dad looked her in the eye. "One day," he said sternly.

That night Chandra helped Animesh get ready for bed. Chandra pulled Animesh's blanket up to his chin and sat down on the edge of the bed.

He looked at her with mournful eyes. "I wish the bear could live here with us."

"Then you could call him Quincy," she said. "He'd probably make a better quarterback than Susan B. Anthony."

"Who is Susan B. Anthony anyway?" Animesh asked.

"She was an activist who lived in the nineteenth century. She fought against slavery, and she helped women win the right to vote. I like her because she knew what she believed, and she fought for it."

Susan B., the cat, jumped onto the bed and curled up at Animesh's feet. "Why do people call it a stray when it's a dog or a cat, but if it's a bear, they say it's on the loose?" Chandra asked. Animesh didn't know the answer, so he just looked at his sister. "I heard this story," Chandra continued, "about a bull that got loose in New York City. It had been brought in for a rodeo, but it got free and went running through traffic. The police chased after it in cars, but they didn't know how to actually catch it. And the rodeo guys ran after it swinging their ropes, but the police wouldn't let them get close enough to use the lasso."

"What happened?"

Chandra realized too late that this was not an appropriate bedtime story. She told Animesh that she would finish the story in the morning.

Chapter 3

Three Ways to Stop a Bear

Sunlight sliced across Chandra's pillow. She threw her arm over her eyes. The first thing that came to her mind was the bear. She needed to deal with the bear. She roused herself and went downstairs. She turned on the computer and found the Web site for the state department of conservation. She wrote down phone numbers for three regional offices and glanced at their wildlife news bulletin board.

A man answered at the regional office. "Roy Barstow here."

"I'm calling to report a bear eating the trash in my backyard," she said.

"Well," he said, "just four weeks until bear season."

"I don't want to shoot it," she said.

"I see. Well, if it comes back again, we can use a non-lethal method of deterrence." He paused. "We can shoot at it with rubber bullets and pepper spray and blast noise right in its ear so it never wants to come near your house again. But the first thing you should do is clean up your trash. Is your trash bin plastic?" he asked.

"Yes."

"There's your problem."

Chandra hung up the phone. Mr. Barstow had given her two things: the number for a store that sold bear-proof garbage bins and the option to terrify the bear instead of killing it. Her dad talked about the bear like it was a criminal. Mr. Barstow talked about it like it was a rat. Nobody talked about it like they did in books or on trips to the zoo.

Chandra sighed. She was hungry. Animesh was making a racket playing football with himself. Just then Dylan stopped by. "Special delivery," he said and dropped a newspaper onto the table. He pointed to an ad asking for help with a research project on bears. It listed the telephone number for a college professor. "Wow!" cried Chandra. "Thanks. Hey, could you do me one more really big favor? Could you go play football with Animesh for as long as you possibly can?"

Chandra looked at the professor's Web site. It had pages of information about black bears. She called the number listed. "This is Lenore Cross," the professor answered. She had a friendly voice.

Chandra told her about the bear and explained that she didn't want to hurt the bear, just move it somewhere else. Professor Cross told her that you couldn't force a bear to relocate because it would always travel back to the place it wanted to be. Her study, she said, was about tracking bears and luring them into better areas where they would want to stay. She asked Chandra if she would meet her the following week and show her where she'd seen the bear. Chandra thought of her dad. "Is there any way we could meet tomorrow?" she asked.

"Tomorrow is Saturday."

"I know," Chandra said. To her delight, Professor Cross agreed.

Chandra called her dad at work. With his permission she ordered a new, expensive kind of garbage can. Then she called Mr. Barstow and invited him to join them the next day. He agreed. Chandra tried to smile, but she felt guilty and confused. What made one animal a pet and another one a pest? And what exactly was the difference between dangerous and endangered? She looked out the window. Animesh was running through the yard with the football under his arm. She tried to imagine the backyard before her house was built, when it was all woods. Did bears live there? Who decides, she wondered, what belongs to people and what belongs to animals?

That night Chandra slept fitfully. The same questions ran back and forth in her head. When she finally fell into a deep sleep, she dreamed she was alone in the woods in the middle of winter. She found a cave of sleeping bears and tiptoed inside. She lay down to sleep and wondered if she too would hibernate and wake up months later. But she stayed awake, cold and lonely, wishing for home.

When Chandra opened her eyes on Saturday, she remembered her dream. She searched for the guilty feeling that had followed her everywhere the day before. It wasn't there. In its place was a new thought. Her job was simple: it wasn't to solve all the problems between people and bears. It was to help one bear find a safe place to live. Once upon a time the bear might have been happy in the woods that were now her backyard, but not anymore. And she could either feel guilty about it, or she could have the decency to help it find a better home.

Roy Barstow arrived in uniform with a can of pepper spray just in case, he said. Shortly afterward, Professor Cross knocked on the Nandis's door. She had brought a tape recorder, a digital camera, and a pad of paper. Chandra smiled. These two were total opposites.

Chandra's father seemed pleased that the problem of the bear was getting serious attention. As they walked into the woods, he told Roy about his new garbage bin, while Chandra, Animesh, and Dylan asked Professor Cross a lot of questions. She explained that it was common for young male bears to be displaced by their mothers. In the process of finding a new home, sometimes they got lost or sustained injury, but usually they succeeded in finding a new feeding area.

When they reached the berry bushes, Professor Cross scanned the ground for bear tracks. Roy Barstow took down the coordinates of their location. Both of them complimented Mr. Nandi on his responsible daughter. Chandra blushed, remembering that she still had to tell her father the full story.

Mr. Barstow offered to drop off a can of pepper spray in case the bear came back, and Professor Cross assured them that she would keep them posted on the bear's movement through the woods.

Brett led the way home. "Do you know what I'm hungry for?" Chandra's father asked.

"Pancakes!" Animesh exclaimed, "with blackberries and raspberries and blueberries."

Chandra was finally feeling good. She had nine days until school started and she was going to spend them however she wanted. And when her nine days were over she would just have to remember, there was more to her life than school. She wasn't just a student. She was a girl who fought for the things she believed in.

As she walked, Chandra remembered a song from when she was little:

"The bear climbed over the mountain / the bear climbed over the mountain / the bear climbed over the mountain to see what he could see. / But all that he could see / but all that he could see was the other side of the mountain. . . ."

Chandra felt hopeful that very soon their black bear would view nothing but woods and mountains as far as he could see.

Comprehension Check

Summarize

Why does Chandra get involved in finding a way to keep the bear away? How is she like her idol, Susan B. Anthony? Use an Inference Chart to help you summarize the story.

Text Clues	What You Know	Inferences

Think and Compare

1. How do the different characters in this story react to the bear? What is Chandra's reaction on page 5? What is Animesh's reaction on page 8? How do Mr. Nandi, Chandra, and Animesh's father react on page 10? *(Make Inferences)*

2. In this story Chandra feels like she's changed a lot from her experience with the bear. Can you think of an experience that changed you? How did you change? *(Apply)*

3. How do people and animals share land? Do they do it peacefully? Do they compete? Make a list of four kinds of animals. Include one that people keep as pets, one that is considered a pest, one that is considered dangerous, and one that is called endangered. How is it different for each of the animals on your list? *(Analyze/Evaluate)*

Write About a Wild Animal

Write a story or a poem about a wild animal that finds itself in the midst of humans. Try writing your piece from the animal's point of view.

Make a Bear Report

Research black bears. Tell what they eat, where they live, and what they are like. Then learn more about how people and bears can live together peacefully by visiting these Web sites:

North American Bear Center:
www.bear.org
Jennifer Jones Whistler Bear Society:
www.bearsmart.com
Then present a report to the class.

People Helping Animals

◇ **GR V** • **Benchmark 60** • **Lexile 670**

Black Bear's Backyard

One day, while picking blueberries by their house, Chandra and her younger brother run into a black bear. Her father thinks the bear is a dangerous pest. Can Chandra find a way to help the bear?

5.2 Week 1

The **McGraw·Hill** Companies

ISBN 0-02-193236-0

9 780021 932368